GODFATHERS

GODFATHERS

LIVES AND CRIMES
OF THE MAFIA MOBSTERS

ROBERTO OLLA

ALMA BOOKS

ALMA BOOKS LTD
London House
243–253 Lower Mortlake Road
Richmond
Surrey TW9 2LL   **09-10**
United Kingdom
www.almabooks.com

Godfathers: Lives and Crimes of the Mafia Mobsters first published in
Italian as *Padrini* by Arnoldo Mondadori Editore in 2003
First published in English by Alma Books Limited in February 2007
Reprinted May 2007
This edition first published in November 2007
Reprinted 2008
Copyright © Roberto Olla, 2003–7
Translation © Stephen Parin, 2007
All rights reserved

ISBN: 978-1-84688-049-0

Printed in Great Britain by Cox & Wyman Ltd, Reading, Berkshire

09-10 BT 14.68

Published with financial assistance from the Italian Ministry of Foreign
affairs.

CONTENTS

GODFATHERS

A Single Entity?

Leonardo was no saint. Not even as a boy, when he still used to go home every day for lunch to his mother's. He didn't remember much about his late father, Francesco Paolo – just enough to feel his absence. Luckily there was his uncle Titta – luckily, thought Leonardo, because his uncle was strong, everyone respected him, he never needed to say much when he gave his orders. Sometimes he didn't need to say anything at all.

In the poverty-stricken, dust-ridden Sicily of 1958, Leonardo was seventeen years old and felt sure his uncle was watching him. Nothing in particular occurred – they met each other on the normal family occasions, and his uncle didn't say anything or look at him more than usual. Yet he was observing his nephew and Leonardo wanted to be observed. It was important not to try to be observed – the best way was to copy his uncle down to the last detail. Doing rather than saying. It wasn't too difficult – a few words, a few gestures. He needed to give an impression of steadiness, solidity, reliability – that was enough for his uncle to understand.

His uncle eventually approached him with a request. Leonardo remained serious, not reacting, just as his uncle was expecting. He was of school age, he could have been studying for a diploma. But when he told his mother he was going to leave school and get a job, uncle Titta just nodded and nothing more was said about the matter.

What does an uncle ask his seventeen-year-old nephew? What can you ask a boy of seventeen? "Are you up to killing a horse?" his uncle asked him. Yes, Leonardo was up to it. A horse – an animal, even one which was large, strong, noble, glossy and groomed – it had to die because that's what his uncle wanted.

An older man accompanied Leonardo on the job. Perhaps he was only two or three years older, but to the boy he seemed like an adult. The man was introduced to him as L.C. Emanuele. They went off to take up their positions near the farm where the horse was going to meet its fate. For a few days the two of them waited, hidden and silent, in the warm shadows. The horse came out, went in again, came out – the right moment to kill it never arrived. Uncle Titta sent a message. They could come back. Leonardo had meant what he'd said – he was obviously ready to kill the horse. With that clear, there was no actual need to shoot the poor beast.

His uncle asked him: "Could you kill a man?" The boy once more said: "Yes." He was sent off to observe the habits and behaviour of the intended victim for a couple of weeks. In the mean time someone stole a rifle for him from a well-known gun shop in Palermo. L.C. Emanuele, who'd kept an eye on him before, came to tell him his uncle wanted to see him.

When Leonardo got to the appointment, there was another man in the room who just watched him and said nothing. His uncle introduced him as Totò L., and gave no further details. They handed him the gun, some overalls and a pair of sunglasses. "F. Giuseppe is coming – you'll be going with him." The new man was to be the driver. Leonardo was to shoot. It was uncle Titta who had taken him on his first hunting trip, using his father's rifle, to make sure the boy learnt how to handle firearms. The driver arrived in a battered purple Fiat Topolino, which looked as if it had been left out in the sun too long or was just dirty, with a grimy dirt that turned it black. But it was perfect – it belonged to a certain widow only the driver knew. Leonardo and the driver stuck a new number plate on the car and drove off.

Perhaps Leonardo was expecting something a bit better than a rackety Topolino for his first mission. But he quickly realized what an effective and essential tool it was. In 1958, Sicily was still a poor country – no one would give a second glance at such a car. It also had a roof you could open, a touch of luxury in a vehicle designed for the have-nots who couldn't afford the real thing.

As soon as he saw his victim, Leonardo stood up through the open roof. The first shot didn't go off. Despite the gun catching, he remained steady and calm and pressed the trigger again; the target dropped to the pavement in a puddle of blood before he could realize what was happening in the purple Topolino. The driver sped away and Leonardo closed the roof. He started to dismantle the rifle and put it in a plastic bag. His uncle took him on a lark-hunting trip as a reward. Shortly afterwards he was initiated as a "man of honour". He was eighteen years old.

From then on he shot and killed every time he was asked to by the man who had been his uncle but was now his "father and godfather", the head of his new "Family". For the next fifteen years, whenever there was some shooting, some burning, some beating-up to do, Leonardo was ready to do it.

Shortly before his thirty-third birthday, on 30th March 1973, he gave himself up to the police. No one realized he was a Mafia killer. He ended up in prison and then in confinement in Sardinia. It occurred to him he might pray. After a few days he realized that it gave him some relief, so he started to spend a lot of time in prayer.

Leonardo was no saint and he was no longer a boy. He was a hardened and ruthless criminal. He took pleasure in killing. No one in the police or the *carabinieri* could have dreamt he would start to talk. But he had turned up at the police station and started to tell everything he knew, for no apparent reason. It was hard to believe he'd been struck by a religious thunderbolt – and harder to believe the more he talked. Yet some kind of motive needed to be found for his extraordinary confession, so the police officials decided to add these words to his statement, at the head of the torrent of accusations which followed: "On reflection and wishing once and for all to unburden my conscience which has tormented me now for some time, for crimes which I committed by myself or with others, as well as

7

for those I knew about as a member of a Mafia organization, I give an account of my sins which I wish to expiate".

They sent him off to a cell, not realizing how essential it was to protect him. The entire underworld knew the traitor was talking. A rumour started to circulate that he was a coprophage. He was a murderer and a religious fanatic, and he also liked to eat shit. These rumours reached the police headquarters: they thought it might be the other inmates who wanted to give an idea of how low Leonardo had sunk – or perhaps not, perhaps there was someone who really knew what Leonardo liked and didn't like to do.

Leonardo talked about the Mafia and described it as a single entity, made up of Families who knew each other, competing with each other to share out business and territory, but remaining united and controlled, ruled by a precise internal hierarchy, interrelated and in contact with Mafia Families in the United States.

After Leonardo's lark-hunting trip, the group that assembled was the Altarello Family, of which uncle Titta was the godfather, the head, the master. He was everything. Totò L. reappeared at the meeting, together with a dozen other men. They drew lots to decide who would be Leonardo's godfather during his apprenticeship: Ciro C., whom Leonardo hardly knew, was chosen. They pricked Leonardo's finger with a thorn from an orange tree, burned a sacred image of St Rosalia and made him swear the sacred oath of the Beati Paoli.[1] As the picture of the saint burned to ashes in his hands he swore he would die rather than betray his new Family. Finally all the men who were there kissed him on the mouth. "But they didn't use their tongues," he was at pains to point out to the police officers, so they could write it down in the statement.

This was Leonardo's initiation. He was placed under a new guardianship, just like a minor who's removed by his uncle from an orphanage and begins a new life. He didn't get a new

---

1   The name of a secret society thought to have existed in medieval Sicily, al-legedly formed to oppose both the Church and the State. It is suggested by some modern sources that the Beati Paoli sect was a predecessor of what today is known as the Sicilian Mafia.

father: his uncle didn't want sons and had no intention of educating him to become a free and independent man. He was quick to grasp the intimate, murky, magnetic nature of the mixture of blood, Mafia and dependence which bound him to his godfather – like some anaesthetic from which he would never awaken and emerge.

From the respect which other young men showed him, he realized that in his new Family any career path was open to him so long as he continued to carry out crimes. His apprenticeship didn't have an escape clause. His independence wasn't even a consideration. Perhaps it might come about if he had the luck to survive the wiping out of his entire Family in some Mafia turf war. Or if he turned traitor, gave himself up to the authorities and was branded as an outcast.

In recounting his frenetic criminal career it almost seemed as if Leonardo remembered the cars better than his victims: the Fiat 1100 torched in Via Perpignano near the Boccadifalco airport belonged to a man who was building the new main post office. The elegant Lancia, on the other hand, had been stolen from Costanzo, the building tycoon and father of a well-known dynasty of property speculators. Leonardo liked to watch them burn.

Building was going on all over Palermo. Business was booming, capital was plentiful, suddenly emerging out of nowhere. Leonardo's uncle-godfather was keen to get in on the sector: the boy was his right-hand man, he admired him like his own father and did to the letter whatever he was asked to do.

A certain Salvatore C. was doing quite well in his market-garden business. In order to get water he had to pay a contribution to the Altarello Family, a proportion of the bill issued by the water company. That's how the territory had been divided up. When the contributions stopped coming, it was Leonardo's job to target his nice bright-red Fiat 1100 family saloon. The burnt-out carcass of the car was left in Via Palchetto for quite a time, as a warning to others.

During a meeting of the Family, when Leonardo was twenty-eight, a certain B. Giuseppe suddenly slapped uncle Titta in the face. The truth of the matter was that when B. Giuseppe had been to collect the contributions the owner of the bright-red Fiat 1100 had to pay for his water supply, he had failed to hand them over to the head of the clan as he was supposed to. But instead of raising this issue, the godfather accused him of being a spy. A spy: he was a marked man. Slapping Titta in the face was simply his way of signing his own death warrant. "We'll deal with it," was all his uncle said when he left the meeting. He then let time take its course – a lot of time.

Leonardo had his own car, a Mini Minor which sped through Palermo's traffic lights and which he liked to think made him the envy of his peers. When the moment finally arrived, he left it parked a couple of blocks away from where B. Giuseppe lived and went to take up his position behind a low wall. He had already examined the spot in detail and, in order not to be visible, had gone back day after day to assemble boulders on the wall. He fired a single shot with the same gun he had used for his first murder. B. Giuseppe was hit in the neck and took a few seconds to die. Then, back in the Mini Minor, Leonardo dismantled the gun, put it in a plastic bag and threw it over a wall into the garden of a villa belonging to a lawyer, as his instructions said he should.

Another time he and three others had climbed inside a light-green Fiat 600 to beat up the owner of a bar. But the driver didn't take to being beaten up, and put up a violent fight – they had no choice but to shoot him and drive off, all four of them inside, in the green Fiat.

On another occasion he poisoned all the dogs belonging to a property speculator with strychnine. It was the time of the so-called "sack of Palermo", when huge amounts of money could be made putting up public and private buildings. His godfather uncle Titta didn't want any competitors in certain contracts, so Leonardo was given a small bag of the poison and carried out his orders.

Leonardo's deposition lasted for hours: one crime after another, he seemed to recall them all. He liked going to the cinema. "Just like everyone, no? Doesn't everyone like going to the cinema?" The police officer didn't reply. He just changed the paper and the carbon sheet in the typewriter. Yes, everyone likes going to the cinema – but only Leonardo got in free. The box-office staff and the usherettes didn't charge him anything at the cinema Imperia. They were "friends of friends", and when they asked for a favour he couldn't turn them down. He agreed to set fire to the manager's brand-new blue Fiat 500 – it seemed his staff found him a bit too gruff and severe.

The Mafia, as Leonardo talked about it, was into everything – petty transactions and multi-million-pound businesses – and it knew everyone, doctors, surgeons, psychiatrists, engineers, civil servants, clerks, cashiers, shop assistants, street-cleaners, nurses, barmen, bakers, grocers, butchers. It was in truth a single entity, and Leonardo had learnt how to move through it with ease.

He listed the Families he knew and the connections between them. He spoke about high-level meetings between the different bosses to reach agreements. He mentioned a certain Totò Riina, one of the leading godfathers, who had managed to solve a dispute between two Families. The firm P. was about to start on a construction project; the Mafia bosses had fixed the sum the firm needed to pay in order to go ahead. Uncle Titta at the head of his Family was in charge of the area round Altarello. Based on the territorial divisions, he should have been responsible for receiving the money. But the Noce Family, in a neighbouring territory, were quick to claim they had the right to it. All Totò Riina needed to say was "The Noce Family is close to my heart" and the dispute was over. Somewhat later Titta sent his nephew to see Pippo Calò, the head of the Noce clan, to let him know they accepted Riina's decision but still thought it might be fair to give something to the Altarellos. Uncle Titta didn't actually expect them to agree. He was just complying with the way things are done under the *pax mafiosa* – giving a signal of friendship and of submission to the rules.

The criminal police handed the long statement as signed by Leonardo over to the judiciary. Leonardo was now an official *pentito* who had agreed to turn State's evidence by telling the authorities what he knew about the Mafia. He was the first of his kind in Italy and, all in all, he'd had more to say than Joe Valachi, whose confessions had been broadcast live on television in the United States. Valachi had been a mere *picciotto*, or foot soldier, in Vito Genovese's clan and spoke only because he was scared of being killed.

Leonardo didn't even know why he was talking. He had broken his oath of loyalty – he knew this very well as he prayed in his cell. The Altarello clan wouldn't stand by and watch – and nor would the other Families. When he came to trial, the judges refused to believe the testimony of this murderer and coprophage. Leonardo's account of the Mafia as a single entity, like some vast fungal growth stretching underneath the society visible on the surface, seemed incredible in the light of the sun which dazzled Sicily in the 1970s.

At the end of the trial, Leonardo was condemned to twenty-five years. When the case went to appeal, the judges decided he was mad and treated him accordingly by sentencing him to a psychiatric prison unit. No further statements were written on the evidence he had provided. He was handed over to the psychiatrists and the staff of the asylum. A heavy iron door clanged shut on all the stories which the madman could tell.

Totò Riina summoned several other bosses to a meeting in Corleone. They didn't give Leonardo's case a second thought. No one said a single thing about it to uncle Titta. There was no point.

Corleone DOC

When they hear the name Corleone, most people think of the Mafia. It doesn't matter much whether the association of ideas comes from the gang based in Corleone, headed by Liggio and Riina, or from the character of Don Vito Corleone, invented by Mario Puzo and played by Marlon Brando in Coppola's film *The Godfather*. The name of Corleone is so famous throughout the world that in 2000 the local councillors thought of using it as a brand name. Why not try to put its negative connotations into reverse and use it to advertise the pasta, jams or cheeses made by honest local producers? In time they might even be contenders on a European scale against other renowned centres for agricultural produce such as Castelnaudary in France.

In novels and films you often see the most violent crimes taking place in restaurants, so making a link between criminals and good cooking. For both crime and food, nothing but the best, just as the godfathers like it. And it's not just a myth: various investigative reports, biographies and eyewitness accounts make it clear that mafiosi like to eat well and that good cooking is part of their tradition.

And it's true that the brand name Corleone on food and drink products would lead potential buyers to expect high quality. Only a process of rather more lateral thinking – linking the Mafia to environmental pollution, with illegal dumping and the trade in toxic waste – might tarnish the image. So it's a good idea then? Cheeses, wines, oils and conserves trademarked Corleone? With a DOC attached and helped along by the cynicism of global trade, the area's hardworking local producers might make their fortunes. It might even break the automatic association in most people's minds of the name "Corleone" with the word "Mafia".

Who would ever associate the name of Corleone with one of the most significant events in Italian history? It would be necessary to show how and why the event was so important. July 1893: the Corleone Treaty.[2] September 1893: Corleone again, where the first great strike in the Italian countryside took place, the movement known as the "Fasci Siciliani's" finest hour. It takes some effort to realize the importance of this. It's possible that the "Fasci Siciliani" don't even merit a mention in the history curriculum as taught in Italian schools. Perhaps an hour during the school year is devoted to the subject, perhaps one of the teachers suggests it as a project. For most people "Fasci" can only mean "Fascist". In Italian schools the students ask you: "But they really had nothing to do with the Fascists? But if they were progressives why are they called 'Fasci'?"

---

2   The Corleone Treaty ("Patti Agrari"), signed on 30th July 1893, is the first example of a workers' union contract in Italy.

1893

The great strikes of farm labourers in Corleone in 1893 are not part of history as it is taught in our schools, nor are they included among the symbolic events which crystallize national self-awareness. Only a few academics and professional historians are interested in the Fasci Siciliani. We need to look again at the dates we choose in constructing our narrative of historical events, and highlight the ones which are most important for the development we want to trace. Mass participation was the key element of the Sicilian Fasci.

In late-nineteenth-century Italy a right and left wing took turns in power, in a struggle to win the votes of a very restricted electorate. The franchise was given only to men who had an income large enough to make them eligible not only for tax, but also for participating in the political machinations of the new nation. The Left, as led by Giolitti, had already abandoned Sicily to its destiny, both as an emotional commitment and as a political decision. Swarming with brigands, resistant to being run by the representatives of the Italian State, the island was only of concern to them as a potential reservoir of votes. The ability to carry out realistic and effective analyses of the political situation has always been part of Cosa Nostra's genetic inheritance.

Another event occurred in 1893 which, unlike the Fasci, has managed to get into the history books: the congress in Reggio Emilia, when the Italian Socialist Party emerged from the Workers' Party. It was born with a congenital defect, hardly noticeable at the time, but destined to have an ever-increasing influence on the fate of the Italian Left over the course of the next century. The new party rejected the popular uprising of the Sicilian Fasci. In thrall to its own ideology, which placed the working class at the centre of the system, it wouldn't or couldn't understand mass movements which emerged spontaneously from below. And despite the presence of many Sicilian Socialists among the leaders of the Fasci, the new party almost wanted the popular uprising to fail.

This political weakness left the way free for the Mafia, which knows how to play the political game. They understood the

Fasci very well and saw in them an opportunity to consolidate their own prestige and power over the mass of Sicilians who were involved in the movement. The left wing in government, on the other hand, abandoned Sicily, its labourers, peasants, artisans, miners, tradesmen, share-croppers, the small – very small – landowners to their fate, just as it abandoned the turbulent mass of intellectuals, anarchists, diehard Mazzinians, ex-Garibaldini and even some Socialists.

Some of the most astute political minds of the period were to be found in the Fasci but, for the Left, there was no trace of that abstract Socialist ideology which they were intent on carrying into action. All they could see was a group of coarse labourers from the deep South in search of land they could farm, men who had no interest in finding more modern types of work, but were content to stay stooped over their hoes in rough farm labour, masses who were inspired by some vague undefined need for democracy, and not by socialist ideals.

The strikes in Sicily were distant events for the leaders of the Italian Left. The Giolitti government turned a blind eye to the organization of the Fasci in rural areas simply because the political price for such negligence was not too high. As for the Right, the Fasci were rejected out of hand – the very idea of a political alliance with a popular movement was unthinkable. The concept of the Right guiding the masses, including the poorest levels of society, was still unformed. Although Crispi was Sicilian himself, as far as he and the other conservative leaders were concerned, all that was needed was enough power to eradicate the movement, by sending the army to shoot the rebels who were protesting against customs duties, taxes and the estate system.

So the Fasci and their leaders were left isolated in a Sicily outside the Italian State, an island which for centuries had been ruled by foreign powers, which survived without any government to whose authority it could appeal, a place where a different mode of being or culture had grown up, an underground form of communication, a hidden and alternative system of power. Italy's government, monarchy, political parties were all so many foreigners in the eyes of the labourers who supported the Fasci and dreamt of land and freedom, food and democracy – or, in more concrete terms, the end of the great estates and the setting up of co-operatives to farm the land. Such a dream was capable of attracting enough men to organize mass strikes.

Several artists and intellectuals began their careers in the climate created by the Fasci, amid strikes and demonstrations, in the face of violent repression, surrounded by the victims of an island which in the course of a few years had lived through a state of siege no fewer than three times, and had had to submit five times to oppressive laws which curtailed its rights and its freedoms. Sicilian-born novelist and playwright Luigi Pirandello was typical: from the experiences he lived through as a young man sprang his deep-rooted contempt for a State which declared itself to be liberal while carrying out bloody repression. His contempt grew into a hatred for the political jockeying in Rome where parties of the Right and Left played at democracy as if it were a game.

Excluded from playing this game, the Fasci grew to have more than 400,000 members; the number of people on the island who were entitled to vote was just 160,000 (and there would have been even fewer if the electoral reform of 1882 had not extended the franchise to thousands more). 400,000 – the overwhelming majority without a political voice; a vast mass of workers to whom the most elementary form of political involvement was denied. Once more, people without a State, outside the State.

But if there was no room for the Fasci in the models of Italy which both Right and Left were trying to create, the Church thought differently. On 15th May 1891 Pope Leo XIII had issued the encyclical *Rerum novarum*, "of new things". It certainly was the epoch of "new things": great engines, complex machines, huge ships, imposing dykes, dazzling ideas – like socialism, which was spreading through the factories and through the countryside, down into the deep South. The Pope launched the Church on the path of social commitment, of political and trade-union activism. At first it took some time for the message to be understood and absorbed; then a vast organization started to grow from the upper echelons of the Church down to the smallest parishes.

In Sicily numerous priests were influenced by *Rerum novarum* – the followers of Don Sturzo, on their mission to support the weakest in society, defending the right to a day of rest on Sundays, accusing those who ruthlessly exploited women and children. The treatment of workers was savage: their lives were at risk during working days that lasted from dawn until dusk, families sold their children to the glassworks of Lyon and Paris, and young boys – *carusi* – laboured naked in the sulphur mines like slaves, subject to all kinds of violence. The great landowners were remote in their noble villas and city mansions; their estates were run by tenant farmers, who held their land on lease and acted as caretakers, who distributed work and exploited those employed under them, who dealt out justice and were criminals themselves, who administered and dictated. They decided who would work in the fields; they controlled the flow of water; they calculated the percentage that was due to the owners; they fixed the price of bread with which the labourers were paid. With blackmail and fear these tenants tortured the men who worked for them: they were the real masters of the labourers who joined the strikes organized by the Fasci. They were the pillars of Mafia power. Even so, when the Fasci movement suddenly broke out, several "men of honour" thought it advisable to side with them, to join them; soon they moved with ease among the Socialist trade unionists, the Utopian anarchists and the first priests influenced by the doctrines of *Rerum novarum*.

Another event occurred in 1893 which is a further justification for including this year on the pages of the history books: the scandal which overtook the Italian banking system, a forerunner of the "Clean Hands" campaign which swept over the country almost exactly a century later.

The year opened with the arrest of the governor and the chief treasurer of the Banco di Roma. The two had been responsible for the involvement of the bank in the most reckless property speculation. The official inquiry established that huge sums of money had been paid to buy off politicians; bribes had even been given to Giolitti and Crispi. Shortly afterwards the director of the Rome branch of the Banco di Napoli was arrested, and other smaller institutions were also implicated in the scandal. Irregularities started to emerge in the Banco di Sicilia, which the director Giulio Benso Sanmartino Duke of Verdura tried to conceal. Finally, when huge capital investments from the Mafia began to be uncovered, the whole investigation ran into a political quagmire for which political expediency demanded a cover-up. What happened in 1893 provided the model for all the cover-ups to come.

There was a certain official, a man of the utmost integrity, a gentleman out of step with the times, even at the end of the nineteenth century, who had undertaken the investigation completely unaware of the forces which had been unleashed. He was called Emanuele Notarbartolo, and he had been the Mayor of Palermo and the Duke of Verdura's immediate predecessor as director general of the Banco di Sicilia. In this position he had started to notice the money-laundering from which the bank drew immense sums. His investigations were on the verge of getting to the heart of the system: the relations between the Mafia, the wider economy and leading politicians. He had been dismissed and shown the door before he caused too much damage, but he continued his investigations privately. On 1st February 1893 he was knifed to death on the train from Messina to Palermo on which he was travelling home.

Just three weeks after Notarbartolo was murdered, Rocco De Zerbi, a member of the Italian Parliament who was on the committee responsible for the reform of the banking system, died in mysterious circumstances. He was under suspicion of having accepted a bribe to defend the interests of the Banco di Roma in the affair. The parliamentary committee investigating the scandals officially reproved Giolitti for his conduct, but stopped short of stating in its final report whether he had accepted any money or not. The man who came out best from the whole affair was, incredibly, the Sicilian Crispi, who had himself been involved in the scandal.

Another Member of Parliament, Raffaele Palizzolo, was accused of murdering Notarbartolo.

1893 seemed interminable, but it brought some good opportunities for changing the national political set-up. The right wing came to power, with Crispi as the new head of government. He launched his period in government by appealing to the country to observe a "holy truce". Having thus gained some time, he didn't waste a moment in sending troops to Sicily to put down the popular uprisings. Dozens of corpses lined the streets of Partinico, of Monreale, of Lercara Friddi.

The New World

Preoccupied as it was with business dealings and criminal dealings, the State paid no attention to remedying the conditions of its own people, a state of affairs that drove the most desperate among them to emigrate. And although it was despair which drove them out, they were filled with courage. They had lost all hope in the new Italy; their only alternative was to look for another home.

This initial period of emigration is important for our story, because right from the outset several "men of honour" managed to infiltrate themselves into the flood of those leaving. These early "pioneer" emigrants were destined, after a few years, when they'd set up their own small shops or businesses, to become the first victims of Mafia extortions and rackets.

In the beginning mass emigration was from the north of Italy – from Lombardy, Liguria, Piedmont, the Veneto and Friuli, all regions which were then extremely poor. These emigrants were the first to make their way to the Americas, but some went even further, to New Guinea or Australia. Many were pursuing the dream of a promised land which would turn out to be as welcoming as their own homeland had shown itself to be cruel. The families with their wagons gathered round Father Bandini in the United States show Italians played a part in how the West was won. They were travelling in their thousands in search of a plot of land to cultivate: they found it in Arkansas and named what became a prosperous small farming town Tontitown, after their fellow emigrant Enrico Tonti. Similar stories lie behind the founding of New Milan and New Tyrol and other places in Brazil, the names of which recall the birthplaces of the men who settled there. Those who chose to remain in the big cities like New York adapted and paid protection money for regular work in the port or as street vendors.

This flood of emigrants contained a bewildering variety of types. There were Utopian anarchists planning on building the new Jerusalem where there'd be no suffering or exploitation, naive labourers who seriously believed the streets of America were paved with gold, speculators and mercenaries convinced they would make money, though not from the gold in the streets, priests and nuns who realized there was a new type of missionary work to be done among the emigrants, old veterans of Garibaldi's campaigns and diehard supporters of Mazzini, ex-patriots who had seen their hopes in the Risorgimento disappointed, and political refugees who had fought for the unity of the country, but had been driven out by the State as revolutionaries. There were factory workers who were regarded as too unionized and troublesome, and got transferred en masse out of the country, like the employees of the Rossi hosiery manufacturers sent by their boss to Brazil. There were criminals, bandits, con men – along with tight-lipped men of honour who were going out to form the bridgeheads for the Mafia in the new world beyond the seas. Indeed their first profit-making venture was emigration itself – the traffic in human beings has always been one of the Mafia's main business interests.

South America at the end of the nineteenth century was a gold mine for some. In 1871 the government of Brazil had passed the "free womb" law, which meant that while mothers must remain slaves, their future children would be born free. At a stroke the future supply of slaves was blocked for good; as a result their cost soared. The *fazenderos*, the proprietors of the great plantations, did their sums and found Italian labourers fitted the bill. A call went out to bring them over from Italy: the traffickers responded by sending over shiploads, with the result that Brazilian farms succeeded in maintaining their high levels of output.

Nothing, on the other hand, came of the Utopias and new

Jerusalems: the harsh violence of the natural world – the rivers, winds, mountains and men – put paid to them. Only those emigrants who had formed a definite plan and had the strength and resources to realize it managed to carry on independently; the rest just replaced the slaves. As soon as they stepped on-board the boat which would take them away from Italy, the trap closed on them. They didn't have a penny to their name. The traffickers encouraged them to seek their fortunes outside Italy and their future employers offered an incentive by paying for the crossing – one way only. The wretches would have to pay back every penny the ticket had cost with their own labour – meaning that in effect they would never pay it off. Added to this was the cost of lodgings and daily food for men who possessed nothing and guessed nothing of what awaited them at the moment of embarkation.

In order to survive, there was one word that had to be learnt very quickly: "boss". Beds, blankets, shoes, soap, food, water – the "boss" supplied everything, deducting the cost from the emigrants' wages. The bosses were often Italian themselves, but it was as if they belonged to a different race, marked out by the name "boss", the first word of slang the new arrivals learnt to speak.

The United States was officially an advanced democracy which protected the rights of its citizens, but the reality there was not so very different from Brazil. Professor Joseph Scelsa, an Italian-American and the son of emigrants, has done a study of the account books of a number of construction sites in Louisiana. He found that there were three different levels of wages: the top rate was paid to white workers; the second for blacks; and the lowest was for the Italian emigrants. This was their new homeland.

The "Romantic age" of Italian emigration, made up of soldiers and adventurers, didn't last very long. Five thousand Garibaldi supporters had fought for the North in the American Civil War in the 39th Battalion, called the "Garibaldi Guard". One of the most important episodes in Australian history is known as the "Eureka Barricade". The government had sent out troops to put down a miners' strike, but the soldiers found themselves facing a well-organized body of men prepared to fight. Behind the men's political leaders there was a military one: Raffaello Carboni, who had fought for Garibaldi and, after emigrating to Australia, endured the hard life of a miner, but never forgot the battlefields where he'd learnt his military tactics.

Back in Italy Piedmontese troops were overrunning the South in pursuit of bandits, but in the Far West no fewer than six Italians were enrolled as soldiers in General Custer's cavalry. Even more remarkable is the fact that all six survived the massacre at Little Big Horn in 1876. One of them was the legendary bugler John Martin or Giovanni Martini. He could have been the real hero of Arthur Penn's film *Little Big Man*. But back in 1970, when the film was released, Hollywood thought that Italians could only play Mafia parts, so a new role was created for the screenplay, the character of Jack Crabb, acted by Dustin Hoffmann, a clumsy bumbling Indian guide, like the real John Martin.

Another surprising figure is Charlie Siringo, the son of emigrants from Liguria, who was a ransom hunter, no different from a gunslinger in the movies. Unlike other gunslingers though, he wrote an autobiography which was regarded as the cowboy's bible and sold in millions, making Siringo a fortune in the process.

And like a character out of a fairy tale there is Anna Rech, a widow from a village in the Veneto. She was tiny of build, with seven sons, one of them disabled; no doubt as she set out from Italy her neighbours thought that all she was capable of was cooking and running a house. But she turned out to have the flair of an entrepreneur, selecting a location for her enterprise and assessing demand: she chose as her destination an uninhabited part of Brazil, crossed by enormous herds of cattle in need of grazing lands, led by teams of cowhands who never came across another living soul in their hot dusty wanderings. She started out offering them a meal and a place where they could rest and refresh themselves – a century later the small town which her children and grandchildren went on to found is named after her in her honour.

New Orleans 1891

Many emigrants had formed plans and showed themselves capable of relying on their own abilities and those of others in carrying them out. They had the capacity to understand their new country and to set up new trades and businesses. In the New World they'd found out how to make money. The early "men of honour" who, attracted by the prospect of money, had managed to infiltrate the masses of Italian emigrants, had similar abilities, supplemented by their use of violence and intimidation.

At the same time as the Fasci were being set up in Italy, a Mafia Family had settled in New Orleans. It was headed by Charlie Matranga and was in control of the port. Officially the Matranga Family ran a business importing oranges, a Sicilian speciality which they had some experience in. Unofficially they controlled illegal gambling, prostitution and rackets. Business was booming, so much so that news got round and the Matranga started to receive visits from the *picciotti* belonging to another Family, the Provenzano.[3]

There were probably enough activities and dollars to go round for everyone, but Charlie Matranga didn't see it like that. A war broke out between the rival Families: they turned from the business of oranges to the trading of bullets. Over the course of the next two years forty murders took place in the city. It was the first Mafia turf war to take place in the US. In 1890 the city's chief police officer David Hennessy was killed. The investigation was complicated: Hennessy had a shadowy past, and it was impossible to rule out his involvement in the struggle between the two Families. Pressure to do something from the newspapers and from the terrified public was high.[4] A dozen Sicilians were

---

3   "They call it a 'Family', probably to soften it. It's not a Family, it's an illegal business organization in which a group of men pledge loyalty to each other, divide up different areas of business and divide up the profits they're making, with a large percentage going to the boss at the top." Rudolph Giuliani, former Mayor of New York.

4   "These Families exist to make money. They will resort to anything in order to continue their criminal operations, including murder. They will even murder innocent people who aren't even involved in the criminal organizations." Thomas V. Fuentes, former Chief of the Organized Crime Section, FBI.

arrested – no attempt was made to distinguish between *picciotti* in the employ of the two Families and ordinary immigrants who were just trying to make a living by working as stevedores. In March 1891 a furious throng of people surrounded the prison where the men were being held: the rougher elements in the crowd threatened to storm the building if the detainees were not handed over to them. The governor opened the gates and the Italians were dragged from their cells. Eleven were lynched outside, nine of them in front of the prison. Two tried to escape but were caught and put to death. Even those on the outermost edges of the mob could see the corpses strung up on the lamp-posts. It was one of the biggest mass lynching in American history: because of it, Italians came second only to blacks for the number of lynchings their community had suffered. One detail the newspaper reports of the event noted was that there were numerous blacks in the crowd baying for the Italians' blood – this in Louisiana where many blacks had already been lynched.

Faced with such fury, the two Families withdrew into invisibility.[5] Complete calm followed on from the murders. The Mafia had been weakened by the conflict: too many *picciotti* had been killed and too much business had been damaged while the Matrangas and the Provenzanos were fighting each other.[6]

But the lynching weighed heavily on the conscience of the United States. The Italian ambassador delivered an official protest to the President and, in an attempt to wipe out the blot, the government sent substantial sums of money as reparation

---

5 "In the history of the Mafia it's always the case that after a turf war the families involved withdraw into their shells. They're acting on the old Mafia saying: '*Calati, juncu, ca passa a china*' – 'Bend down, reed, and let the river tide wash over you'." General Angiolo Pellegrini, former head of Direzione investigativa antimafia (DIA) operations in Sicily.

6 "The history of Cosa Nostra shows us that the recourse to violence and to murder occurs either when the relations within each Family have reached a stalemate or when the organization needs to send a message to the outside world. This is the case with so-called 'third level' crimes. Violence isn't a game for Cosa Nostra, it's a necessary method of discipline, to be used sparingly, only when absolutely needed, in order not to offer any openings for possible police investigations." Colonel Mauro Obinu, *Carabinieri*, former deputy commander of the special unit."*Raggruppamento Operativo Speciale* (ROS).

to the families of each of the men who had been lynched. The money couldn't eradicate all traces of the event – several documents still survive in scrupulously organized American archives – but it managed to cancel it from collective memory.

The Godfather

Vito Cascio Ferro was already a man of honour when he infiltrated the Sicilian Fasci. The protest had infected his own village Bisacquino. Ferro was thirty and liked to think of himself as an anarchist; he acted the part so well that he convinced himself he was one. It seemed the natural thing to do to approach the more advanced members of the movement and start making his own proposals. He'd been born in time to absorb all the contentiousness left behind by Garibaldi's "Thousand" in their progress through Sicily. All kinds of causes sprang up in the wake of the red shirts: vague impulses towards social justice and the first stirrings of socialism, seeds of anarchist uprising as well as authoritarianism. Costumes for every occasion could be fashioned out of the ideas left behind after all the battles had been fought.

Since he'd been a boy, Ferro had been exposed both to the Mafia influence of his own family and to the desire to organize protests and even rebellions in true Garibaldian spirit. These were opposing tendencies, but in Vito Cascio Ferro, thanks to the peculiar Sicilian mix where they didn't have to cancel each other out, they merged and formed a new type of mafioso. If intelligence can be defined as the ability to solve a series of problems arising from a particular situation, then having to keep his wits about him in that social laboratory made Ferro a very intelligent man. With his fiery impetuous character, his liking for making rousing declarations and for inciting the masses to action, Ferro soon made his way up the hierarchy to become the leader of the Bisacquino Fascio. To succeed in this enterprise and to maintain close contacts with the most capable and best-informed leaders, Ferro needed more than a liking and instinct for rebellion. He was given the responsibility for maintaining links with other villages and towns, and he became a sort of reference point – the ideas he expressed must have carried conviction, since nobody seems to have suspected there was anything else behind his motives. He soon developed a loyal following.

"Property is theft" was the basic anarchist principle. By dint of thinking it and repeating it, Ferro must have found it easy to take to cattle-rustling: it was with the trade in stolen livestock that he first started to make money. But like the good mafioso he was, he soon found other opportunities beyond the limited confines of Bisacquino. By day he mixed with the labourers in the Fasci, by night he consorted with the local brigands. By keeping company with both he quickly realized what he needed to do to become a *padrino*.

He learnt the skill and distributed favours to everyone. It wasn't a straightforward skill to learn: a precise set of ideas needed to be applied consistently: "I eat and I let other people eat". If a godfather enables others to eat, no one has the right to go and see how much he's eating himself. The system seems simple: a web with the godfather at the centre. But instead he's on the outside, perfectly camouflaged within ordinary society, awaiting his prey.

The important corollary to the law of "I eat and I let others eat", the one which determines how it's actually put into practice, is "There's no such thing as a free meal". Once you're inside the godfather's web, in one way or another, sooner or later, you will have to pay for "eating".

The Republican constitution was a key moment in the history of Italian society: it established work as the basic principle of the new republic. It is work which gives each individual dignity and autonomy over "eating", the wherewithal to live: through work individuals can provide for their own needs and for their own families. But the Mafia paid no heed to the Constitution: the godfathers with their webs went on doing what they'd always done, denying dignity and autonomy to others. It's hard for people to realize this is what's happening when, driven by need, despair or rage, they commit the venial sin of asking for help from the friend of a friend. Everything can be transformed into a favour, and a favour always leaves someone in the position of having to repay it.

Mafioso and anarchist-socialist, Don Vito proved to be a master at his art: recovering a letter which had disappeared, returning a stolen horse, providing a badly needed sum of money: the recipients of these favours started to feel in debt and ended up entangled in the godfather's web. On the one hand, he led a trade-union organization, the Fasci, which brought together labourers, tradesmen, peasants and the self-employed entrepreneurs of small businesses. And on the other, he headed a secret organization, the Mafia, which immersed those same labourers, tradesmen and other ordinary folk in a web of fear and mystery.

The illiterate and the poor in the countryside didn't even have the courage to call it "the Mafia". They didn't give it a name. The slightly more educated in the villages and towns whispered about it, careful to make sure they were out of earshot.

If there is a motto made for the figure of Don Vito Cascio Ferro, it's the one made famous in Lampedusa's *The Leopard*: "Change everything so that everything stays the same". The godfather saw that Sicily was passing through a momentous period, and made up his mind that he'd be ready to meet history in the making. No one in the Fasci thought he was an infiltrator, and even he didn't see himself in this way. "Change everything so that everything stays the same": so he was within the movement, ready to seize every opportunity which came along to reinforce his own personal power, his own role as a Mafia boss.[7] He waved the hammer and sickle flag of the proletariat in one hand, and in the other he wielded the Mafia shotgun. He put up pictures of the Madonna, of St Joseph,

---

7 "The Prince had one of his usual sudden visions: a scene of guerrilla combat, gunshots among the trees, his son Tancredi lying on the ground with his guts hanging out like that wretched soldier. 'You're mad to go off and join those men, my boy. They're all mafiosi and con men. A Falconieri should be on our side, for the king.' A smile reappeared in his eyes. 'I agree, for the king – but which king?' The boy suddenly had one of those customary fits of seriousness which made him so inscrutable and lovable. 'If we don't join them, then they'll form a republic. If we want everything to stay as it is, then everything has got to change. Don't you understand?'" From *The Leopard* by Giuseppe Tomasi di Lampedusa.

King Umberto and Queen Margherita, while preaching that "the land belonged to the people who worked on it". There was even a legend in Bisacquino, passed down from mother to daughter, that some women preferred to go to confession with Don Vito rather than with the parish priest. Bakunin plus the Royal family plus the Madonna: a heady brew to bewitch the ignorant. But it's not as simple as it seems. The labourers in Bisacquino, like the others who belonged to the Fasci, perhaps knew only enough to let them dream: the land should belong to the men who worked on it, social justice, dignity for everyone. Yet among the leaders of the movement, the intellectuals, no one gave a thought to plans for educating the masses. Mobilizing the masses was always the topmost priority. In every period the margin of ignorance which separates leaders from the masses seems to be a mere venial sin of politics.

But the women in Bisacquino, lining up for confession with the godfather, rather than telling their sins to the parish priest and obtaining absolution from him? Vito Cascio Ferro was known to everyone as "Don" Vito: no one in Bisacquino could remember a time when he wasn't called this.[8] "Don" like a priest or a nobleman – and that's because a *padrino* is an aristocrat of crime, a count, or rather a prince of the world of evil. Yet, unlike titles of nobility, it was difficult to inherit. It was possible for a son to inherit it from his father, if his father had been a *padrino*, but this wasn't enough. You needed to prove your rights to the title again and again, by your deeds.

The long Mafia tradition had taught Don Vito that direct conflict with the State was to be avoided: in the long run the Mafia was bound to lose. He'd learnt how to make himself inconspicuous, never attracting the attention of the police or the judges, never doing anything to shake the officials and administrators from their institutional torpor. A godfather should if possible have no criminal record, in order to pass

8 "Mafia godfathers are like godfathers to everyone. Down to the lowest ranks everyone recognizes him as the person who dispenses justice and rights wrongdoings. You can also go and ask for his help in finding employment. But what you must never forget is that, if you didn't obey their orders, the godfathers were also the men who sentenced you to death." General Angiolo Pellegrini.

unseen and uncaught through the nets laid by the law. Don Vito was a model for the Mafia, the first great godfather of modern times, the times of "new things", when business travelled on great ships powered by huge engines. His way of life was out of the ordinary, and in choosing it he fashioned a new model of the man of honour. It was essential to respect the rules if you wanted to be respected – and honoured – yourself.[9] A man of honour could threaten, torture, rob and kill, but only according to precise rituals which would demonstrate both his power and his respect for tradition. Violence was a weapon which was always to hand, but it was a weapon of last resort, to be used when other ways of enforcing authority had failed.

Don Vito wore a beard, but made sure it never grew so long that it covered his gentlemanly cravat; he had an aquiline nose and large hands; his clothes were smart but always creased. But none of this mattered: a godfather could be short and fat, or thin, or ugly and unattractive. His power lay in his intelligence combined with his unscrupulousness. With intelligence Don Vito built up a troop of armed thugs, like the *bravi* who surround the "Unnamed" in Manzoni's novel *The Betrothed*.

Don Vito also knew how men behaved, their vices, their flaws, their deep-rooted fears. Well before the insights of psycho-analysis, he had a kind of intuitive knowledge which enabled him to identify the weak points in any character that he could exploit. When the government in Rome sent in the army to suppress the Fasci, Don Vito had already acquired all the skills and all the power of a Mafia boss. He moved to Tunisia, which has always provided a nearby secure refuge for many men of honour – only sixty miles across the Mediterranean, a stretch of water he had crossed many times before as a young mafioso dealing in stolen horses and cattle.

---

9 "But why 'godfather', why *padrino*? Because their authority is so complete. It's like a dictatorship. There's no legislature, no rule-making body, they don't consult, they don't go to the flock, to the voters. It's the Boss: the Boss tells people what's right, what's wrong, and people follow him." Mario Cuomo, former Governor of the State of New York.

With the army in Sicily, the forces of progress were running out of steam: it was time for Don Vito to remove his Socialist mask. Other leaders of the Fasci realized this immediately and drove him out of the organization, blocking his contacts with other Socialist groups. It didn't much bother him: Don Vito was already off across the Atlantic in order to participate in the huge trade in emigrants – whether they were legal or illegal didn't matter. In his eyes America was the golden land of organized crime. Using the violent language of anarchism which was now instinctual in him, he managed to get himself welcomed as a political refugee by several anarchist groups in the United States. Property might be theft, but by theft you acquire property: Don Vito didn't care about legal documents signed and stamped officially. Real possession was achieved through the power and authority that came with being a Mafia boss.

He'd been forced to leave Sicily, expelled from the Fasci and pursued by their enemies. But what did this matter? Soon the Fasci would be washed away, just like our sins. "Change everything so that nothing changes": this was the principle which had led Don Vito from the Mafia into the Fasci, from the Fasci over to America, to take charge of the wretches who'd been forced to emigrate. It was and still is a principle in the business world, still invoked in the big firms, even as a way of saving the business. Politicians too adopt it, careful though they are to conceal it a little so they don't appear too cynical. No one goes to the stake because he wants to change everything in order that everything stays the same. Often there are those who explicitly espouse the principle as the best way of conserving power, like the cynics who declared that the Fasci supporters were mere dreamers and looked on impassively as their backs were broken.

All of the Fasci groups were smashed up, with loss of blood: many of the members died, many ended up in prison. The masses were brutally reminded that they were born to labour in the fields. And those who couldn't even do that left for the New World – the great estates didn't have room for everyone.

The Little Bird's Beak

Emigration was born from defeat, and developed into a vast phenomenon.

The emigrants didn't find any sympathy towards them in the new world: one of them once wrote to the Americans: "We were born where you wouldn't want your dogs to be born, and we came to find work here, where we've learnt that living a dog's life is the only way not to die like one."

Probably no one can take the credit for inventing the *pizzo*. In the criminal underworld it must have seemed a discovery waiting to be made, a device to extract money illegally and unjustly from any activity undertaken in the daylight world. But Don Vito can be said to have been responsible for elevating the practice into a theory, for developing it into a system which could be applied on a large scale. His was the cunning which masked the practice under the pretence of helping immigrants who were poor and clandestine. *Pizzo* means the beak of a bird: all that was needed then was for the beak to take a little sip from the huge American soup bowl. A small feeble bird in a city like New York, full of concrete skyscrapers rising up on steel frames, road tunnels roofed with steel beams, steel bridges over the rivers and rail tracks disappearing into the distance. All the little bird wanted was to peck its beak into every immigrant's daily pay packet, each small tradesman's daily takings, every business's profits.

This was Don Vito's project. He passed through the immigration controls on Ellis Island, apparently like any other emigrant, unrecognizable to the authorities – though it's fair to say they were efficient enough to know about his arrival and to attempt to follow his tracks. But they didn't know who they were following – how could they? They had an image of a kind of bandit, an anarchist hell-bent on fomenting disorder, a murderer, a robber, or even the head of a gang of criminals. A figure from the underworld in other words. But not a "Don" in jacket and tie, surrounded by a crowd of ordinary supporters.

The police forces had made a serious and common mistake. They thought the Mafia didn't have a history and didn't exist in history. The Mafia for them was a problem of public order: they were a gang of bandits who had to be arrested and suppressed. A century later, the Italian magistrate and Mafia prosecutor Giovanni Falcone would again single out this mistake as the principal misconception in trying to understand the Mafia.

It's also the case that during the years of mass emigration very few people actually believed in the existence of the Mafia. The bandits the American guards had in mind were gunmen. No one had informed them that Don Vito didn't carry guns. His cynicism and intelligence were the weapons he used. His strength lay in the network he had built up around him based on the principle that there is no such thing as a free lunch. All those who ended up entangled in Don Vito's web knew that sooner or later the *padrino* would demand repayment for the favours he had bestowed.

There's a word which encapsulates the deepest fears of ordinary Americans: "underworld". The American imagination, fed by its film industry, sees a dark side everywhere, behind or underneath the town streets with their rows of neat houses and gardens and curtained windows. Giant worms, sharks, icebergs, bionic monsters, extraterrestrials, bodysnatchers who suck the life out of you. There is a whole hidden plot underneath the surface. The least imaginary, the only real world among all these figments is the underground world of organized crime.

In Don Vito's time, the police thought it was a question of hunting out criminals in the lower depths of society, but the Mafia moved in the world above, emerging from the underworld as and when they pleased, going about their business freely. The police were looking for "outsiders" when they should have been searching for "insiders" who resembled any other citizen. The men of honour could do this because they came from a long-established tradition of running a secret state; within a few years this secret state would invade and control the unsophisticated American underworld.[10]

---

10 "In the original structure of the organization, the bosses were very experienced criminals. They were older, more mature, and had engaged in racketeering basically throughout their lives, from the time they were teenagers through to their mature years. They did pass that on to the younger generations of criminals." Thomas V. Fuentes.

The American investigators knew of course that anybody could enter a bar and sit down next to someone who'd stuck a knife into another man. Ordinary people had the right to be left in ignorance, but they had to be capable of identifying and arresting the criminal. However, the arrival of the Mafia with Don Vito upset this simple strategy. The United States, with its clear distinctions between the good and the bad, its rigorous ethical code apparent in the way people behaved and how they thought, was unprepared. It had no idea how similar the Mafia was to ordinary people and their way of life. It wasn't just that the mafiosi wore suits and ties. It had nothing to do with wearing masks. It was the Mafia's hybrid mix of morality and immorality which generated a type completely unfamiliar to them – men capable of carrying out the most savage crimes while at the same time showing the utmost respect for religion, of organizing massacres while in ordinary life defending traditional principles and ways of life.

In trying to explain what respect and honour meant in the Mafia, Giovanni Falcone chose the example of a Sardinian life-convict called Peppino Pes. Pes wasn't a mafioso, but he came from another Mediterranean island with a similar centuries-old culture, one which had also given birth to godfathers who dispensed rudimentary justice under the village oak tree and exercised authority in the absence of a distant and oppressive State. In Sardinia there were godfathers and bandits, but they didn't form part of a Mafia because of the different social conditions which prevailed on the island: limited trading links and restricted commerce, a smaller proportion of the population with the vote and, most importantly, the much greater role played by real – blood – families who succeeded in keeping criminal activities under their own control, employing and arming their own members to extort money and obeisance from the other inhabitants of their village.

In the prison kitchens Peppino Pes was given the job of preparing meat for the canteen meals. Falcone asked him if he ever took advantage of his position to give himself a bit more than the standard ration. Pes was indignant at the suggestion: "Your Honour, I don't steal meat. I commit murders." People might brand him a murderer and kidnapper, but he still wanted them to respect the moral code which guided him and meant that he would never stoop to pinching rations of meat like a common thief. The America in which Don Vito had arrived was a tumultuous social magma of morality and immorality, respect and bullying, honour and violence, in which he could turn every opportunity which came his way to his own advantage. With the clear-sighted analysis of a sociologist or a historian he decided to enter the big businesses of gambling, prostitution and racketeering.

The White Hand and the Black Hand

The White Hand fought against the Black Hand. The American ports were the front lines of the battle between the Irish and the Italians. The Irish came from earlier immigrant stock and refused to make way for the new arrivals. They enjoyed several advantages: they spoke English and they'd been in charge of organized crime first. Many of their compatriots were accepted and prominent members of the community.

The numbers of Italians – the Black Hand – were increasing all the time with the arrival of immigrants from the south of the country. After only a few years had passed, the millions of immigrants gave rise to increasingly large numbers of gangs.

But it didn't matter whether they were Italian or Irish in origin, whether they worked on the railways or in the docks, whether they were fishmongers or greengrocers: if they didn't want their market stall or shop destroyed, they always had to pay the *mazzetta*, a small percentage of whatever they earned. The racketeers threatened them with dangers of various kinds: their boats could be sunk, their windows shattered, their shops torched. Their children too were at risk: who would protect them while their parents were at work?

The Irish thought it "normal" to pay protection money to the White Hand gangsters, just as the Black Hand had the right to occupy themselves with their own immigrants. But given the vast influx of Italians the balance of the situation was increasingly unstable. A war broke out over new victims to pay protection money, new shops, new stalls or carts: a long-drawn-out war for the domination of the world of organized crime, fought with machine guns and bombs, alliances and betrayals and corrupt practices to avoid police ambushes or to lay them for one's enemies.

And so in the early years of the twentieth century corpses began to be found on the streets of American cities like New York and Chicago. The advance of the Italians was unstoppable: the Black Hand included everything – street bandits, con men, men on the run, robbers and murderers, Neapolitan *camorristi* as well as authentic mafiosi from Sicily.

At a Christmas party in 1925 at the Adonis Social Club in Brooklyn, two mafiosi asked a couple of Irish girls to dance. A boss belonging to the White Hand saw them and threatened them. In a moment all the lights went out and then two flashes of machine-gun fire lit up the darkness. When the lights were turned back on, the Irish boss and his men were lying dead on the floor. Someone present said he had seen "a man with a long scar on his face": "Scarface", otherwise known as Al Capone, who'd come back from Chicago with the aim of exterminating his old enemies. The police were left as usual counting the corpses and looking for witnesses. No more was heard of the White Hand, and the few remaining Irish gangsters managed to find a way of co-existing with the new American Mafia.

Lieutenant Petrosino

In 1906 a silent film called *The Black Hand* was being shown in American cinemas. Several of its cinematic features were new: cutting between alternate episodes, various open-air sequences shot on the busy streets of New York, a special use of lighting for indoor scenes. Like many films of the time it took its inspiration from a recent event: in 1905 a butcher by the name of Gaetano Costa had been the victim of a Black Hand racketeer. Costa had come over with one of the first waves of immigrants from northern Italy; with hard work he opened up a shop which did well. He'd finally started to make good profits, when he received a letter with the request for protection money and the usual threats if he failed to pay up. Gaetano Costa was merely one of many victims, but his story made the newspapers because he decided to resist and contacted the police. A trap was arranged, and when the criminals turned up at Costa's shop for the money, they were arrested.

The forces of law and order in the United States had quickly reorganized to confront the criminality which had arrived with the new wave of immigration from southern Italy. Several Italian immigrants had been enlisted to create a special squad of the New York City Police, known as the Italian Bureau. It was led by an investigator who was well known for his intuitive flair, tenacity and courage: Joe Petrosino.

He'd risen through the ranks, managing to infiltrate anarchist groups in New York where, according to the secret services, some of the more dangerous characters were planning to assassinate the President, William McKinley. Theodore Roosevelt had recognized Petrosino's qualities and promoted him to sergeant as early as 1895. At the time Roosevelt was the Police Commissioner, but shortly afterwards, in 1901, he was elected President. As President therefore he had direct knowledge of, and a personal trust in, this robust and sturdy Italian policeman.

Petrosino and his team worked undercover: out of uniform, they mixed with Italians in their social and festive gatherings and all the time maintained close contacts with the secret service. There was also an Irishman in the team, who was particularly useful because he knew both White Hand slang and Italian.

The Black Hand gangs continued an increasingly violent and out-of-control campaign of crime. They were fighting among themselves as well as against the White Hand gangs. Petrosino identified a building on East 107th Street which early reports suggested was the headquarters of the Black Hand gang. Various victims and enemies of Ignazio Saietta's and the Morello brothers' gangs converged on it. Saietta was a man so notorious for his ferocity that his fellow criminals called him "Lupo the Wolf". The Black Hand didn't restrict itself to torching shops and beating up their owners; kidnapping was one of their methods for getting people to pay. The threats of torture and violence were such that it was extremely difficult to gather witness statements and accusations.

In the film *The Black Hand*, Costa's little girl is kidnapped in an effort to persuade her father to pay up. Today, a hundred years on, the film seems crude and naive, but it was sufficiently developed to get its message across to the public who went to watch it. The kidnappers gesture theatrically just like the Italian street traders who could be seen everywhere in New York. The Black Hand gangsters pass the time playing cards with a bottle of wine on the table; their women too helped with organizing the crime. The bottle of wine, which in the shots just seems to be a stage prop, was on the contrary a precise connotation of being Italian; this was long before drinking wine became an American habit. The film ends as the case did in real life, with a success for the police.

But the most significant result for the police was their entry into the apartment block on 107th Street, named by the press "the murder stable". The Italian Bureau were able to arrest many of the members of the Black Hand including "Lupo the Wolf", who ended up in jail. But when Petrosino found himself face to face with the criminal, his investigative intuition immediately led him to realize that the man was no more than a common murderer; he didn't have the ability to be a Mafia boss.

Someone else was pulling the strings of the Black Hand, someone much higher up than Lupo. The victims of the Mafia's extortion rackets were increasingly to be found in other sections of American society, while the methods of blackmail and the ways in which payments were requested became more subtle. Among those arrested, the *picciotti* stood out for a particular way of behaving, almost for a certain style. Somewhere there had to be someone who was attempting to take control of the racket, the extortions, the prostitution, the gambling and the myriad other channels through which the illicit earnings of the underworld were flowing.

In 1903 Enrico Caruso had made his debut at the Metropolitan Opera House; then, as now, an appearance at the Met meant the beginning of a world-famous career. So it turned out for Caruso: an unprecedented success here led to numerous tours in the United States. In 1906 he sang in *Carmen* at the San Francisco Grand Opera House, and escaped the earthquake which destroyed the city shortly afterwards. He also sang in Chicago in a place called Colosimo's Café, ignorant of the fact that the café's owner, Peter Colosimo, was the leading Mafia boss in the city.

At the end of one of his return performances at the Metropolitan, where the public now adored him, Caruso found a note waiting for him in his dressing room. It was a demand for two thousand dollars from the Black Hand. Caruso paid up, thinking that was the way to settle the matter, but a few days later he received a second note, again from the Black Hand, but this time asking for fifteen thousand dollars. Someone advised him to go and see an Italian who worked in the police force: Joe Petrosino. Petrosino persuaded Caruso to lay a trap; he would agree to pay and go to the arranged appointment. So, with hardly any risk to Caruso, the gang's messengers were arrested. The lieutenant and the tenor became great friends, but from then on Caruso had to live with an escort: there was always the danger of a revenge attack or a reprisal, and he was by now too valuable a commodity on the stage.

Sending Caruso a second demand for payment just a few days after the first had been a bad mistake; Don Vito Cascio Ferro wouldn't have allowed his men to make a similar false step. From the moment he'd arrived in America he realized that if he could succeed in bringing the various gangs of the Black Hand under single control, his power would be immense. So the boss set to work building alliances, but it was far from easy; he had to deal with common bandits who didn't obey any rules, very different from the disciplined and obedient foot soldiers in the Sicilian Mafia. Also, America, with its vast spaces and its tumultuous economy, was not an ideal ambience for Don Vito's undertaking. And two further obstacles lay in his path.

The first was Joe Petrosino's investigations and his team of undercover agents. The second problem was back in Italy, where the trial for the murder of Emanuele Notarbartolo had caused serious damage to the innermost structures of the Mafia organization.

Don Vito left behind some of his men in America, giving them precise instructions about the management of his various business affairs, and turned his attention to Sicily. The best approach was to tackle the problems one by one, starting with the most urgent.

A Right Honourable Member Accused

Emanuele Notarbartolo was highly respected, and his murder provoked wide consternation. His body had been found close to the railway lines a few kilometres outside Palermo; it was full of knife wounds and battered by the fall to the ground after being pushed out of the window of a moving train.

An unenergetic inquiry held by the court in Palermo had led to charges being brought against the train driver and one Giuseppe Fontana, who was identified as the actual murderer. But Giuseppe Fontana was no ordinary murderer: he was a man of honour from the Villabate Family, a mafioso trusted by Don Vito Cascio Ferro, who was always ready to call on his services.

For three years the inquiry dragged on aimlessly and ineffectually. The judge who had been appointed to oversee the inquiry in Palermo in 1896 had thought of closing the investigation and releasing the accused. This plan would have gone smoothly had it not been for a prisoner who, a short while after this, requested an interview with the police, maintaining that he had some precise information about Notarbartolo's murder. With new evidence pointing to them, the train driver and Fontana were charged for the second time, but now there had also emerged in the shadows behind them a new figure, a member of the Italian Parliament no less: the Right Honourable Raffaele Palizzolo, whose power was such that he had been returned to Parliament uninterruptedly for sixteen years and was indeed still a sitting MP.

In the mean time Notarbartolo's eldest son Leopoldo had taken up arms on behalf of his murdered father: in the course of a long naval career he would become an admiral in the Italian fleet, but at the time he was still a young midshipman. He put all his energy into obtaining justice and succeeded in stirring up public opinion. He pressed vigorously and successfully for the trial to be moved from Palermo to Milan, and on 17th November 1899 took the witness box with his evidence prepared. He knew that a crime had to be reconstructed and re-enacted in the courtroom: only by making it real again with documentary evidence and testimony would it mean anything for the jury. Leopoldo's stand in the witness box was reported in detail in the *Corriere della Sera*, and then by all the other papers. He spoke openly of the Mafia and of the hidden machinations behind the banking scandal which reached as high as the government itself. He roundly accused Palizzolo of instigating his father's murder. Public opinion in the country was shocked: Leopoldo had revealed not only the extent and danger of the Mafia and its contacts with politicians, he had openly accused an important politician of belonging to the secret hierarchy of the organization.

Shortly after the young naval officer had testified in court, the Italian Parliament voted by a large majority to open a trial against Palizzolo, who was sent to the Ucciardone prison. So the country's first great trial against the Mafia opened in 1901, once again far from Sicily, in Bologna. Public opinion increasingly wanted to know more about this hidden underground world. It was no longer simply a matter of a killer and a train driver who belonged to some local Mafia gang; now a Member of Parliament stood handcuffed beside them in the dock.

Palizzolo's lawyers adopted an ill-considered tactic in his defence: they chose to deny the existence of the Mafia, asserting instead that it was all an invention of certain Socialist circles. But the jury didn't believe them and decided the accused were guilty. In Sicily meanwhile, opinion was gathering against the trial and its possible outcome: the island's intellectuals, politicians and industrialists – including the extremely powerful Florio Family – rallied to defend regional pride. Some declared themselves offended by the accusation that the Mafia had any influence on the island's day-to-day life; for others the idea that the shadow of the organization fell across everything and everyone was absurd. Behind this mass reaction to the trial the theory began to circulate that Palizzolo was the victim of a plot against Sicily and its inhabitants, cooked up by Northerners and the government in Rome. This wave of public feeling reached its climax at the same time as Palizzolo's lawyers appealed against the guilty verdict: the Court of Appeal duly allowed the appeal. Apparently dismissing the numerous procedural and technical problems involved in the decision, they ordered a new trial to go ahead, this time in Florence. It opened in September 1903, ten years after Notarbartolo's murder. The hearings continued for ten months, at the end of which the court acquitted the accused on grounds of insufficient evidence.

Sicily greeted the news of Palizzolo's liberation in triumph. Don Vito Cascio Ferro had already arranged secretly to send Notarbartolo's murderer Fontana to America, where he would manage a drugstore and oversee some unfinished business matters with the Black Hand gangs. Now Don Vito could turn his attention to the real business of Palizzolo, and once again make sure that everything changed so that nothing would change. He decided attack was the best strategy, to transform Palizzolo not just into a martyr, but a hero who would redeem Sicily and lead a new mass movement in the island. Don Vito was after all no stranger to techniques of rousing the masses: he knew how to mix ideas and slogans in such a way that even the most recalcitrant came out of the houses to cheer.

After Palizzolo had been acclaimed and applauded throughout the island, Don Vito arranged for him to undertake a tour of the United States.[11] He made sure a large crowd was there

---

11 "It is grievous to have to confess that forty-eight years on from 1860, in the land which gave birth to Romagnosi, Beccaria, Vico and Filangieri, the administration of justice is sadly deficient. Look at the innumerable scandals involving trials which take place in every important city, the inquiries ordered by the ministry, the grave revelations and debates held in both Houses of Parliament, and the beneficial reforms initiated, to universal acclaim, by the young minister Orlando – a native of Palermo – who has shown himself to be a great statesman and to whom I ask you – for I see many from his constituency in the audience – to send a cordial greeting in the hope that his work will be remembered with gratitude for a long time to come. But will Orlando's reforms be enough to heal the sicknesses which afflict Italian justice?" From a speech given by Raffaele Palizzolo in America.

to greet the politician who stepped off the ship in New York on 8th June 1908. The American secret services had been alerted to Palizzolo's arrival by their Italian counterparts, but when he disembarked they could do little more than hold him for a couple of hours in a room on Ellis Island. This was the land of liberty, and they had no legal grounds to detain him. He had been acquitted at his trial, he was a free citizen, and he had come – travelling first-class with his staff – to undertake a lecture tour of the country. Undercover agents followed him as he moved from Chicago to St Louis, Pittsburgh to Boston, Philadelphia to New Orleans.

All Don Vito's most secret and seemingly irreproachable contacts were instructed to protect Palizzolo and make sure that the halls where he lectured were full. He gave the same speech everywhere he went. The Sicilians must organize themselves, he declared, and form a state within the State with its own rules. He proposed the idea of setting up a "Sicilian Union" which would defend the immigrants against all the accusations and prejudices others laid at their door. He never named names, preferring to let his audiences guess who these "others" might be. His speeches seemed clear and irreproachable, but they were full of ambiguous turns of phrase which contained hidden messages. The proposal for a "Sicilian Union" concealed an invitation for political engagement on the part of the Mafia. Those who could read between Palizzolo's lines understood what he was really saying.

Palizzolo had been saved from a prison sentence by a carefully orchestrated mass protest. Now he was touring the United States appealing to Sicilian immigrants to think of politics as a fundamental tool. Camouflaged among the immigrants who flocked to his speeches there were those who could understand what he really meant. If they wanted to develop, then the new American godfathers had also to be politicians, and not just in the sense of maintaining contacts with those in power. They had to learn how to create the wide social support which would protect their businesses and conceal their crimes.

Sicilian Mission

The American secret services followed Palizzolo's lecture tour and kept cuttings of the articles on him published in the immigrant press. But his speeches were too carefully crafted to let slip even a hint of criminal activity. Petrosino and his team were also tracking the ex-parliamentarian's every move. Perhaps it was now that the celebrated police lieutenant began to understand what or who was in control of the criminal underworld. Faced by men such as Palizzolo, the rooms full of applauding crowds, the welcoming toasts, Petrosino saw that the investigation needed to change method and widen its focus. It was pointless trying to find the real faces of the Black Hand among the crowds of Palizzolo's supporters. Petrosino understood the Sicilian dialect, as he knew other dialects spoken in the rest of southern Italy, but he wasn't merely linguistically prepared: he was capable of understanding the culture which was transmitted through a language. He was able to grasp the nuances of concepts which were communicated and see that a single phrase could have two different meanings depending on who heard it. He was able to decipher the hidden messages behind seemingly innocuous words.[12]

His investigations made him sure there was a mind working behind the racket, a brain bringing the various gangs together into one organization. The criminals who belonged to the Black Hand made themselves indistinguishable from other immigrants, but the man who controlled them was not so close. He could even still be where the Mafia originated – back in Sicily.

Petrosino must have had a rock-solid conviction that this was the case, since he started to look for financial support towards a mission which would strike at the heart of the Mafia. He was by now an eminent police chief; his career was a list of successes which had won him praise and renown. Americans liked him because he was self-made and had battled his way up

12 "The important thing about Petrosino is that he was quintessentially anti-Mafia. If you did an analysis of the Italian-American experience, the children of those giants, the immigrants, the numbers would show that there is a great disproportion: there are many more Joe Petrosino types – not as policemen, but as legitimate, honest Italian-Americans – than there are Mafia types." Mario Cuomo.

through the ranks. He had won the trust of men like President Theodore Roosevelt. So when he began to ask for financial support many were generous in contributing, above all those Italian immigrants, like the butcher Costa, who'd started up successful businesses and were increasingly vulnerable to extortion rackets. Petrosino accumulated a pile of dollars, set sail from New York across the Atlantic and the Mediterranean, and disembarked in Palermo. He was alone.

He'd judged that going with men from his Italian Bureau would only have attracted attention. He didn't even ask for the collaboration of the Italian Police and the local authorities, since he believed that the police and legal system in the island were corrupt and infiltrated by the Mafia. Hadn't Leopoldo Notarbartolo just a few years before referred to the chief of police in Palermo as a "Mafia chief of police"?

Petrosino thought he had taken all the necessary precautions in going to hunt down the brain behind the criminal underworld, but an article appeared out of the blue in the *New York Herald Tribune* on why he was in Sicily and what he hoped to find out. Unperturbed by the risks he was taking, he continued his investigations: his mission was now public knowledge, but he believed he'd already made good progress and had some useful cards to play.

Don Vito Cascio Ferro didn't need to read an article in a New York daily newspaper to find out what Petrosino might be up to on his home territory. All he had to do was to set his *picciotti* like bloodhounds on the trail of dollars Petrosino was leaving behind him. In 1909 Sicily was still wretchedly poor and dollars were out of the ordinary. Farm-labourers, carters, blacksmiths, shepherds – all those who'd been paid by Petrosino for the help and information they'd provided – came to change the notes they'd been given. The game moved into the open: Don Vito knew and Petrosino knew that he knew. The police lieutenant and the boss of bosses circled increasingly closer to each other. But then the godfather made a pre-emptive move.

What actually occurred has, as so often happens with Mafia crimes in Sicily, got clouded over as rumours pass from person to person: at each stage someone adds a detail to weaken or

44

lessen or mock or just distort the events and the men involved. The best-known version goes like this: Don Vito sent his men to invite Petrosino to supper in a *trattoria* in Piazza Marina. Opposite the *trattoria* was a magnolia tree; today its thick-clustering branches create an interior dome of shadow. Petrosino accepted. It appears that Don Vito told him that, yes, he was the godfather. When they'd finished dinner, Petrosino took his leave; as he exited he was shot down by Don Vito's henchmen standing in the shade behind the tall magnolia tree, as tall as the apartment blocks in central Palermo.

Today there is no plaque, no obelisk, and certainly no statue to help recall the Italian-American police lieutenant from New York who back in 1909 managed by himself to discover who was at the top of the Mafia hierarchy. But if you look closely along the low wall which marks the perimeter of the Piazza Marina public gardens, you can find Petrosino's name carved like a graffiti mark with a nail or penknife a few inches above ground level. Next to the name there is a cross more as a sign of his death than as a pious gesture. Even on the exact spot where he fell there is disagreement – different places in the piazza have been indicated by those who've written about the event. So the memory of Petrosino's murder has disappeared along with the man himself.

Petrosino had made several mistakes because he'd failed to appreciate how widespread the secret society of the Mafia actually was. He hadn't understood that it wasn't simply a matter of hunting down the controlling brain behind it all. But he committed an even more obvious error, perhaps because he relied too much on his own admittedly exceptional investigative skills: he'd risked his life before he'd had time to communicate what he'd found out to others. If his success in identifying and tracking down Don Vito Cascio Ferro had been handed on to subsequent investigators, the long struggle against the Mafia would have taken a large step forwards.[13]

---

13 "Investigating organized crime entails two risks. The first is that if you are identified as an investigator you are in danger of being killed. The second is that if this happens then all the knowledge which has been acquired in the course of the investigation is lost." General Angiolo Pellegrini.

In the archives of the American House of Congress there's a 1909 film which is listed in the catalogue as "A policeman's funeral". It's a shot of a street taken with one of the early movie cameras fixed on a tripod, with occasional breaks each time a new reel of film had to be inserted. It shows a vast and solemn procession, with thousands of policemen on horseback and on foot, officials in ceremonial dress, the coffin draped in mourning colours.[14] It's an impressive event, taking place in the heart of New York watched by a huge crowd. Such was its importance that it was thought worth recording for posterity: a cameraman and his equipment were hired – at the time this would have been expensive – to film the procession for the archives, as a document or testimony more vivid than any stone monument could ever be. The film has aroused the interest of the archivists in the Library of Congress where it is kept, and they have attempted to do further research on it, but despite their efforts the description in the catalogue has remained the same non-committal "A policeman's funeral. New York 1909".

Yet the funeral procession in the film can only be Petrosino's, an event which was so significant for the Italian immigrant community, as well as for New York as a whole. It was an event which brought together the various nationalities and races which had emigrated to the metropolis, as if to test their relations.

The body lay in state in a room belonging to the Republican League club on Lafayette Street in the third district. Twenty thousand people queued patiently from dawn to pay homage to the murdered policeman. The room was to open only in the afternoon, so the newspaper reporters had ample time to observe and describe the mass of people waiting to enter. There were many Italians, obviously, but the long line also contained, as they mention in their accounts, Russians, Armenians, Greeks, Bohemians, Slavs, Turks, Syrians, Irish, Jews, Scandinavians, Chinese and blacks. When she saw how many people were

---

14   "His body was flown back to the US. A funeral was held for him in Manhat-
     tan, and I think more than 250,000 people went to that funeral. He was the
     first Italian-American to be killed in the line of duty." Bernard B. Kerik,
     former New York City Police Commissioner.

waiting to file in, Petrosino's widow decided to open the room much earlier than planned. Floral tributes sent by clubs and associations and private individuals flooded Lafayette Street. Next to the coffin lay the wreath from the seventeen police officers and three detectives in Petrosino's squad, the Italian Bureau; lilies, roses and carnations tied together with a ribbon on which the one word "Comrade" was written. When the long procession was ready to set off, the police band struck up Chopin's *Funeral March* while the carriage with Mrs Petrosino positioned itself immediately behind the hearse. Six police lieutenants walked alongside the hearse, together with a guard of honour made up of twelve members from the city's traffic squad, who were to carry the coffin into St Patrick's Cathedral.

Father Ferrari and Father Polozzo had been called from the parishes in Little Italy to celebrate mass with the Revd John F. Kearney. It was a solemn ceremony with a hundred-strong children's choir; when it was over, the procession made its way towards the cemetery, even longer than it had been on its way to the church. On either side of the streets, the New York crowd watched in silence as the long parade passed by: twelve hundred police officers, five bands, the representatives of sixty local Italian immigrant associations, as well as ordinary folk from every section of the immigrant community.

Ellis Island

Many of the immigrants who watched in astonishment Petrosino's coffin pass by were recent arrivals, but they'd still heard of him. He was the most famous Italian immigrant in the city. They still had vivid memories of being kept in quarantine on Ellis Island and of the undignified medical checks they'd been forced to undergo. And before that, they could recall the voyage over the seas with the ship shifting and rolling as it made its way towards their new homeland. For such men and women the ocean was still frightening, much as it had been several centuries before for the crew that sailed with Columbus. The world was still terrifyingly large.

A few years before, in 1906, a small boy called Salvatore Lucania and his parents had embarked on one of those rusting steamers. In the ship's hold the families slept one above the other on stacked-up beds. People got seasick, gave birth, fell ill and died, never moving from their beds. The air was unbreathable.

Salvatore was nine years old: he realized the need for a space up on deck, even if that meant being in the cold and breathing in the air damp with salt water – at least it was clean. During the month-long voyage he learnt to identify the other passengers who were not, like him, from Sicily: Poles, Turks, Greeks, people who were accustomed to enduring hunger and fatigue. There were Jews escaping from the terrors of the pogroms, who had seen their own homes burnt to the ground and who had trailed across half of Europe to reach the sea.

All the passengers were escaping from lives which were not worth living or from certain death. They had not, like many of the immigrants of a previous generation, planned their journeys and paid for them with their savings in the hope of reaching a better land; they were not, like Garibaldi's ex-soldiers who had come to fight in the American Civil War, in search of battles and glory. These people from southern Europe, packed together on slow boats making their painful way across rough seas, were simply searching for a life.

Up on deck Salvatore watched as the women hung the washing out to dry and the men slaughtered the livestock. The calves were still living when they embarked – in this way a fresh supply of meat for making soup was guaranteed. Imitating the adults, Salvatore ate his portion in silence, his hands dirty with rust and a bitter taste, like salt mixed with iron, in his mouth. The life of the community onboard only paused to mark in silence the funerals at sea of their fellow passengers who'd not managed to survive. As the ship's engines throbbed on, two centuries met in one great exodus of populations from the Old to the New World.

There were countless Italian children onboard those ships: Carlos Marcello, just ten months old, was one of them, Francesco Costello, four years old, and Giuseppe Bonanno, only a little older, were others. And there was a small Jewish boy by the name of Maier Suchowljansky.

This last name proved impenetrable for the immigration officers on Ellis Island: they kept asking his parents to repeat it but only succeeded in understanding "Lansky". The family was fleeing from Poland: not only were they impoverished Poles, they were impoverished Jewish Poles. But the boy was healthy, and finally he got through the border controls with the name of Meyer Lansky. In New York he discovered that his ghetto bordered on the Italian one, and he found himself playing in the streets with Salvatore Lucania. They soon became the best of friends.

Their new homeland, despite its size, was already concerned about how to restrict or stop the floods of immigrants. Well-to-do Americans, conveniently forgetting that they were the children of immigrants themselves, were scared of all the others now arriving in their thousands; the fear changed into hate; and the hate led to outbreaks of racist violence. Ordinary people decided to resist the newcomers who brought crime, prostitution and disease with them; these ordinary people also had the duty every four years of electing their governors, who were asked to ensure that there were tight controls against the foreigners.[15]

In the 1900s many Italians had emigrated to Tunisia: it wasn't America, it couldn't be called a "new world", but it was easy to reach and you could start a new life there. Several Tunisian ports provided Don Vito Cascio Ferro with bases for his fleet of fishing boats engaged in the illicit trade in stolen livestock and other goods. But the Mafia trade started to displease the local authorities. The country was under French control, and the government in Paris sent out some officials with the task of driving out ten thousand Italians from the colony. The soldiers and police employed to do the job didn't use a light hand: they forced women and children to abandon their homes without

---

15 "Historically, in every ethnic group that has migrated, other than the honest people seeking a new life in the United States, there was always a small percentage that were just criminals. In fact, with each wave of immigration, those criminals actually victimized their own community." Thomas V. Fuentes.

question, they requisitioned and closed down shops, they hunted down criminals. Many Mafia Families had to make a sudden escape. Their network organized crossings to America for their own *picciotti*, with their wives and children following on. But suddenly the United States government issued a severe restriction on the number of immigrants allowed into the country: in the course of 1906 Italians practically found themselves denied entry. The ten thousand chased out of Tunisia, criminals or poor, found themselves for the most part sucked into the illegal-immigration racket run by the Mafia.

Don Calogero Vizzini

If they were to survive in the United States, illegal or clandestine immigrants needed a protector. The way this "protection" worked is well described in an American silent film, *The Italian*. The hero is a young man who leaves behind a picture-postcard Italy, full of people in holiday costume dancing to the accompaniment of guitars. The audience never learns why he wants to leave such a splendid life to emigrate and end up as a shoeshine man in New York. The episodes in America are dominated by a godfather surrounded by a court of thugs and flatterers. The screenwriters present this local boss as a respectable middle-class citizen who is fond of his little granddaughter and lives in a large, well-run house. We learn nothing about his activities or how he earns his money or how he's managed to clean himself up after the dirt and dust and cut-throat gangs which roam the immigrant ghettoes, nothing of how he's acquired so much power. The poor Italian shoeshine boy has need of him, seeks him out and asks for his help.

The first thread in weaving the web of favours came from below: it was the immigrant who found himself in difficulties and so set the mechanism of protection in motion. Once he had reached a certain degree of strength, all the godfather had to do was spread his net round him and wait for the little fish to swim in. The godfather even had the luxury of choosing the ones he wanted to keep and tossing the others back into the sea. Among the millions of Italians who needed to build a new life in the new world there would always be some recent arrivals who were ready to get caught in the Mafia's nets.

Alongside fictional films like *The Italian*, there were also those which showed the reality. The Library of Congress in Washington has in its collections a short reel which is attributed to Thomas Alva Edison himself. The catalogue entry says that it was shot in 1903 in Siracusa in Sicily. Edison was travelling in Europe with the aim of trying to sell his film cameras in the new market opened up by the coming of the cinema. It's thanks to his business sense that we now have a short documentary film showing a long row of women hard at work in a laundry, rubbing the dirty clothes with rapid gestures made even jerkier by the low number of frames per second in the film of the period. Towards the middle of the sequence a man appears in the top right-hand corner of the frame. He doesn't appear to be an inquisitive passer-by who just happens to look in; he has all the air of someone in charge of the women employees. In charge of them and exploiting their labour.

In early twentieth-century Sicily new godfathers continued to emerge from the so-called *gabellotti*. *Gabella*, or tax, is a word which comes into modern Italian from either medieval Latin or the Arabic *qabala* – it refers to the tax which is paid to acquire the right to farm a piece of land. *Gabellotti* were the parasitical tenant farmers on the great estates. In learning to become godfathers, such men extended their rule over all the forms of production on the land, and on all the products – on flour and on the bread which was baked from it, on horses and carters and herdsmen, on salt and sulphur and the water which watered the fields and filled the drinking troughs and laundries.

When Edison's camera was filming the washerwomen of Siracusa, Calogero Vizzini was twenty-six years of age. He had two brothers who were both priests, Don Salvatore and Don Giovanni. They had every right to the title "Don", but Calogero also aspired to it, not in its religious and canonical form, but in the secularized version based on a person's social standing and criminal power. Being born in Villalba at the centre of an unchanging world of great estates didn't seem to him to restrict his ambitions: the long miles of scorched yellow fields did not make the prospect of power appear more distant.

There were also two bishops in his family: his uncle, Monsignor Giuseppe Scarlata, and his nephew, Monsignor Giuseppe Vizzini. Calogero never missed mass and was always given a prominent position in church processions. He lit the candles on the high altar and stood close enough to breathe in the incense.

In the history of the Mafia there is not one mafioso who has been a self-declared atheist. Giovanni Falcone pointed out that "mafiosi follow traditional Christian values more closely than average believers". In the same way, mafiosi have often found clergy who are willing to give them spiritual aid. Traditional religious behaviour promotes invisibility: a mafioso stands out more if he doesn't attend Mass or novenas accompanied by the whole family. There have been mafiosi who have played an active part in parish life, participating in assemblies as well as in the torch-lit processions against drugs organized by Christian youth associations. Perhaps their fellow churchgoers didn't know that the boys in those other families were apprentice *picciotti* who sold contraband cigarettes on street corners, or that the local pawnshop was run from their homes with loans offered at extortionate rates of interest. Or perhaps they knew but thought such matters need not prevent them looking after their souls, hoping perhaps that their religious practices would eventually lead them to see the error of their ways. When all is said and done, the laws of God and of religious faith are not those of men: it is possible for an honest priest to find himself dealing with mafiosi who are also genuine believers.

The fugitive boss Pietro Aglieri had a chapel built for himself in his hideaway. It contained pictures of the Madonna and of Jesus, a kind of altar with a crucifix and flowers and candles underneath. There were dozens of sacred images on display, and even benches for kneeling down to pray, just like in church. Aglieri regularly read the Catholic weekly magazine *Famiglia Cristiana* as well as the Bible. In short, he was an active and devout Christian and as such a perfectly normal Mafia type.

In 2002 the boss Antonino Giuffré, regarded as the right-hand man of the boss of bosses, Bernardo Provenzano, announced he was sorry for his past deeds; his decision to collaborate with the police had come to him, he said, from watching the ceremony for the beatification of Padre Pio on television.

A century earlier, Calogero Vizzini's brothers had belonged, together with Don Sturzo, to that wing of the Church which tried to protect working people from the dangers both of socialism and unbridled capitalism. Leo XIII's encyclical *Rerum novarum* had had a profound influence on the Church: Catholic movements attracted an increasing number of clergy who appealed to the authorities to favour small and middle-ranking property owners, to ensure that women – like the washerwomen in Edison's film – and children did not become victims of unrestrained exploitation, and to encourage the observance of religious holidays.

Rural savings banks and Catholic workers' associations sprang up, but the encyclical also worked to ensure that modern progress did not lead to revolution. This was an aim with which Calogero Vizzini was in perfect agreement. Under the protective cover of such a powerful Family, he felt at liberty to seize every opportunity and take his share of whatever was going.

Within such a Family he had learnt to think like a leader of men. The Italian State had irrevocably abandoned Sicily to its fate. The island's representatives shut themselves up against the sirocco in their north-facing rooms in the palaces of Palermo and the other cities. On holiday evenings they would venture out to receptions held in the gardens of the local aristocracy's villas. Swarms of local officials saved them from having any direct contact with ordinary Sicilians. In the countryside the only real authority belonged to the godfathers. A network of favours, large and small, trapped the whole island and influenced even the election results: the Mafia made sure their voices could be heard through the deputies sent to represent Sicily in the Parliament in Rome.

Calogero Vizzini quickly grew up in this atmosphere. He disguised himself as a trade-union activist, and organized co-operatives, with the blessing of the Church.[16] The *Rerum novarum* was the encyclical of modernity, of the new century and of a new mentality. Extraordinary things were occurring with the advent of the new century: everything seemed to be changing. Vizzini succeeded in riding the changes: in the end he was known as "Don Calogero" more than his four clergymen relatives had ever been.[17] He became a new kind of godfather, mafioso and trade unionist, a figure of authority and a demagogue, capable of uniting around himself a vast consensus which rested on the solid alliances he had built with the political world, while in secret he presided over the initiation rituals for new *picciotti*, with the pricking of fingers and the hot drop of blood and the devotional image. History enabled Don Calogero to wear the costumes of the politician and the trade unionist, and he continued to dress up in them whenever the appropriate occasion presented itself.

The Great War

The New World too was creating its own type of godfather. In New York the most powerful godfather controlled the docks. He disliked the title "Don" and preferred to be called the "Boss" instead – it sounded more American and was more appropriate for his business affairs in the city.

Uncouth and cruel, Joe the Boss Masseria had become fat from the food and alcohol which were so plentiful and easy to obtain in the United States. He passed the day slumped in an armchair; when the evening came, he had to be helped up by his *picciotti*. Bright lads, all of them – and quick with their guns too. They'd done spells in prison. They knew how to kill a man. Their names were Salvatore Lucania, Vito Genovese,

---

16 "There were pretensions of grandeur in the Mafia, they thought of themselves as recreating the Roman legions. Maybe that insulated them from the reality of the fact that they were pretty vicious criminals." Rudolph Giuliani.

17 "Vizzini's life was always out of the ordinary. He never married. He was only interested in giving orders and in being shown respect. But this is also true of all godfathers. They become powerful when they exercise command." General Angiolo Pellegrini.

Frank Costello, Albert Anastasia and Carlo Gambino. They were all aged about twenty when the Great War broke out in Europe. They could have been called up, but America was still keeping its distance from the conflict, and their old homeland Italy didn't think itself ready to intervene. There was no cause for concern, the battles in Europe had not yet turned into a world war.

Their boss, Joe Masseria, was certain he was the undisputed authority in the criminal underworld – to all intents and purposes, the boss of bosses. But he didn't realize how cunning the *picciotti* were who surrounded him. He thought they were useful for delivering and collecting, always ready for action if needed – but only for that. After all, they were *picciotti* on the lowest rungs of the Mafia hierarchy. The boss hadn't caught on to the fact that they were more loyal to themselves as a group than they were to him. They were obsequious and respectful in his presence as if he were a sultan; it didn't come to his ears that they were nicknamed by others the "Young Turks". For the present they were sitting in rows at the school of Joe the Boss. A godfather after all educates his men in a life of crime; like any other secret society, the Mafia has its own school to train its younger members.[18]

---

18 "When the Mafia is most united, then training is given to those who are going to become men of honour. A school exists. In the Calabrian Mafia one becomes a member because one belongs to a Mafia Family. The son of a mafioso has to become one himself; from the moment he's born and his upbringing begins, he's a member. I remember very well a thirteen-year-old lad, whose father was a mafioso who had decided to collaborate with the police. The son didn't want to leave his birthplace – he said everyone respected him there because his father belonged to the Mafia. I managed to persuade him that respect is not something you earn by belonging to something, but because of what you do. But it was an uphill struggle to make him understand this because, like all children in such Families, he'd been brought up to become a mafioso. In Sicily it's different. There, apart from the sons of bosses who are destined to follow in their fathers' footsteps, the typical man of honour enters the organization when he's practically an adult. He comes under the supervision of a branch of the Mafia who control a certain area. They want to see how he behaves, how he functions, if he's got a natural feeling for Mafia principles. He's given various small crimes to perform as a test. On the threshold of adulthood he's shown what the Mafia is, what the concepts of respect and honour entail. Then he enters the ranks. There's always a long period of training in the Mafia gangs when he's kept under observation and examination by the older mafiosi. Only subsequently does he become a 'man' within the organization." General Angiolo Pellegrini.

The real Young Turks were a group established in Geneva in 1891, supporters of liberal ideas with which they hoped to shake up the Ottoman Empire. History was on their side: in the course of only a few years they'd grown strong enough to be able to depose the sultan, Abdul Hamid II. The "Young Turks" at the court of Joe the Boss Masseria also had their own ideas about running the Mafia empire. But they didn't tell anyone what they were thinking – their view of things was not the same as that of the fat sultan they were serving.

In Chicago another godfather was similarly so taken up with the demands of his business affairs that he had no time to spare for the young men he used for carrying out his crimes. Big Jim Colosimo had created a fortune for himself by controlling the city's prostitution and gambling rackets. He'd opened Colosimo's Café and had even managed to get Caruso to come and sing in it. It became a fashionable nightclub, frequented by gangsters and industrialists, a place where the city's two worlds could meet and make contact – the ordinary world where decent people worked for their living, and the underworld with its gangsters who had business of their own to manage.

Meanwhile immigrants continued to flood into the United States through Ellis island. The influx seemed endless, epoch-making. In the fish markets, on the building sites where new skyscrapers were rising up, along the quays on the dockside, among the crowds on the pavements where the street vendors set up their stalls, young men were emerging who were determined to get ahead in the new American Mafia. Since they'd set foot in their new country, they'd attempted to camouflage themselves; as soon as they could, they changed their name, sometimes their family names too. Joe Profaci, Joe Magliocco, Joe Bonanno wanted to rise up the ranks by fighting in the streets of Little Italy.

Then Italy decided to enter the war: the call went out for emigrants to return. This posed a serious problem; countries where the emigrants had settled – the United States, Brazil and Argentina – didn't want men who were classified and pursued as deserters in their own populations. For American morality the idea was unacceptable. But for the immigrants, returning to fight meant losing their jobs, leaving their families behind and, most likely, never coming back. The national governments were deaf to all pleading: those who'd been called up had to return to their own countries. Many asked for help in going into hiding; the godfathers were ready to oblige. Europe was putting increasing pressure on the United States to enter the war. A delegation from the Italian government arrived in Washington to discuss how many cannons, how many men and how many dollars were needed for the Italian front. The gift of these was obviously out of the question; they would need to negotiate a loan.

When the United States finally entered the war, there was suddenly a flood of money for arms. Many Italian-Americans enrolled voluntarily in the forces, like Fiorello LaGuardia, a young man who was just beginning to get noticed on the political scene. He served as a pilot in Italy, gunning and bombing the Austrian lines from the air. He was later awarded a medal for valour by Victor Emmanuel III.

The infantrymen who set out for Europe in their thousands were given a promise that in the case of their death their widows would receive a pension which would allow the families they had left behind to survive. There were brothers who found themselves fighting in the same battles; one serving with the Italian army, the other with the Americans.

The first American soldier to be killed in Europe was in fact an Italian, an immigrant who had become a US citizen: Rudolph Rubino, private first class in the American army serving in France. He was killed in Dannes-Camiers by a German bomb at 10.55 in the morning on 4th September 1917, while helping out with the rest of his section in a British field hospital. He was part of a mobile unit, the United States Base Hospital No. 5. His body was shipped back to America and his funeral was held in the church of Our Lady of Pompeii in Little Italy. Three other men who were with him died of the wounds they'd received from the bomb: the commander of the unit, Lieutenant William T. Fitzsimmons, and two privates, Oscar C. Tugo and Leslie G. Woods.

By now the war had become a world war – a war various countries had been waiting and preparing for with armaments, munitions and victory plans. The Mafia too was not unready: any war brought new business, and this was the biggest one yet. The fronts where the war was being fought were in need of everything: weapons, vehicles, fuel and meat, men and animals.

Don Calogero Vizzini was the undisputed king of cattle-rustling in his territory. He made profits he could hardly have dreamt of from the new opportunities in the trade in stolen livestock. He contacted some high-ranking officers in the Italian army and became its official supplier. All the horses, mules and donkeys which vanished overnight from the Sicilian countryside turned up the following day in military wagons: they'd been sold, as could be read on the officially stamped delivery note, "for military purposes".

Among his network of "friends of friends", Vizzini found someone who needed to pay back a favour and who was also in a position to persuade officials to turn a blind eye to what was going on. The result was that the same animals filed past the military registrar twice, multiplying as if by miracle, and multiplying Vizzini's profits too. He was even arrested in 1917 for having sold the same horses and mules twice over; he was brought to trial in Sicily and promptly acquitted. The celebrations which broke out on his acquittal reinforced his power.

But there was an even more profitable business than supplying donkeys and mules to the armed forces: sulphur. Up in the frozen trenches of the Alps, every soldier knew that if the supply of sulphur suddenly ran out, then the fighting would have to stop or they'd have to resort to fighting with bayonets and swords. Without sulphur the guns wouldn't fire in the First World War.

Now Don Calogero Vizzini happened to be the tenant in control of large deposits of sulphur among the sun-scorched Sicilian hills. Just like the relationship between the tenant farmers and the great landowners, the man who held the lease on the sulphur mines replaced the real owner, who merely drew an income from the money made from the lessee's exploitation of the resource. And, in the name of business, it was a ruthless exploitation. Even in distant Sicily the war was the priority, and the war needed sulphur.

Sulphur was practically a Sicilian monopoly. In the underground mines the workers slaved away, naked because of the heat and the mineral dust. The men who mined the sulphur were not the bottommost rung of the industry; below came the *carusi*, the young boys who were enslaved to the slaves, totally dependent on them. Despite all the Church's appeals, children – sometimes not even ten years old – were sent to work in the sulphur mines. They were sold to the miners by their parents; they were subject to every form of violence, including sexual abuse.

The world market for sulphur was huge, and the war served to increase its price continually. This was one of Don Calogero's most successful lines. As a godfather he exploited the opportunity and amassed huge profits. Despite this, his wealth appeared to mean little to him: he continued to live in a modest house with his sister, who was devoted to him and ran his home.

While the war was continuing, while nerve gas blowing about on the winds was decimating the front lines, revolution broke out in Russia and Communism seemed about to spread round the world. The politicians and generals were immediately aware of the danger and planned to send entire armies of battle-weary soldiers to fight against the Bolsheviks. But the initiative was feeble and lacking in conviction: the few forces who went to combat the Communists came back in defeat. Every nation turned in on itself to count its dead, to heal its wounded.

But ideas moved more quickly than the ships and trains which were taking the demobbed soldiers back home. Communist groups sprang up even in the United States, where several of them united to form a new political party.

The Great War was over, in part thanks to American soldiers and American dollars. American troops paraded in front of the Duomo in Milan or entered alongside the Italians in Trieste and Fiume and the other cities which had been won from the Austrians. Some newspaper reports comment on the derisory whistles which greeted the Italian soldiers while the Americans received only warm applause. Official history in its version of the events, however, preferred to gloss over the American contribution. Even the Colosseum in Rome was co-opted for propaganda purposes, and opened and decked out for a victory ceremony. However, the head of the Italian forces, General Diaz, still felt obliged to visit New York, where crowds of Italian-Americans acclaimed him.

Italy had won the war, but it was exhausted. In its need to find fresh resources to drive Austrian and German troops from its territory, it had incurred debts towards America – and debts, especially those incurred in wartime, have to be repaid. The immigrants considered it their duty to contribute to a fund to pay back the Italian debt towards the United States; their former homeland hadn't a penny, and accepted the contributions which arrived from Italian-American associations. The collection was seen favourably by public opinion in America: patriotism – and respect for the dollar – always won plaudits.

For a brief period there was a new atmosphere of trust between the immigrants and their motherland. Some of the wealthier among them sent money directly to the men they regarded as the heroes of the Italian victory: Attilio Masone in Argentina, for example, sent fifty thousand lire to the poet and patriot Gabriele d'Annunzio to support the Italian cause in Fiume. But the euphoria of a victory which had left such crippling poverty in its wake soon evaporated. In Italy a period was ushered in when the outbreak of revolution seemed just around the corner. For two whole years Sicily was shaken by an occupation of the estates and a struggle against the great landowners. The soldiers who had waded through mud to storm enemy trenches, who had disembowelled enemy soldiers with their bayonets or cut their throats before they could resist, had now returned home and were marching in demonstrations which once more, as in the days of the Sicilian Fasci, demanded that the land be given to the people who worked the land. They were perhaps more determined; they were certainly more aware of what they were demanding.

The Mafia remained unperturbed. Don Antonio Milletarì, agronomist and godfather, decided to put on the Socialist cassock and take part in the demonstrations, marching alongside the same peasants whose livestock he'd stolen, the same labourers he exploited in the businesses and firms which were under his control. Don Antonio Ortoleva didn't bat an eyelid at the creation of a strong and well-organized Italian Communist party. He'd already established his own organization in the criminal underworld, a kind of Mafia "super government" designed to bring the different provinces together, supported by its own army of armed thugs, and even a court to examine rule-breaking and betrayals and pass the appropriate sentences.

Johnny Torrio and Al Capone

While poverty and revolutionary uprisings held Italy in their grip, the immediate post-war years in the United States seemed to hold out the promise of riches for all. And whenever there was money to be divided up, the American "cousins" were ready to make the division.

In Chicago, Big Jim Colosimo's business affairs were booming. Earning money from brothels and poker tables was proving almost too easy. Out of the blue, however, the boss got a letter – from the Black Hand. One of the gangs had dared to write to Colosimo demanding a kickback from his activities. Colosimo realized he'd let his attention wander, preoccupied as he had been in managing the city's prostitution racket, together with his lover Vittoria Moresco. Now there was a confrontation brewing and he didn't have enough "troops" to deal with it.

The boss of Chicago found himself in need of protection. He decided to appoint a right-hand man called Johnny Torrio, known as Johnny the Terrible, for the city. His well-deserved nickname had been earned in action. Colosimo heard no more from the Black Hand.

Torrio was successful in protecting the business interests of his new boss – he was so good at it that Colosimo presented him with his own bordello, already furnished and equipped with prostitutes. It was a nice gift for a young mafioso, especially one as intelligent as Johnny Torrio had already shown himself to be. He made the women in the brothel dress up as students and middle-class young ladies, with check skirts and scrubbed faces. They all looked like virgins; in just a few days the number of clients shot up. But a new money-making concern, much bigger than prostitution, was about to appear in the criminal underworld: on 16th January 1920 the 18th Amendment to the Constitution became law. People referred to it simply as "prohibition": it was prohibited to sell alcohol and to consume it in public places.

A new market opened up, fuelled by a continual demand; the clandestine supply of alcohol became a source of untold wealth for the godfathers. There was no comparison with the earnings from prostitution. For those who were quick and determined, who could distil and distribute in a continuous cycle, who were forthright about corrupting the police – especially the local squad, who might notice the insistent smell of basement distilleries wafting up from the pavements of Little Italy – there were mountains of dollars waiting to be made. But Big Jim Colosimo was slow in catching on. He held things back; he needed to be removed. The new game required everyone to be onside, especially because FBI agents were playing in the opposing team. They were only too ready to have themselves filmed whenever they made an arrest or destroyed the equipment they'd found in an illegal distillery. Their careers could only gain from the newsreels which were shown nightly in American cinemas before the main programme. Some agents were corrupt, but the others fought to the end. Transporting illegal alcohol demanded new organizational skills from the Mafia Families.

Yet Colosimo didn't understand what was at stake. There was no time to lose. Johnny Torrio asked a young man to come to Chicago from New York, where he'd become well known for his cynicism and violence. He was called Alphonse. He wasn't particularly bright, and he had a fairly serious failing: he liked to show off. But he would do – for what he had to do.

Torrio transformed him into a loyal companion-in-arms. Five months after prohibition was introduced, Alphonse Capone killed Big Jim Colosimo.

On 11th May 1920, the corpse of the one-time boss of Chicago was carried out of his nightclub. Now Johnny Torrio the Terrible and Al Capone Scarface could dedicate themselves to the illegal trade in alcohol. They paid the police off: no one came to sniff the strong smell of alcohol which wafted up from the cellars.

Torrio provided the brains – from now on he was known as Johnny the Brain – while Capone just continued to be known as Scarface. Brains were not his strong point. He liked to show off and strut by the footlights; Johnny worked away in the wings, trying to create an alliance between the rival gangs in the city, all excited by the prospect of the money prohibition could bring in. Al Capone's great good fortune was his partnership with Johnny the Brain. One brain was more than enough for the two of them. It was a question of meeting the various bosses and dividing up the territory. Everyone in the city's criminal underworld stood to gain if only The Brain could forge an agreement among them. On 24th April 1925 he was mown down by a hail of bullets; he was lifted up from a pool of blood and taken to hospital. Al Capone set a guard of thirty armed men round the building to protect his partner. Johnny survived but was in a coma for ten days. When he came round, he realized that he'd survived by a sheer miracle and decided to retire from public life. With the money he had accumulated he went and spent two years in the Mediterranean sunshine. He continued to advise many godfathers; his advice on tricky matters was often considered valuable. But that was all. He no longer had the physical energy for the job and he never assumed control of the business again.

Left alone at the commands, Capone, far from becoming invisible, encouraged the press to turn him into a legend. Johnny the Brain would never have allowed him to terrify Chicago with the St Valentine's Day massacre in 1929.[19] But that's what Scarface

---

19 "It was four of us who went, it was Valentine's Day. We arrived at one. The guys from the other gang were in the car park. We went in with our machine guns and killed them. We were wearing police uniforms. We killed them because they didn't want to accept orders from Al Capone." Frank Frigenti, one of the killers involved in the St Valentine's Day massacre. From an interview given during his exile in Italy just before his death.

was like. He was amoral, ruthless, and he liked showing off how powerful he was. He was proud of being called "Public Enemy No. 1". His intrinsic stupidity was concealed by the press and by corrupt police officers and judges. He became a "supergangster": pompous and self-important in an armchair in his suite in the Lexington Hotel, he liked to give interviews to journalists who would then recount to their readers the epic tales of his crimes. The newspapers and journalists were trapped in a mechanism which demanded new bloodshed and new violence to fill their pages with sensationalism. And then the cinema joined in, turning Capone into the "negative hero" of film noir. But in reality Al Capone only managed to glimpse with a kind of half-intuition what a real godfather should be. He knew that a Mafia godfather needs to create consensus; he realized that he had to construct the usual network of "friends of friends". He opened a free canteen for the unemployed during the economic crisis which followed the Wall Street Crash. He boasted that he employed and paid the salaries for many men.

Someone had probably told him that a godfather needed to be politically astute. He had his own ideas of what this entailed. He offered to advise the President; he tried to get into the good books of good society by urging them to unite against Communism, which in his view was about to invade the United States. He'd heard somewhere that real godfathers behave as if they're the defenders of the people, so he launched an attack on the entire capitalist system. He wanted to distribute favours. He wanted to have ideas on a grand scale. That's what real godfathers did, so that's what he would do too.[20] But his greatness was all show. He attempted to take part in several meetings convened by the

20 "We must keep America whole, and safe, and unspoilt. If machines are going to take jobs away from the worker, then he will need to find something else to do. Perhaps he'll get back to the soil. But we must care for him during the period of change. We must keep him away from Red literature, Red ruses; we must see that his mind remains healthy. For, regardless of where he was born, he is now an American... I believe Mr Hoover may make the text of his December message to Congress a suggestion that the nation's legislators raise the percentage of the alcoholic content of liquor. That will be his best card for renomination. Besides, you know he has always called the Volstead Act 'a noble *experiment*'." From the interview given by Al Capone to *Liberty* magazine, 17th October 1931.

American Mafia bosses, but was always rejected. Once in Florida a gang of armed *picciotti* prevented him from even getting off the train – they waited until it set off back to Chicago.

It can never have crossed his mind that he would end up in Alcatraz for not paying his taxes. The toughest prison regime in the United States soon deflated him. The other inmates beat him up and insulted him. If he'd never been particularly bright, once he was behind bars syphilis caused a rapid decline into complete idiocy. When he was released in 1939, he was no longer capable of hurting a fly.

Charlie Lucky

But there were other figures, very different figures, moving around the Eldorado of the American underworld which Al Capone had thought was so easy to conquer.

Don Vito Cascio Ferro continued to work, methodically and patiently, like someone who is prepared to wait for the emergence of the right conditions in his ascent to power. Once his Sicilian affairs were in order, he could turn his attention to his project of bringing the Mafia gangs in America under his control. He had sent one of his most determined and ruthless aides to New York: Salvatore Maranzano's assignment was to make contact with the local Mafia Families and reach agreements for dividing up the territory. For ten years after the end of the Great War Maranzano travelled back and forth over the Atlantic, working to build the bridges between Sicily and the United States which his godfather wanted to realize.

Yet the situation in Italy suddenly changed. The Fascist party emerged and took power before Ferro had time to assess its significance. He was arrested in 1928. Any mafioso was expected to put up with periods in prison, and a godfather was perfectly capable of controlling his business from his cell. On this occasion, however, silence ensued: no orders or messages were received from Don Vito Cascio Ferro's cell. Maranzano thought his great opportunity had come; it was 1929, and he thought it might be his year.

Joe the Boss Masseria had realized immediately that Maranzano was seeking control over the American Families. Apart from a couple of skirmishes, Masseria and Maranzano had held back for a long time. Both of them were making preparations; both wanted to reinforce their Families with new recruits. Many of the recruits were to be found among the young immigrants arriving from one of the most beautiful towns in Sicily, Castellammare del Golfo, which had become a new base for various kinds of illicit trade.

Masseria might have been slow on his feet because of being fat, but he wasn't slow-witted: he saw that his rival was preparing to take over power. Maranzano's foot soldiers were invading every territory; they approached the shopkeepers and made their way into building sites. It was obvious what they were up to. Maranzano wanted to give the orders; he wanted to become the boss of bosses, the biggest godfather of them all. But he lacked Don Vito Cascio Ferro's skills. He wasn't ready, and he unleashed what is known as the "Castellammare War".

Like all Mafia wars, it was carried on underground and out of sight, but it was as bloody and ferocious as any normal war fought in the ordinary world. The foot soldiers belonging to the new Families fought with no holds barred. No street was safe; every car might be booby-trapped; any friend could attack or betray you. On 16th October 1929 Salvatore Lucania almost lost his life. He entered without thinking into a dockside warehouse and realized immediately he had walked into an ambush. He forced himself to stay calm. The killers left him hanging from a meathook with his throat slit. He seemed done for, so much so that they didn't even bother to give him the finishing blow. And they were wrong, for Salvatore somehow managed to find the strength to crawl back from death into life. He managed to get free of the hook, and dragged himself out of the warehouse onto the street. His wounds were stitched up. As soon as he could speak, he told the police he had no idea who the thugs were who'd attacked him. The police officers, echoed by the "Young Turks", told him he'd been really lucky.

The news of Salvatore's luck soon spread through the underworld. He'd survived when anyone else would have died; he'd managed to get free of the meathook on which he'd been left hanging and begin a new life. He deserved a new name. From then on he was known as "Lucky", "Charlie Lucky" to his friends, Lucky Luciano for everyone else.

He was good at understatement: he could take a step back, withdraw a little into the shadows, make a tactical retreat, not get worked up, make light of events when they were getting overheated. This is a quality great statesmen need – as well as important godfathers.

Lucky himself maintained that he owed his nickname to the horseshoe tattoo on his arm. The people who tried to eliminate him thought they were dealing merely with one of Masseria's foot soldiers – Joe the Boss and Maranzano, locked in the Castellammare War, thought the same. But Luciano was born to command, and he was already busy building up a "third force" with men he recruited from both the opposing factions. The "Young Turks" were part and parcel of his plans, and together with these there was also his old childhood friend Meyer Lansky, who had since become the boss of organized crime in the Jewish ghetto.

As soon as he felt sure of himself, Luciano put his plans into action. He went to dinner with Joe the Boss Masseria, who was accompanied by his most trusted bodyguard. The three men agreed they would play cards at the same table after they'd finished their meal. At a certain point Luciano got up, as if casually, to go to the bathroom. His henchmen entered the restaurant: they were real professionals, gunmen belonging to the Jewish gang controlled by Luciano's loyal friend Lansky. The shooting took a few seconds. Masseria was so fat he remained wedged in his chair, simply slumping forwards, with his face in the plate of pasta he was eating.

Luciano was good at keeping his cool. He came out of the bathroom only when he heard the police arriving. When they questioned him he said he'd seen nothing; he'd remained in the toilet while the shooting was taking place, only venturing back out into the restaurant when he was sure it was all over. The police officers kept asking him the same questions, as if at random, in the hope of catching him out in an inconsistency.

But Luciano just repeated his version: after all it was the truth, he'd set the whole episode up very carefully. He'd managed to make the police officers the best witnesses to the fact that he'd had nothing to do with the murder.

Salvatore Maranzano was delighted when he heard that Fat Joe had been killed – he thought he'd won the turf war. But everyone in the criminal underworld knew what had really occurred and what part Luciano had played in the killing. Maranzano knew it too of course, and decided to bring Luciano over to his side with the offer of making him his deputy. The conciliatory gesture pleased him: he was acting like an authentic godfather, re-establishing peace after war and bringing the Families together. He crowned himself *capo di tutti i capi*, the boss of bosses, but his reign was short-lived: just five months.[21] Five months were enough for Luciano to put phase two of his plan into action. Maranzano was killed in an ambush, and this time the killers made sure they got it right.

Maranzano's murder was the signal for a massacre to begin. The night of 10th September 1931 has gone down in the annals of the American Mafia with the picturesque name of the "Sicilian Vespers". Luciano eliminated all the men who'd remained loyal to the two dead bosses and couldn't be persuaded to fall in with his plans. The newspaper reports of the time found it impossible even to put a figure on the number of people killed in the massacre: Charlie Lucky had ordered his killers to destroy the corpses of their victims in the time-honoured Mafia tradition which seeks to erase all traces of a murder.

The episode of the "Sicilian Vespers" was the last great Mafia war fought on the streets of American cities. The Castellammare

---

21 "They were all a tremendous success. And they owe it to two things: to this marvellous engine of opportunity called the United States of America, and they owe it to their legacy, as Italians. There's something about the culture, about the values that these immigrants brought with them: their commitment to hard work, their commitment to family, their commitment to their own crude, simple religion, but a beautiful commitment. All those things helped them, and the success has been immense. You can't tell that from the way we've portrayed them on television – you'd think that the most successful Italians were the ones who got to be *capo di tutti i capi*, but that's not true. It was improbable, because one or two generations ago, the people who came here were very humble and modest of means." Mario Cuomo.

War had ended with the elimination of its two opposing protagonists, leaving the field clear for Lucky Luciano's total victory. Now his constant aim was to get rid of those *picciotti* who weren't up to the mark, and those bosses incapable of performing like real godfathers.

Sacco and Vanzetti

Luciano had won because he'd put a lot of planning into his victory. The American Mafia knew it, and had also taken the time to regroup. In 1929 the various godfathers, accompanied by their entourages of underbosses, advisers and bodyguards, had gathered, like heads of State, at what is known as the "Atlantic City Conference". The delegates strolled in and out of their hotel in this fashionable seaside resort next to unwitting families taking their children to play on the beach or paddle in the sea. All the business of the conference was carried out over lunches and dinners and informal chats. The Mafia bosses seemed like a group of business colleagues and friends determined to have a good time on holiday. The camouflage was impeccable: no one would have dreamt that the criminal underworld was meeting in conclave.[22]

Luciano explained, or rather attempted to explain his vision of the criminal underworld. What he said amounted to the principle that the State is responsible for the organization of public virtues while the godfathers can be tolerated as the organizers of private vices. In a sense, Luciano sought to institutionalize criminality.

It was an ambitious project, but not unfeasible – it just needed some intelligence to make it work. Not many in Atlantic City understood, at least among the bosses. Some kind of agreement needed to be reached with the State authorities. The agreement would never be signed and sealed on official paper, but it would still exist because it would be put into practice and

---

22 "Cosa Nostra is a secret organization, and its rules have always been those of a secret organization." Francesco Gratteri, Italian Police, Director of the "Servizio Centrale Operativo".

adhered to. Over time the new "arrangement", or way of doing things, would become habitual.

Luciano's Atlantic City proposal was to make the Mafia equivalent to a licensed brothel. It earned its licence so long as it didn't give the authorities too many problems. But to achieve this status, alliances needed to be formed and the mafiosi needed to be disciplined and follow rules. The corruption of the police and the judiciary was useful in blocking their investigations, so long as it was realized that it was just a tool to stop the situation getting out of hand. The authorities should not become targets for attack, since this would only provoke reprisals which would damage the Mafia's interests. Precise rules should be adhered to before there was any recourse to violence.[23]

The repercussions of the Sacco and Vanzetti scandal had not yet died down. Such an event must never be allowed to happen again. It had involved two poor Italian immigrants, a cobbler and a fisherman, who in 1920 had been accused of armed robbery and murder. In Italy, Fascism was beginning to emerge as a movement, but the country was also known as a nest of anarchists and Socialists. Sacco and Vanzetti had come to the United States in search of a better life. They had passed through quarantine on Ellis Island and had only recently settled in the country. They'd been accused of a crime they had not committed. Part of the country sprang to their defence, but demonstrations, public committees and rallies had divided public opinion in two. The case of the two men was widely followed outside the United States.

Nicola Sacco and Bartolomeo Vanzetti could hardly speak any English. Vanzetti had managed to declare: "I am suffering because I am Italian." The Ku Klux Klan had taken advantage of the situation to attack Sacco and Vanzetti in particular and immigrants in general. In the list of enemies to be exterminated, these Catholics were white "niggers", in third place after blacks

---

23 "Cosa Nostra wouldn't be what it is without the respect for rules. The rules regulate what goes on inside the Mafia and its relations with the outside world. They're straightforward and at the same time harsh. There are those, for example, which determine the structure and the hierarchy of the organization, or those which set out the different territories and the regional commissions." Colonel Mauro Obinu.

and Jews. The whole episode had given rise to a wave of racism against the immigrants arriving from the poorest regions in Italy. Fear prevented the incomers from taking part in politics, trade unions and public life in general.[24]

Despite the impassioned demonstrations in their defence and the incontrovertible evidence of their innocence, the fisherman and the cobbler were arrested, condemned and executed in the electric chair. Many years later, in the 1970s, the Mafia boss Vincent Teresa, known to his colleagues as "Fat Vinnie", decided to turn State's evidence and tell the truth about the affair. The Morelli gang was responsible for the murder of which Sacco and Vanzetti had been accused. On 15th April 1920, during an armed robbery at the Slater and Morrill Shoe Company at South Braintree in Massachusetts, one of the Morelli brothers had shot and killed one of the employees. Luciano didn't need to wait for Vinnie Teresa's confession to find out what had really happened. The two sides which had come into conflict over the affair – even holding opposing demonstrations at the funeral of the two immigrants – were both hostile to the Mafia. The whole episode had been damaging to the interests of organized crime: too much police interest, too much noise, too many clashes in the streets. In future the underworld would need to make sure that the actions of gangs did not provoke such mayhem.

The Knights of Crime at the Round Table

When the Castellammare War had ended, Luciano was able to think in more detail about his project for the Mafia: in future the organization's business interests, rather than its internal hierarchy, had to take priority. Luciano wanted an organization

---

24　"When the Italians arrived and tried to work their way into the society, they were met by great hostility. They were called 'guinea', 'greaseball', 'day-go', 'wop'... Every immigrant group has been treated that way... Each wave of immigrants to the United States seems to settle in, achieve success, win the battle of survival, and then turn and say, 'take up the gangplank, we don't need any more.' Each wave seems to resist the next wave that comes after it." Mario Cuomo.

in which no one was the boss; the position of being the boss of bosses had to be abolished. Even the word "boss" was forbidden. The running of the organization was instead to be entrusted to an oligarchy made up of the various bosses, a kind of round table at which the knights of crime would gather *inter pares*.[25] No longer a monarchy, but a republic governed by a group of godfathers who had acquired their position through the use of arms and intelligence. They needed to be acknowledged as godfathers, and control a territory, to be admitted on to this administrative council. It was as if the American political system had influenced Luciano's thinking.

He saw the Mafia as an organization which should adapt itself to the rules of the country where it operated, so much so that he regarded the old ethnic divisions as redundant. After all his own best friend was a Jew who'd fled the pogroms in Poland. Joe the Boss Masseria had always advised him to "get rid of that little Jew", but Luciano chose to get rid of Masseria and remain loyal to Lansky. The new-style organization would bring together Sicilians, Jews, Irish, Poles and whoever made a name for themselves in the criminal world. Only by opening out like this could real criminal talent be recruited. Lansky was an example: an FBI report on him declared that if he'd pursued an ordinary career he could have ended up as the chief executive of General Motors.

The Mafia under new management: governed by a round table at which there was room for men like Lansky. The underworld had no problem in understanding the concept, also because they respected Lansky, but there was scepticism among the godfathers and the foot soldiers. "The Mafia is 'our thing', it belongs to us, Sicilians. What have Jews got to do with it?"

---

25 "The reality is organized-crime figures are all different. They're human beings, and human beings have endless varieties of the way in which they act, and complexity. Some of the organized-crime figures are among the most vicious, horrible, awful human beings you'd ever meet – they have an almost animalistic quality to them. And some of them, except for the criminal part of their life, can be very nice people. They can be good friends, good fathers, good and loyal in other areas of business, and then they also have this other side of them in which they sell drugs, or kill, or whatever. So there's no one description of an organized-crime figure. The rest of their personality is not unlike society at large, which is very strange." Rudolph Giuliani.

But Lucky Luciano was insistent: "Our thing is our business interests and there are no barriers in business."

So the Commission was born. The first meeting of this body, which would coordinate and control the activities of the American Mafia, was like the establishment of a criminal equivalent of a holding company. Even a man as unintelligent as Al Capone had the right to a seat on the Commission, where he represented Chicago, though not for long.

Luciano was *primus inter pares*, a kind of president of the criminal republic. The other members wanted to give a new name to the new organization, but Luciano wanted no names: "If it isn't called anything, no one else can call it anything either, and we'll be invisible."[26] Real godfathers worked in silence and with understatement. But the others were insistent: the organization needed a name. Someone proposed "Sicilian Alliance", but Luciano cut him short. He didn't even want to keep the initiation rites. The ridiculous habits of burning religious images, pricking your finger till it bled, kissing each other on the lips, were inappropriate to the Mafia's new way of doing business.[27] It was Lansky who intervened to persuade Luciano he was wrong: those rituals were necessary because they helped to strengthen the commitment of the new recruits, gave them something to believe in and something to fear, a sense of belonging to a vast secret organization.

Luciano probably didn't change his mind about the rituals, but they stayed. No name was chosen however, especially not "Sicilian Alliance", which sounded to him like a political party or the literary evenings of some cultural association. "It's better our thing doesn't have a name," he concluded. In the outside world, the official world, everything would remain calm and favourable to them: "There's no such thing as the Mafia."

---

26 "Joe Bonanno described it in his book – and described it to me when I interviewed him and questioned him – as being like the United Nations, which is a rather exalted way to describe it. But he thought of it as the heads of State coming together and trying to create a peaceful environment in which they could make the maximum money." Rudolph Giuliani.

27 "Without its rituals the Mafia wouldn't survive from generation to generation, it would lose its historical and cultural roots and become just like any other criminal organization, people without a religion." Colonel Mauro Obinu.

An opportunity to try out the new rules immediately presented itself. The new Mayor of New York was a small energetic Italian, Fiorello LaGuardia. He liked showing off, but at the same time succeeded in charming the city and its inhabitants. He had a programme on the radio in which he read popular comics aloud, imitating all the noises – crash, pant, gulp – which were drawn in bubbles. He had himself filmed destroying slot machines, which were being used as a gambling racket, with blows of a baseball bat. He'd promised to eradicate crime from the city.[28] It was better not to take on LaGuardia; the rules of the Commission were clear, it was best not to come into conflict with anyone in official authority.

Luciano and Lansky watched while the Super-Mayor performed his antics: when he impounded thousands of handguns and melted them down to make a new coat of arms for police headquarters, or when he dumped heaps of rifles and machine guns into the Hudson River. They reached an agreement with the new godfathers of New Orleans, Sylvestro Sam Carolla and Carlos Marcello, by making them such an advantageous offer that Carolla and Marcello, though extremely reluctant, had to accept. So the slot-machine business moved south, and not a shot had been fired, in a perfect example of what the rule of using violence sparingly entailed.

"There's No Such Thing as the Mafia"

No one named the thing which had been organized by Luciano, and the thing didn't exist. Judges, police officers, politicians and priests throughout Sicily and America went on repeating: "There's no such thing as the Mafia."

J. Edgar Hoover, the powerful head of the FBI, said it. He didn't believe in organized crime and even less in the existence

---

28 "LaGuardia came in as the mayor and wanted to see change, he was someone that reached out to the communities. He created a change and made New York City a better place. When that happens, people take note, and they memorialize those figures in time, and one of the ways to do that is to name an airport, name a street, things of that nature." Bernard B. Kerik.

of a vast underworld dominated by godfathers. The real villains were gangsters like Dillinger, and Hoover and his team dedicated all their resources to them. He declared Dillinger to be "Public Enemy No. 1", and set a whole army of federal agents – as well as a large team of cameramen – to track him down.

It was a question of priorities. Propaganda and furthering his own career came at the top of the list. The American public were expected to come out of the cinemas pleased with the Hollywood film they'd just watched and impressed by the images of the FBI in the accompanying newsreel. When Dillinger was captured, the FBI's success was flaunted, so that no one could be unaware of it. Now Americans could sleep peacefully in their cosy houses; the criminal world had lost its leading figure. The images of the solitary bandit and the brave federal agents could be delivered to the cinemas. Hoover set his network of public relations into motion, had himself filmed and photographed on every official occasion – but above all, next to his men during target practice, when they were shooting at the silhouette of some imaginary enemy.

The head of the FBI was so confident his success made his position unassailable that he continued to spend days when the weather was good at the racecourse. He was passionate about betting on horses, and ended up in the network controlled by Frank Costello, a godfather who thanks to Luciano's lesson had become invisible. But for Hoover there was still no such thing as the Mafia: when someone pointed out to him that it might be a good idea to send one of his agents to investigate the business of illegal horse-betting, Hoover agreed that there was probably some shady business going on in the racecourses, but the FBI had more important problems to deal with. Hoover was always ready with a reply, as much as – if not more than – any politician. It was absurd to imagine a criminal network, a secret organization with a centralized command, a government of superbosses directing criminal activity. It was the kind of fantasy scenario you'd find in a B-movie, all just a lot of talk. So in silence the Mafia went from strength to strength, leaving the police forces far behind them. The Commission was able to do its work undisturbed for a long long time.

The Racket's "New Deal"

It was while Luciano's "thing" was making the most of prohibition and the FBI believed it didn't exist that the course of history suddenly generated another golden opportunity. The stock market in New York crashed, plunging everyone into panic and despair – everyone, that is, except the criminal underworld. 1929 ushered in the Great Depression. Among so many millions of unemployed it became easier to find new recruits for the gangs, but strengthening the Families wasn't the main point. The stock-market crash had changed America, and the godfathers were ready to make sure their Families were prepared for the changes.[29]

Luciano and his fellow members on the Commission knew their earnings from the clandestine trade in alcohol wouldn't last for ever. Already some politicians had started to speak out against prohibition. A certain Joe Kennedy, a wealthy Irish-American, had obtained a licence to import and sell alcohol "for medicinal purposes". The situation developed rapidly: with the Democrat victory and the arrival of Roosevelt in the White House, the prohibition era came to an end in 1933.

The new President announced his "New Deal", although not many of his citizens, even among the newspaper reading classes, understood what it meant. Lucky Luciano was not one of them: he knew very well what it entailed. The government would play a leading role in the management of the economy. In order to create employment it would construct new dams, bridges, railways, roads and parks with a series of huge public contracts.

---

30 "In the history of modern crime, Cosa Nostra is a model of originality and efficiency. It's not a gang of bandits or a federation of gangsters who prey on various local communities. It's a social organization which gives rise to a complex criminal phenomenon, driven by an unending search for power and profit. The complex alchemy of Cosa Nostra and its history must be known in depth and in detail, because without such knowledge it is impossible to fight it effectively. In Cosa Nostra too over the course of time events repeat themselves, former strategies re-emerge for use, periodical crises break out. It is very dangerous for the State to underestimate the Mafia's history, because if it does, it has no means of progressing in its struggle against the organization, it will simply go on repeating the mistakes it's made in the past. Emergency measures against the Mafia are pointless... expertise and continuity are needed, which give rise to a coherent and practical set of laws which will support police investigations into Cosa Nostra." Colonel Mauro Obinu.

Roosevelt was in favour of signing national contracts in order to create a new workforce. The initial result was a growth in the union movement and an increase in its power. The cudgels and tear gas which had been used to quell social tension during the crisis now gave way to a more reasoned and programmed approach. If the New Deal meant that business in the United States would start to move again, then the mafiosi were ready to take advantage with their own New Deal.[30] Without a hitch, Luciano's "thing" became part of the new ferment of activity among the busy picks and shovels. The Commission had realized some time ago in what direction the United States was heading, and the Families had made their preparations. It wasn't some hunch that made these knights of the criminal fraternity change course while they were still making huge profits from prohibition; it was an indication that the "thing" was working properly. It had shown itself capable of making accurate political and economic analyses. After only a few years, Roosevelt's New Deal, with its public contracts and labour market, was a cow waiting to be milked by the godfathers. Controlling the labour force, timing strikes – when to start them, when to end them – to the best advantage, infiltrating and taking over firms and trade unions, extending the racket's network to every new construction site: this was the real big business concealed behind all the activity of the New Deal. Al Capone's free canteen for the unemployed had nothing to do with it.

After he'd lost Johnny the Brain Torrio as a mentor, Capone had done his best to persuade himself that he too had the makings of a great godfather.[31] He wanted to create a general consensus

---

30 "Economic activity is one of Cosa Nostra's main interests. The methods they've used to infiltrate this activity have been adapted and improved over time (think of the various ways which have been devised for recycling money, for example) and have built up an entire illegal economic system under the direct management of Cosa Nostra." Francesco Gratteri.

31 "When Al Capone started his La Cosa Nostra Family in Chicago, he wasn't Sicilian, so he didn't believe in the ceremony, he was very independent. He used criminals from many other ethnic origins, so he didn't strictly require that the members even be Sicilian or Italian. He went into existing ethnic neighbourhoods, used the criminal organizations and brought them under his power. So historically in Chicago there never has been a ritual to designate someone as an official member of a Family." Thomas V. Fuentes.

among the Families, but never realized that he simply wasn't clever enough to achieve this. As a godfather he was an anomaly among his own criminal fraternity, while in the public world his notoriety was excessive. Someone must have taught him the rudiments of Mafia culture, but it was as if he was incapable of transmitting them to others. He couldn't apply the rules he'd learnt; he may have wanted to, but his innate violence overcame everything. Being known as "Public enemy No. 1" seemed to give him satisfaction, but if he'd known how to listen to the rank and file of the mafiosi, he would soon have realized that, in their world at least, he was far from being regarded as "No. 1". His period of rule in Chicago, aimless and rudderless, led to a situation of complete chaos, with the result that none of the Mafia Families in the city were represented on the Commission.

Even after the arrest of Al Capone, the local Families didn't adhere to Luciano's rules and the city's criminal gangs ran riot in fighting against each other. The Mafia seemed to have lost its traditional capacity to control its own territories. The new Mayor of the city used his police to target those who'd taken over from Al Capone; under increasing pressure, the Chicago Families were powerless to do anything as other criminal organizations sprang up. They had to choose: whether to continue losing business and dying out, or react to events.

Assassination Attempt on the President

Not every mafioso in America was in agreement with Lucky Luciano's new vision of things. In the Families where the god-father's authority was weak, the usual solution to problems was armed conflict. Chicago – or rather its mayor, Anton Cermak – was just such a problem. Contacts across the Atlantic with the criminal world in Europe held out the possibility of new arrangements for carrying out a killing.

"Zip" was the name given to a Mafia killer who arrived from Sicily with the job of killing someone. It was usually part of an exchange of favours: someone might have gone out from the United States to solve a problem in the island. The so-called "zips" worked rapidly and discreetly.[32] They arrived and did the job, and didn't leave any traces. In this way the local mafiosi didn't run any risks themselves, and the police were faced with insoluble puzzles when they came to investigate the murder.[33]

Joseph Zangara came over from Sicily during the 1930s. For a while he lay low down in Florida. Then on 15th February 1933, he shot at Roosevelt. The newspaper headlines screamed "Assassination attempt on the President". In actual fact Roosevelt was unharmed: Zangara's bullet had not even grazed him. The resulting inquiry was able to establish that the young Sicilian had been one of the best marksmen in the Italian army and knew a lot about firearms; nonetheless he missed Roosevelt, even though he fired from only a few feet away. The shot had seriously wounded the Mayor of Chicago, who was standing near to the President at the time of the incident.

Another interpretation of this event exists. A woman happened to be standing next to Zangara at the moment the killer fired his gun. Reading her statement carefully, it's clear that at first she thought he was aiming at the President, as anyone present at the parade would have thought. But then she realized that he "was shooting at someone": she doesn't repeat "the President", she says "someone".[34]

For the journalists and photographers and cameramen who recorded the woman's testimony, the news that an assassination attempt had been made on the President would have had an

---

32 "We've heard many cases of when hired killers were brought in that way, where they would have no identity or criminal record within the United States. They would commit a murder on behalf of an American La Cosa Nostra Family and then return to Sicily." Thomas V. Fuentes.

33 "The murder of Judge Livatino is an example. Police evidence, also presented during the trial, showed that Cosa Nostra had used men of honour from Germany to carry out the mission of killing one of the organization's enemies. The killers were arrested. They had been living in Germany for a long time and had become part of the society there; however, they still maintained their links to Cosa Nostra and obeyed its rules." Francesco Gratteri.

34 "My first thought was that – I knew he was shooting at the President – so my first thought was to get the pistol up in the air so he wouldn't hurt any of the bystanders. When the first shot was fired, I realized he was shooting at someone and I took my right arm and pushed the pistol up just as hard as I could. And the gentleman beside me helped me push it up." Transcription from the witness's statement a few hours after the assassination attempt.

incalculable professional and commercial value: it was the kind of scoop that occurs once in a lifetime. An assassination attempt on the Mayor of Chicago, although still notable, paled into comparative insignificance, especially as he didn't die on the spot but only after a few days, in hospital. In the sheer excitement of the moment when they recorded the woman's statement, all that counted was the idea that someone had tried to kill the President of the United States.

It's obvious that in that kind of situation, the eyewitness herself might well have been swept up in the excitement and confusion of the crowd of reporters who wanted to talk to her, in the belief that she'd been right in the front row at such an historic event. Yet watching the film clip of her interview, there can be no doubt as to what she says: at first she thought the shot was aimed at the President. Only afterwards did she realize that Zangara "was shooting at someone".

In the light of this version of what occurred, Zangara's real target was the Mayor of Chicago. On his deathbed, hardly able to speak, the Mayor himself admitted that he could have been the target. He said that he was glad that he and not the President had been hit.

Before the shooting, Cermak had been behaving strangely. He'd been away from Chicago – the city he ran and where a turf war between local gangs continued remorselessly – for over two months. Was Zangara then a "zip" who'd been commissioned by the Chicago Families to come from Sicily to kill the Mayor? Had they asked for a favour which couldn't be refused?[35]

In the eyes of American public opinion Zangara was seen as an anarchist. As such it was obvious why he would have targeted one of the world's most powerful men. There was a lot of discussion in the papers about the two possible versions of

35 "I think the nature of the criminal business has changed a little bit in the way they conduct their partnership between the Sicilians and the American La Cosa Nostra. Also, they're well aware that we have established the closest of working relationships with our Italian colleagues. So we are sharing the membership lists and a great deal of information continuously. So it would be much more difficult for a Sicilian to enter the United States without our Italian colleagues alerting us that this individual has come over. It would also be very difficult for the Americans to ask for a murderer or hit man to come over without us being aware of it and trying to stop it." Thomas V. Fuentes.

the event: the incongruities and inconsistencies of interpreting it simply as an attempt on the President's life were obvious. Then Cermak died, Zangara was condemned to the electric chair, and the discussions faded away.

Why didn't the Sicilian killer admit to wanting to shoot the Mayor of Chicago? He never did, not even when he was about to die, with his wrists and ankles tied, when the presiding officer asked him if he wanted to make a final statement. His lack of response meant that what had become the official version of the story – that it had been an attempt on Roosevelt's life – stuck.

So Zangara climbed into the electric chair, and waited for the charge while silence closed around him. No one bothered to think that he'd left a family behind him in Sicily. No one pointed out that the Mafia traditionally likes to cancel out even the memory of a killing: in this particular case they couldn't get rid of the corpse, but the killer and his real motive disappeared. Zangara died thinking of the family he'd left behind to come over to the United States on this difficult mission. A family that could be killed or kept alive by the Mafia – it all depended on him.

Trade Unionists and Politics

"*Calati, juncu, ca passa a china*": "bend over, reed, and let the tide pass you by". The Mafia let justice take its course. Roosevelt had been unharmed, the New Deal was continuing and the godfathers were making the most of the many opportunities to increase their income that were coming their way.[36]

The turf wars between the Families were a distant memory. The peace which had been established by Luciano's new

---

36 "We've felt that labour-racketeering, control of major labour organizations and the industries related to those organizations was more important to them as their base of power and source of income. By controlling labour unions, they were able to control the trucking industry, the construction industry, the docks along the eastern seaboard, and many other areas that were very lucrative over the long run, along with traditional racketeering, such as gambling, loan-sharking and extortion." Thomas V. Fuentes.

framework, and which was protected by the Commission, gave rise to new opportunities. Now the territory could be divided up without having to resort to pointless shoot-outs. Within the unions the Mafia was perfectly camouflaged and utterly invisible. From the period of the Sicilian Fasci onwards mafiosi had learnt how to disguise themselves as trade unionists. Over time they'd become experienced in managing to keep afloat during a strike and navigating the stormy waters of an uprising. After all, hadn't Don Vito Cascio Ferro been an anarchist and a socialist? Men with Italian surnames began to emerge as leaders in the more powerful unions. In many places they had no scruples about seeking and obtaining election, at one and the same time holding forth passionately at political gatherings and meeting secretly with the – still officially non-existent – Mafia's men of honour.

With contracts and corruption, Luciano's "thing" managed to infiltrate the associations of American workers: the emergence of a man like James Hoffa was a result. He was the acknowledged chief of the nation's freight-industry workers; he could have brought the whole country to a standstill. He should also have been able to ensure the godfathers went about their business in the utmost secrecy. As it turned out, he ended up on several occasions being put on trial. He became highly inconvenient: instead of understating, underplaying, avoiding, mediating, he took to talking too much, to making too many threats, to getting rather too carried away in the glare of publicity.

He disappeared. There were rumours in the criminal underworld that he'd been buried in the concrete foundations of a skyscraper, one of the American Mafia's classic methods for getting rid of a corpse. Without a corpse or a motive, faced with a rapidly fading memory of the man, the FBI investigators never succeeded in solving the mystery. The official line was that there was nothing certain to go on; only the persistence of the FBI Organized Crime Investigation unit managed to keep the inquiry open. In 2001 a hair was found in the car from which the truckers' leader was thought to have disappeared; its DNA matched Hoffa's. The investigation took a new turn just at the time when Hoffa's son was emphasizing his father's prominence as leader of the powerful truckers' union.

It was also in the 1930s that the American godfathers realized that the unions represented a way of opening up contacts with the political world.[37] By means of maintaining a presence inside the unions, indirect approaches were made to several up-and-coming members of the Democrat party.[38] Once more the Mafia showed it could act with political instinct. Politics helped to protect business: the great public works had to continue while the "tax collectors" quietly went on their rounds to collect their share of the money. Wherever the great factories showed signs of emerging from the depression, the godfathers were on hand to control who was taken on for employment. The purpose of the Mafia's political activity was to encourage all this, while keeping it under wraps.

Lucky Luciano Gets Arrested

The economic crisis was at its height, the depression was dragging American down, but Lucky Luciano was living the high life, visiting nightclubs, striptease parlours and luxury restaurants. His new management style had changed the way the Mafia did business in every sector of activity: prostitution too was no longer a home-grown affair of brothels run by owners working independently, responsible for recruiting the girls and negotiating prices with the clients. One by one the brothels were turned into sex supermarkets; their owners were "approached" by mafiosi and "persuaded" to agree or leave. And many did agree, perhaps reluctantly, to join the

---

37 "How do they corrupt you? With money. They give you money for your campaign, and in return you're supposed to forget about what's good for everybody and do what's good for them, because they give you money. A lot of that is done very successfully by big money in the US. So it should be no surprise that the Mafia, which has its own organized crime, its own desires for its business, should do the same." Mario Cuomo.

38 "The Mafia regards politics as a means of achieving what it wants. Cosa Nostra has a long history which feeds on anti-values which are on occasion shared by the general population. It's this which sustains Cosa Nostra's real power and enables it to interact with State authorities and regional politicians and administrators. The Mafia and politicians have a kind of physiological relationship... a mutually advantageous co-existence." Colonel Mauro Obinu.

new chain stores of vice where quantity became the overriding priority. Access to the women was to be straightforward, with no haggling on the price: two dollars was to be the agreed amount. Whenever and wherever you went to a prostitute for her services you'd pay two dollars – it was as simple as that.

For Luciano prostitution was small beer in comparison with the Commission's new interests, yet nothing could be overlooked and everything needed to be rationalized. He picked out a few old friends – people he'd known when he ran about the streets of Little Italy as a kid – who'd remained at the lower levels of the organization, and got them to bring the prostitutes into line with the new rules. He didn't have the time to deal with it himself – nor, probably, the inclination: traditional Mafia culture had always avoided getting involved with prostitution. It was an old Mafia rule that a man of honour shouldn't exploit prostitution, largely because of the ill-feeling it could create, and the belief that the money it brought in was not enough to justify the potential damage to the image of the honoured society. In the past brigands and fugitives had to observe the so-called F-rules: in order to escape capture they should avoid festivities and fountains, where people gathered, and females. Prostitution was entirely about women, and this was a potential source of discord and disorder and, generally, of insecurity which could turn out to be a man of honour's undoing.

Lucky Luciano thought that this rule might be obsolete in the New World; it was to become the reason of his undoing. It was precisely the women in the brothels who led to his downfall; under the new system they now found themselves having to work harder without any increase in earnings. Yet still Lucky Luciano would have stayed lucky if he'd not had the bad luck to come up against a new Attorney General, Thomas Dewey.

Dewey was a puritan, a dyed-in-the-wool Republican, with strict and inflexible conservative convictions. He was a tough nut to crack, and he'd decided to wage unremitting war on organized crime. He was moreover capable of the most painstaking methods. He was also well aware that he was playing a political game, since it was obvious that the Mafia's money ended up for the most part in certain sectors of the union movement and subsequently in the pockets of politicians – Democrat, and certainly not Republican, politicians. Dewey had certain brothel owners and their prostitutes arrested. He was clever enough to see that they were under increasing pressure both from the new economic organization of brothels and from puritanical public opinion, which led to increasingly severe laws against them.

He persuaded some of them to testify. They were young women, girls from poor families in the most backward regions of the country, with names like Nancy Presser, Betty Cook, Thelma Jordan. They told Dewey how Lucky Luciano was the big boss. He controlled everything; prostitution, the racket, drug-trafficking, extortion money, smuggling.

It might seem incredible that a handful of prostitutes should come out against the great godfather who managed the business affairs of the criminal underworld, those same business affairs which once led Meyer Lansky to boast, in a rare public declaration, that the Mafia was "bigger than General Motors". Dewey was well aware how implausible it might seem. He and his assistants had difficulty in believing it, so it was easy to imagine the problems a jury might have. So he bided his time until he could come up with a valid pretext for bringing Luciano to trial. With his characteristic patience, he tried over a long period of time to reconstruct – in so far as this was possible – Luciano's daily life. He knew that in the courtroom he would need to back up the prostitutes' testimony with detailed and believable descriptions of the kind of ambiences in which Luciano lived. After they'd spoken, the prostitutes had started to cry and complain; they'd said they'd withdraw everything they'd told him. But Dewey knew that he and his team of investigators were getting near to the heart of organized crime. Mildred Harris, the bolshiest of the brothel owners, told him he didn't have the faintest idea who he was dealing with: "Luciano can do anything, he's in charge of all the others, his hitmen are everywhere, in every city, all over the States."

But Luciano had his Achilles' heel; he liked to receive prostitutes when he felt the need in the hotel apartments he always kept reserved for himself and his escort. In Miami he was down in the register with his real name, but in New York at the Barbizon Plaza he was known as Mr Charles Lane, and at the Waldorf Astoria as Mr Charles Ross. Large tips and burly bodyguards managed to keep any curious hotel staff quiet. Like all important businessmen, Luciano had no time to waste; once Betty or Nancy or whoever had provided her services, she had to disappear back where she came from.

When Dewey had managed to extract a convincing story from his witnesses and, above all, when he'd succeeded in pressurizing them to overcome their fear of the big boss, Dewey sent out a warrant for Luciano's arrest and had him brought to trial.

For the "President" of the Commission to find himself in handcuffs was a real humiliation. Luciano was taken to prison for the most trivial, least dignified aspect of his business interests, and not even one which he controlled directly. When they saw the "big boss" surrounded by federal agents, some of the older Mafia members must have thought that the old Sicilian Mafia had it right when they told new recruits to keep away from prostitution. Luciano lost his invisibility as photographers and cameramen waited for him to enter and exit the court each day, but he retained his calm and his ability to think clearly.

The Attorney General's prosecution tactics worked like clockwork, putting Luciano's defence lawyers to the test. The "President" of the Commission hadn't foreseen how detailed and well-planned his opponent's strategy would be. When the time for the verdict came, the jury foreman pronounced the word "guilty" 549 times for each of the indictments. Luciano was sitting in the dock together with some low-ranking members of the Mafia, who in ordinary circumstances would never have dared even to approach the great Charlie Lucky at the top of the hierarchy.

All were found guilty, but the heaviest sentence was reserved for the boss. Dewey had succeeded in drawing up an endless list of indictments and in keeping them all distinct and numbered, one by one. So the judge went through the list as the jury foreman replied "guilty" to each.

Luciano received a cumulative sentence of imprisonment for a minimum of thirty years to a maximum of fifty. A simple mechanism of United States law allows this kind of sentence. Since there was a risk of reprisals against the witnesses who'd testified for the prosecution, the sentence would automatically be set at the maximum if one of them were threatened or attacked. The indictment centred on illegal earnings from prostitution, and the older court reporters were astonished at the severity of the sentence. The court had backed Dewey's theory: "Get Luciano – he's the really dangerous one!"

All the cameras were pointed on Lucky Luciano as he was taken to prison to start serving his sentence. But he always remained calm. For the Mafia, a spell in prison could also be a way of showing strength; imprisonment seemed to awaken their genetic instinct to behave as if they belonged to an army, the hidden military force of the criminal underworld. A soldier needs to know that, if he is wounded in battle, his comrades won't abandon him, but will carry him off the field and look after him. If he is captured by the enemy, then his command will try to arrange an exchange of prisoners or will ask that international law on their treatment be respected. If he is killed, then his family will receive support of some kind. This trust applies equally to the soldiers in the Mafia.

They need to know that their bosses will negotiate at the first possible opportunity to obtain better conditions for them in prison and will try to get the verdict "adjusted" so that they are given early release. They must feel that their principal needs are being met. If a boss lands up inside, then he needs to communicate with the members of his Family in the outside world so he can continue to manage his affairs.

The images of Luciano that you can see on the newsreel of the time don't suggest he's a man who's lost his freedom. He was so wealthy that he managed to direct the Commission even from the confines of his prison cell by bribing anyone who might be an obstacle. He delegated the running of day-to-day business to two of his best "pupils", Frank Costello and Joseph Doto, both of them experienced men who knew how to act silently and invisibly, although Doto, nicknamed Joe

Adonis, was known for his vanity and love of elegant clothes. However, Luciano's real "delegate" was his old friend Meyer Lansky: it was Lansky who informed Luciano of the shifting relations between the various Mafia Families and who reported the boss's orders back to the world outside the prison walls.

Luciano's commands might have seemed bizarre, but it was best not to question them. Take for example the command which had gone out just a year before the trial in 1935, when Luciano was informed by Lansky that one of the New York bosses, Dutch Schultz, who led a gang of dozens of armed men, was planning to kill Dewey. Schultz had acted by the new rule book: he had gone to the Commission to ask for permission to murder Dewey. Only Albert Anastasia, in a sudden gesture of irresponsibility, had agreed, but when he had listened to Luciano's arguments against ("No attacks on politicians"), he understood what the consequences might be and changed his mind. Schultz's request was turned down. Luciano knew that Dewey was pursuing him, but the order was clear: the Attorney General was not to be killed.

It was again Lansky who told Luciano that Schultz was going ahead in planning the attack. So a group of hitmen was sent out. They burst into the restaurant where Schultz was eating with his bodyguards, three of the toughest men in his gang. The three of them died immediately. Schultz was rushed to hospital: the Commission's gunmen waited, unseen, outside until his death too was certified.

So Luciano had saved Dewey's life and had also made it clear that the new rules had to be obeyed. He himself applied them, even though the federal agents had closed on him and his freedom was at stake. No attacks on politicians.

Fascism Versus the Mafia

Italy now had a Fascist government. In the early years of his regime, Mussolini won the plaudits of American political observers, who saw him as a bulwark against the advance of Communism. He was also a favourite type of many American journalists: he was a self-made man, he had started off as a primary-school teacher and had become head of State, he'd abandoned the socialism he'd once espoused and gave the impression of being a man of action focused on facts. Many immigrants could feel proud of the reactions to Mussolini which they read in the American press. It was a good thing for everyone if the Americans liked Mussolini, and Italy enjoyed a new prestige. The diminished Italy of the past was finished with. Now people were waiting to see what changes the Fascist revolution would make.

During a visit he made to Sicily in 1924, Mussolini visited various towns and met the local authorities. Banquets and receptions were organized for him, and crowds turned out to greet him. In the small town of Piana dei Greci, the Duce met Don Ciccio Cuccia, the godfather, the boss and – it goes without saying – also the mayor of the place. Don Ciccio knew nothing about Fascism, but he was well aware of the prestige which a visit from the head of the government would bring. He had a great banquet prepared for his illustrious guest. It was not an important stop for Mussolini – he was merely on his way to somewhere else – so no formal accounts of the visit exist. All we know about it comes from eyewitnesses who were there, whose accounts have been passed down to become the stuff of legend.

Don Ciccio was more than impressed, he was amazed by the number of cars and staff accompanying the Duce. "Capitano, you really don't need all this escort – here you're under my protection, and I can make sure nothing happens to you." Mussolini was taken aback. So there was another power in Sicily in addition to the Fascist authority. He, the Duce, was to be protected by some wretched provincial godfather! He looked round attentively and realized that the Mafia was indeed a state within the State.[39]

---

39 "Cosa Nostra is a state with its own laws, which co-exists with the legal State in order to exploit it. If there weren't a State to distribute public contracts, then Cosa Nostra wouldn't be able to use its criminal power to turn those contracts to its own advantage. It's a state which is parasitic on the real State. It comes into conflict with the legal State when this is on the point of defeating it: then open warfare and Mafia terrorism break out. When co-existence is possible, then Cosa Nostra may even accept there will be losses, so long as its own survival is not threatened. It has to live within the State, causing as little damage as possible, drawing attention to itself as little as possible, if it wants to exploit the resources of the State." General Angiolo Pellegrini.

Don Ciccio didn't even have time to realize what he might have said to so offend the great man who'd come from Rome, before Mussolini's fleet of cars sped away down the dusty road out of town. Like all the other mafiosi, the godfather-mayor of Piana dei Greci was accustomed to the absence of the State and couldn't begin to understand the new totalitarian State which was emerging round the figure of the Duce. For him it was a straightforward matter: the number-one man who ran that distant State had decided to come and pay a visit, so a welcome was prepared with a banquet and a toast and official thanks, and he was sent on his way. What was the problem?

As soon as he got back to Rome, Mussolini decided to strike. He wanted a man who was tough and inflexible to head operations in Sicily: the prefect Cesare Mori's name was proposed. Mori wasn't in fact a Fascist; he was a leading civil servant who was ready to serve the State. And he possessed all the qualities Mussolini was looking for, including a knowledge of Sicily, since he'd been posted for several years to Trapani, where he was known as the "Iron Prefect".

Like a general in wartime, Mori was given full powers. Parts of Sicily were put to the sword, as if it were under enemy occupation. He mobilized not only the police, but brought the army in. His troops seemed like invading mercenaries. He knew he had the total backing of Mussolini's regime, and laid siege to entire villages. He took Ganci, for example, by storm after a brief siege, and had a monument put up in the main square in memory of his victory: a lion leaving a cave.

The men he arrested were tortured. Rumours spread throughout the island of Mafia foot soldiers forced to drink salt water, being beaten or hit on the testicles, or wired up and electrocuted. The wives of mafiosi on the run were hidden away after they'd been raped, but the doors of houses which had been demolished as Mori's men rounded up the mafiosi were left standing as a reminder of his methods. They were methods which could only have been used in a country which was no longer democratic. There was no possibility of defence, no recourse to law. The island's godfathers were left in a state of shock; they'd been used to an absent State, with which, every now and then, they'd needed to come to terms in order to fix the result of a trial.

The danger increased daily. Their men were being subjected to torture and were talking. Mori's brutally direct methods soon started to give results. He found that the Mafia had its own statutes, its laws and rules. It was, exactly as Mussolini had feared, a state within the State. The situation for the Duce was intolerable: no other power could exist in the Fascist State.

The Mafia started to understand what Fascism meant. About five hundred of them were helped out by their American cousins and fled to the United States. Sicily became a no-go zone for the Mafia. The ordinary folk of the island also began to understand what Fascism was about and some were grateful to it for making it into such a no-go zone.

On this occasion the Mafia had got things wrong. They were not prepared for the turn taken by historical events – or perhaps it was Fascism which had been too rapid in seizing power and taking decisions, above all in deciding to deal in such a thoroughgoing way with Sicily. But whatever the truth, the men of honour had failed to understand Fascism. Many tried to find a way of negotiating and reaching an agreement, but the dictatorship seemed to offer no possibility of compromise. In the attempt to defend their "territories", the godfathers created huge problems for themselves. Genco Russo was arrested and all his business suddenly terminated. Antonio Galera was sent to prison, where he didn't receive the usual privileges given to godfathers, but died while awaiting sentence.

The Iron Prefect's campaign also affected Don Calogero Vizzini. He was put under arrest in 1931 and swiftly brought to trial. But he was saved by his own character, his sangfroid, his family and the wide network of friends and favours he had built up, even his personal way of life – that of an important godfather in the traditional mould. He proved much more astute than the others of his kind; his family, full of leading churchmen, also came to his defence. He was acquitted. Despite this, Mori used his special powers to send him into exile, from the island to Tricarico in the region of Lucania.

There Don Calogero started to mend his by now rather tattered network; it was all a question of time, of patiently weaving favours and bribes. Time would eventually bring success. Once again he applied the old Mafia maxim, to be used at times of high danger: "Bend over, reed, and let the tide wash over you". The fundamental law of the Mafia is the use of power in order to control a territory.

Violence or the use of force is a State monopoly: no one apart from the State is authorized to use violence. Whoever commits a violent act has to face justice. No citizen is given the right *a priori* to use violence; *a posteriori* the use of violence can in exceptional cases be absolved if there is evidence that it was used in legitimate defence. But the Mafia refuses to accept this State monopoly: being a state within the State, it arrogates to itself the right to the use of force. The violence practised by Mafia Families extorts a payment on all the economic activities which are carried on in a given territory, as if it were imposing a tax which has to be paid to the authorities of the anti-State. Mafia firms use armed gangs to put their competitors out of business, doing what some entrepreneurs perhaps have guilty dreams of doing – using their internal security services for external purposes against other firms. It's the dream of a savage capitalism which has only recently started to appear wicked.

"Bend over, reed..." is ultimately a demonstration of strength – the strength of being a good tactician, of knowing how to arrange a retreat in order to avoid definitive defeat; the strength of knowing not only how to exercise authority over one's own men but also, while still in hiding, to recruit others so that the territory can once more be reconquered; the strength in waiting – perhaps for many years – for the right moment.

Deftly slipping between all the obstacles to his return, in 1937 Calogero Vizzini went back to Villalba, where his presence was "tolerated" by means of a tacit agreement with the local police and *carabinieri*. Nothing seemed to stop the Iron Prefect however: by dint of torture and violence, Mori finally arrived at Don Vito Cascio Ferro, who was put under arrest and kept from any involvement in the multifarious interests of his Mafia empire. Mori understood very well that even from their prison cells

1. Anna Rech
(Anna Maria Pauletti Rech, 1828–1916)

2. Lieutenant Giuseppe (Joe) Petrosino
(1860–1909)

3. Petrosino's coffin arriving
at his widow's home

4. Giuseppe (Joe) the "Boss" Masseria
(1879–1931)

5. Giovanni (Johnny) the "Fox" Torrio
(1882–1957)

6. Mayor Fiorello Enrico (Henry) LaGuardia (1882–1947)
speaking on WNYC radio

7. Soup kitchen for the unemployed financed by Al Capone
at 935 S. State St., Chicago

8. The first page from the FBI
investigation file on Al Capone

9. Alphonse (Al) "Scarface" Capone
(1899–1947)

10. Ed Diamond, Jack Diamond,
"Fatty" Walsh and Lucky Luciano

11. Charles "Lucky" Luciano
(Salvatore Lucania 1897–1962)

12. Lucky Luciano, handcuffed, leaving
New York Supreme Court

13. Meyer the "Brain" Lansky
(Maier Suchowljansky, 1902–1983)

14. Meyer Lansky
in 1958

15. John Edgar Hoover
(1895–1972)

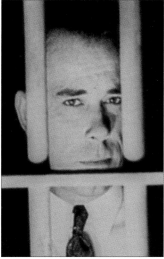

16. John Dillinger
(1903–34)

17. James Riddle (Jimmy) Hoffa
(1913–75?)

18. Frank Costello
(Francesco Castiglia, 1891–1973)

19. Joe Adonis
(Giuseppe Antonio Doto, 1902–1972)

20. Benjamin "Bugsy" Siegel
(1906–47)

21. Bugsy Siegel
c.1940

22. The body of Bugsy Siegel on a sofa
in his Beverly Hills house after his shooting

23. Salvatore Giuliano
and Vito Genovese

24. Vito Genovese
(1897–1969)

25. The corpse of the bandit
Salvatore Giuliano (1922–50)

men of honour manage to send out messages and control their Families; he'd realized that prison is simply another dimension for the Mafia, an alternative strategy for winning power.

No messages emerged from Don Vito's cell. His foot soldiers were left without orders. With the arrest of the big boss, Mori's operations had finally infiltrated the secret area where the contacts with the banks, the American Families, the most elusive men of honour took place. The world of high finance, and the financiers who moved vast amounts of capital around, began to feel the Iron Prefect looming over them. In certain documents highly placed politicians were named, such as the ex-nationalist and now Fascist Alfredo Cucco, and even army generals who might have come into contact with the Mafia, such as Di Giorgio, who was related to the Milletarì clan. There was no proof as yet, but it was best not to give Mori any more time to find out: he'd arrived too high up the hierarchy. "*Promoveatur ut amoveatur*" – give someone a promotion if you want to get rid of them, as the Roman emperors' councillors used to advise when some official started to make a nuisance of himself. A few more steps and Mori would have reached the summit of the Mafia's secret organization and revealed its connections with the banking system, with the United States and, above all, with the politicians in Rome. The Duce declared himself satisfied with the results Mori had obtained – as indeed public opinion was too; the Iron Prefect was made a senator, and left Sicily.

Handsome Bugsy

In the following years Fascism had its own triumphs to celebrate; Mori's Sicilian campaign was no longer mentioned. Only the Mafia remembered and transmitted the memory at its secret meetings down through the generations.

While they had bent their heads and waited for the tide to pass over them, godfathers and foot soldiers had had the time to do some thinking. They had been taken by surprise; no one had really understood what Fascism was about. But one thing was certain: dictatorship – and in particular that dictatorship

– not only restricted the Mafia's room for manoeuvre, but threatened their very existence. Once the full tide of Mori's campaign had passed away, the bosses and the ranks in the Families could get on with the business of learning to live with a triumphant and widely popular Fascist regime. They survived by keeping their heads down and giving up more lucrative ventures which might have attracted attention and made them targets once more.

Out of the blue, in 1937, Vito Genovese arrived on the island. He got entangled with the most recent of the murders he had planned. He'd been one of the "Young Turks", very close to Lucky Luciano – indeed he was his pupil and ally. But he'd not learnt how to make himself invisible. In any case, the maestro himself was in prison and couldn't be expected to keep his eye on everyone and everything. In his heart of hearts, Genovese thought that Luciano's temporary removal from the scene was a chance for him to make headway in the organization. But he'd been clumsy and had made a bad mistake. Now the New York Police was on his heels; with the help of the Commission he managed to get onboard a transatlantic liner to take refuge in Fascist Italy.

He was forty years old and regarded himself as an experienced and ruthless boss. He saw that good business was waiting to be done in Italy. He ordered some imports of cocaine, a fashionable drug among artists and intellectuals. He managed to have a meeting with the young Count Ciano, who was married to Mussolini's favourite daughter, Edda. He associated with portly Fascist officials and ex-members of the party's paramilitary squads, in an attempt to ingratiate himself with the dictatorship and define himself as one of the regime's benefactors and friends. He put up the money for the building of a local "Casa del Fascio", the party headquarters, and gave conspicuous financial support to various public initiatives. And when he found that supplies of cocaine and dollars were not enough to win the approval of the leading Fascist politicians, he decided to try with a murder.

The editor of the anti-Fascist periodical *Il Martello*, Carlo Tresca, was living in exile in New York. Tresca was a personal enemy of Mussolini. Genovese ordered his assassination, convinced that he was doing the Duce a favour. He chose as the killer Carmine Galante, at the time a lowly foot soldier, but destined for advancement, becoming for a certain period the godfather of the Bonanno clan. Carrying out the murder proved to be easy: Galante took up his position on Fifth Avenue on 11th January 1943; when he saw Tresca pass by, he shot him and disappeared before the police could arrive. But the killing brought Genovese no benefit: Mussolini and his government had more pressing concerns, embroiled as they were in a war which increasingly appeared to be hopeless.

Benjamin Siegel was another mafioso who decided to pay a visit to Italy. He had been one of the killers in the Jewish gang of gunmen under the command of Meyer Lansky. Staying loyal to his boss, he'd made a career for himself; he was as handsome as a film star, and changed his name to Bugsy. When he wasn't on some job for Lansky, he was chasing women: he was as notorious as a Don Juan as he was as a ruthless mobster. He became the legendary Bugsy, depicted in films by the likes of Warren Beatty.

Two years after Genovese left for Sicily, Benjamin Siegel decided to cross the Atlantic as well. It was a reckless voyage: he was in pursuit of one of his lovers, even though he didn't have much confidence in the affair continuing. She was the Countess Dorothy Di Frasso, who had decided to assassinate Mussolini with a bomb. Bugsy had a weakness for beautiful women – and Di Frasso was fascinating, blue-blooded and an adventurer. But she didn't have a clue what a bomb was made of, and so missed getting into the history books since she simply gave up the assassination attempt.

In the mean time Bugsy found himself inside what the Nazis called Fortress Europe, now almost entirely under their control. Rumours among the criminal fraternity made out that glamorous Bugsy had met Hermann Goering and Joseph Goebbels. Seen from close up, perhaps the Nazi leaders seemed to him like criminals, but of a kind he wasn't used to. These criminals had taken over the State – one in which there was no room for him, a Jew and a mobster. Bugsy wouldn't even have got as far as the gates of a concentration camp. If they had guessed who he was, this Jewish gangster or gangster Jew would have been dispatched on the spot. Confronted with the violence of Nazi anti-semitism, Siegel decided to abandon the Countess and go back to America. He reported back to Lansky on his trip, and the legend of his travels began to circulate among the foot soldiers.

Something was afoot in the underworld, something which neither Bugsy nor Genovese knew anything about. Luciano and Lansky, a Sicilian and a Jew, had worked to bring the Commission over to the side fighting the Nazi and Fascist dictatorships. This had nothing to do with ideology; it was simply a question of business. If their business was to go on growing, then the bosses needed democracy, needed to exploit the freedoms and civil rights which only democracy guaranteed.

Smoke over New York

The United States had entered the war on 8th December 1941. Lucky Luciano was still in prison and continued to direct the clans from his cell. Al Capone had been freed from Alcatraz, but syphilis had left him a wreck. The bosses were asking themselves where money might be made as the conflict developed.

The Americans found they faced two significant problems. Strikes were still endemic in the factories, and enemy submarines were able to approach their coasts and even take on new supplies. But now a third and even greater problem emerged. A number of attacks showed that ships were an easy target for sabotage. The navy needed independence of action to guarantee the security of the ports – which were now enormous naval dockyards – at whatever cost, and the army needed to know its troops could leave and arrive on schedule as they were moved to the various battle fronts.

The attacks provoked a sudden alarm over foreign spies. In an unpopular measure that didn't solve any problems, the government interned thousands of Italian, German and Japanese immigrants. Australia and Brazil followed suit. Propaganda asserted that spies and saboteurs could easily infiltrate them, but the episode broke up entire communities. Parents were sent off to internment behind barbed wire while religious boarding schools took in their children. Sixty years later, in 2000, the American Senate was forced to set up a commission to inquire into the episode and the damage it had caused, and to investigate possible compensation for those who had been victimized.

Obviously, as in every war, there were also real spies operating in the United States. Mussolini and his regime had long asserted that communities of Italian immigrants, whom they preferred to call "Italians living abroad", and regarded as outposts of Fascism, would by force of numbers cause upheaval in the various countries where they had settled. Now, all over the globe, from London to Sydney, Italian-owned shops and restaurants were smashed up by crowds who accused their staff and owners of working for the enemy. Nazism had taken a more practical approach by trying to enlist various German immigrants in the United States, bringing them back to Germany for training and then sending them back as spies. The operation failed: several of the immigrants continued to prefer the American capitalist system over the German National-Socialist one.

Hoover set the FBI into action and – making sure as usual that the cameras were on hand for propaganda purposes – managed to identify and arrest several spies. They were brought to trial almost immediately; their executions, by hanging or shooting, were also filmed. The voice-over on the newsreel repeats that the United States had to defend itself from spies and saboteurs. The commentary in the films also mentions the interest which the Axis powers were taking in South America. If a country like Brazil decided to back the Fascists, then the United States would be vulnerable to invasion. There was an American Nazi party which had also succeeded in holding a rally in New York, with thousands of supporters waving the stars-and-stripes together with the swastika in the belief that a superior Aryan race could purify America.

While all this was happening, strikes continued to bring some of the large factories to a standstill. Luciano and the other bosses could have intervened to stop them, but why should they have done this? What was in it for them? The Commission was not unaware of the tensions affecting America but, before they made a move, whatever that move might be, they wanted to know how it might benefit them. They soon found the answer and worked out what to do accordingly. Luciano and the others decided to transform the war into "Our Thing"; the Commission acted as if it were an independent State. Once again the Mafia was able to play a leading role in the course of historical events.

The French transatlantic liner the *Normandie* was in the naval dockyards in New York undergoing work. It was the fastest boat in the world and held the Blue Riband award for the fastest transatlantic crossing, which in 1933 had been won by the legendary liner the *Rex*.

The Germans had seen the *Normandie* escape from under their noses when they invaded France. Now the huge liner was filled with American labourers who were transforming it into a troopship. The navy believed that the liner would be fast enough to escape submarine attacks on transatlantic crossings. On the morning of 11th February 1942, New Yorkers woke to see a column of smoke rising over the port. It was coming from the *Normandie*, which was lying turned on one side along one of the quays: it had been bombed. Fire engines on the quayside were dousing it with water, rows of sailors rolling hydrants along were climbing up and down the ladders placed on the ship's sides, tugboats with water cannon onboard surrounded the liner as if to defend it from another attack.

The idea of sabotaging the *Normandie* had occurred to Albert Anastasia; from his prison cell Luciano had given the idea his approval. The dense cloud of smoke hanging over the liner was intended to show the American armed forces that the port of New York was in the hands of the Mafia.

As the military always say, there was no time to lose – action was urgent. Contact was made immediately with the Mafia. They looked through some of the dossiers which an official inquiry into organized crime had started to compile, identified the names of the men they needed to talk to, the bosses who commanded the clans. The Chief of Staff of the American Navy, Admiral Haffenden, and the Attorney General himself, Thomas Dewey, gave their approval to the top-secret plan code-named "Operation Underworld". The Mafia had to be negotiated with, the war meant there was no time to lose.

The name at the top of the list of the "right" men to talk to was Polakoff, Lucky Luciano's unscrupulous lawyer. He practised his profession in the normal world, but his work also took him down into the deep byways of the Mafia underworld. Starting with Polakoff, the Navy's secret-intelligence officers identified the boss of the New York port and also the godfather who controlled the city's fish market. His name was Giuseppe Lanza. His real nature as a ruthless boss was hidden by his taciturn air and his vast weight, caused by his addiction to huge meals of pasta and beefsteaks swimming in butter. The criminal world knew him as Joseph "Socks" Lanza – not because he wore nice socks, but because he was capable of landing heavy blows. It could be said to be his speciality. Often he would beat his victims to death, finishing them off – so some said – by strangling them with a sock, so perhaps the other meaning of his nickname is relevant.

But these myths didn't interest the men from the United States Navy. When Lanza was confronted by these officers with their mysterious air, he passed them on to Frank Costello, who in turn, after they'd told him what they wanted, sent them to Meyer Lansky. Like the managing director of an important firm, Lansky received them and listened to their proposal. He made a rapid calculation of the pros and cons; he asked himself what the benefits would be for the organization. The matter was serious, and only one man could make a decision: Luciano. During the night of 11th May 1942, Luciano was transferred in great secrecy to the prison at Great Meadow, near Albany. His transfer was the first condition the boss had set – fulfilling it was a token of the authorities' goodwill – so that discussions could begin.

The Mafia had an appointment with the course of historical events, and this was the first step.

Pact with the Mafia

Lucky Luciano opened the negotiations by immediately raising the stakes. He knew that at all times and in every country, when the fear of defeat in war is looming, ethics go by the board when it comes to supplying military requirements. He was behind bars, like many other bosses and foot soldiers. If the Mafia entered negotiations with the State, then the first point to discuss was the possibility of adjusting the trial results and helping out the men who were incarcerated. Now this meeting with the official representatives of the United States held out significant prospects for progress.

The results of the agreement were immediately apparent. New York and other American ports became secure overnight, guarded by military patrols and Mafia foot soldiers. In the huge factories no one dared to agitate for a strike.

After this, Operation Underworld went on to fulfil the other points in the top-secret protocol. The Allies had been joined by a secret state: "Cosa Nostra". The state within the State, the criminal underworld had entered the war.

Shortly after the sabotage of the *Normandie*, the Governor of New York State fell seriously ill, too ill to carry out his official functions. At such a critical and delicate moment, his deputy had to take over provisionally: a young Italian-American, the son of a stone-cutter from Novara who had emigrated to the United States in 1895. He was called Charles Poletti and he'd been much praised in the local Italian press. He had enjoyed a brilliant legal career after graduating from Harvard, making his way up the ladder in important legal firms in the city. At the same time he had pursued a political career in the Democrat party and had taken part in official commissions inquiring into social welfare and organized crime. In 1938 he'd been elected as Governor Lehman's deputy in the Democrat victory in New York State.

Then suddenly the governorship became his for a provisional period of twenty-nine days. The newspaper reports of the time mention his presence, accompanied by his beautiful American wife from Buffalo, at some civic receptions. There are no official documents from his time in office in the archives – apart from a few papers which Poletti managed to sign during this period, even though he was only responsible for day-to-day administration.

Operation Underworld was being put into effect, the Mafia was mobilizing in secret, America was reeling from the shock of sabotage and spies – and the young Italian-American lawyer was exercising his right as governor to pardon some prisoners and free them. It's easy to identify who the Italian-Americans are in the list signed by Poletti: men imprisoned for murder, for extortion, for setting fire to shops and warehouses, even for practising as a doctor under false pretences – all of them saw their sentences wiped out with a stroke of the pen, and the doors of their prison open to release them.

The name of Francesco Gambino can be found on Poletti's list. He had been condemned for murder back in 1933 for twenty years to life imprisonment. He'd killed his cousin "during an intense family quarrel" about money. The reasons given for his release read: "His opportunity for rehabilitation is exceptionally good. The sentencing judge expressed his opinion that there is considerable merit to Gambino's application for clemency". Another name on the list is John Santapaola, sentenced in 1933 for culpable manslaughter for fifteen to thirty years. The reasons state that "he has an excellent prison record. He has been in the prison hospital for many months and his health is failing. His children are devoted to him and he intends making his home with them".

Another interesting name is Peter Tusa, condemned in 1937 for murder for twenty years stretching to life imprisonment. The explanation: "District Attorney O'Dwyer of Kings County recommended executive clemency in return for the 'invaluable assistance' rendered by Tusa in connection with the investigation of a number of murders committed in Kings County".

Poletti signed other measures to cancel "minor" sentences, for cases in which the period of detention had been completed, but whose provisions still prevented the released men from exercising certain professions or setting up new businesses. In this category we find the names of Maurice Buonomo (armed robbery), Mario Pece (robbery), Anthony Gerardo (attempted robbery), Filarginio De Pasquale (practising as a doctor under false pretences).

The press, especially the conservative press, rushed to the attack: Poletti found himself the target of the *Herald Tribune*, the *Daily News* and the *American Journal*. The crime reporters demanded an explanation for the pardons. The clever young lawyer gave a number of reasons: the men who'd been set free had behaved well in prison, many were repentant, the magistrates had approved their release.

The day before his provisional period in office ended, Poletti wrote a policy document intended for the Democrats in which he outlined what he thought should be future party policy on social welfare, child benefits and anti-discrimination laws. He was clearly preparing himself for the next step in his political career. In fact, once the governor had returned, Poletti remained unemployed for precisely three days. To the surprise of everyone, a government press release tersely announced that Poletti had been appointed special assistant to the Minister for War, Stimson. He would now be working directly for the War Department; no further details were available, since the nature of his work, in the words of the government communiqué, was confidential. The secret-intelligence services asked him to make anti-Fascist propaganda broadcasts in Italian on the radio channel Voice of America.

On 18th April 1943, it was discovered that Poletti had been given the rank of lieutenant colonel and assigned to the Civil Affairs division of the military government in countries occupied by the Allies.

The Sicily Landings

Thomas Dewey had been told that he owed his life to Lucky Luciano, who'd not only blocked the plan to kill him, but had also eliminated the boss who, despite the Commission's opinion to the contrary, had tried to organize and carry out the assassination by himself. But Dewey didn't need to be told: the pressures of the military situation more than justified collaborating with the Mafia on the invasion of Sicily, the biggest naval operation ever undertaken. It was too big: blockages were created among the two thousand vessels which, coming from ports all over the place, had to take up their positions at the scheduled time just off the coast of the island. Teams of parachutists got lost, gliders ended up out of action before they'd fired a single shot, hundreds of soldiers arrived more dead than alive, but from seasickness rather than enemy fire. General Staff then decided to reduce the number of ships involved in order to send some to the Normandy landings. But Sicily remained the place of the first real attack on "Fortress Europe", and no one quite knew what they would find.

Waiting with a short stretch of sea between them and those uncertain shores, the Americans wanted to make sure of two points before beginning the landing on 9th July 1943: they didn't want their men to die unnecessarily, and they didn't want any problems with the populations they left behind as they advanced across the island. They made their plans accordingly.

As the front advanced, a military government run by the Allied Forces was set up in the territories they occupied: AMGOT. General Alexander and his staff assigned the position of governor to a lieutenant colonel serving with them, an Italian-American. Charles Poletti re-enters the story.

Vito Genovese managed to infiltrate himself – as an interpreter – among the staff employed by this military government. After the war, Poletti would distance himself from this irregularity by saying that he knew Italian and didn't need to employ an interpreter. Some American war reporters were told by officers on Poletti's staff that on one occasion during the rapid military advance he found himself in a small town which had only just been abandoned by the Germans. He realized that he was the only American so far to have arrived, and gathered the population of the town together in front of the town hall. He stood on top of the few steps so that he could see the caps of the peasants on the edge of the crowd and held a political rally there and then, telling his audience that if they behaved obediently everything would be well and all of them would benefit. "The crowd applauded – it was just like some ordinary political meeting in peacetime," Poletti's amazed officers reported. A few days later Poletti repeated his harangue, this time in Palermo: it became a standard turn of his, and he repeated it in several towns in the island.

Poletti was right in saying he didn't need an interpreter. But while he himself didn't, other officers on his staff did. Whatever the case, Genovese worked undisturbed for the military government for a long period before General Staff discovered the irregularity and dismissed him. But, while he was serving as interpreter, no doubt Genovese had provided his services for all the kinds of business which had to go through the military government – establishing authority over the territory, the town halls, the public offices, the factories and firms, the provision of military supplies, petrol, tyres, uniforms, medicines, cigarettes and tinned food. It was all, more than ever, "cosa nostra". It was all business, just business.

The advance of General Patton's troops in Sicily, like General Clark's advance on the Italian mainland, was helped by the enthusiasm with which the inhabitants welcomed them. The help consisted only in this: no armed Mafia foot soldier played a role in the military strategy. The defensive strategy adopted by the German forces meant that Patton reached Palermo in record time, while the English in the eastern part of the island met with dogged resistance. The Germans had built a series of fortified lines to prevent the Allied advance, which very skilfully took account of the terrain and exploited its defensive possibilities to the maximum. They had taken up their defensive position in the east of the island, gradually retreating towards the Straits of Messina in order to ensure their troops could withdraw. So Patton encountered little real resistance moving towards Palermo. The American troops were greeted everywhere by joyful crowds. Behind such receptions there were the godfathers. Sometimes someone would shout, "Hurrah for the Americans, hurrah for the Mafia!"

The British commanders thought this sympathy for the Americans wasn't a normal reaction. It seemed more like an inexplicable passion or love for the invading forces, so much so that their intelligence officers were asked to find out the real reasons which lay behind such sudden and over-demonstrative enthusiasm. But military considerations, as always, took priority; no one could deny that the friendliness and helpfulness of the Sicilians made the generals' life much easier. Several Mafia godfathers could say they'd been the persecuted victims of Fascism, even anti-Fascists: they'd been imprisoned or interned, and could prove it.

Some of them were nominated as town mayors by Poletti. Rapid inaugurations were held, often in the street in the midst of festive crowds; the new mayors were asked to raise their right hands and swear a brief oath. Once the short ceremony was over, they were handed charge of entire villages. Don Calogero Vizzini became the mayor of Villalba. Control of the territory that had been liberated and occupied was an essential part of the Allies' military strategy. It didn't much matter if this control was exercised by the Mafia bosses. In this way the godfathers' authority, which had survived the fall of the Fascist State, re-emerged among the ruins of war. The rest is legend.

Legend tells of a solitary armoured tank arriving in Villalba shortly after the Allies had landed, but a good while before the other troops had reached the town. A soldier emerged from the turret and called through a megaphone for Don Calogero Vizzini. When he appeared, he handed him a token of collaboration with the Mafia: a yellow handkerchief with a large "L" embroidered on it. The token had been sent by Lucky Luciano. But the legend tells us nothing we couldn't already find out about the role played by Luciano and the Mafia in the Second World War.

Poletti certainly never said anything to prove the legend. The former governor of occupied Italy was never shy of giving interviews to newspapers and magazines and on television, but he always denied any connection with the Mafia. Throughout his very long life – he died peacefully aged ninety-nine in his villa in Marco Island in Florida on 11th August 2002 – like a true intelligence officer, he always maintained complete secrecy on clandestine operations.

Documentary film footage, shot by army cameramen, has been discovered in archives which shows various Sicilians taking the oath to become mayors under the hurried supervision of officers. Other footage shows Italian civilians wearing their customary caps, accompanied by small fishing boats, climbing up and down from the warships, directly in the battle zone.

The special teams set up to conduct "psychological warfare" did what remained to be done by easing the way for the new civil authorities, making sure the right messages reached the right places, and asking the whole population to show obedience and collaboration. The former victims persecuted by the Iron Prefect might have been delinquents, but they knew what order meant, and had no problem in showing they also knew how to maintain it. For the generals that was enough. "Hurrah for the Americans, hurrah for the Mafia," someone shouted again, as the people of Villalba celebrated the appointment of their new mayor.

Salvatore Giuliano, the Warrior Bandit

In reality Lucky Luciano was rather more sceptical than the American generals were about the capacities of the Sicilian godfathers. He saw them as they truly were, anchored in the past, to the old honoured society, and incapable of understanding the new "thing" which the immigrant mafiosi had built up in the New World. Luciano developed a real relationship only with Don Calogero Vizzini, the godfather who'd survived the pressures of Mori and now showed he was capable of coming to terms with history even in his small town of Villalba.

The war front moved away from Sicily, but it did not leave peace behind it. The island was full of disturbances, demonstrations and uprisings. The regular distribution of wheat and flour rations was always a tense occasion, when conflict could erupt at any moment. Once more labourers were on the march, and men and women occupied the great estates. Once again revolutionary slogans and strikes were everywhere. Other unionists marched at the head of street processions.

The end of the war brought a wind from the North across the country. Representatives from the partisan movements joined the government; among them were members of Togliatti's Communist party. The public squares were full of clenched-fist salutes and graffiti in praise of Stalin. If someone still raised his hand in the customary Fascist salute, all a militant had to do was close the hand and the gesture immediately changed its political meaning. No one knew who Stalin really was, not even the Communists, who in the packed streets always spoke of him as of some benevolent father figure.

This was what the wind from the North brought with it. It seemed the only wind to blow over the devastated country. But any American soldier stationed in Sicily could see that there was also a wind from the South and predict what its effects might be. It was a movement sweeping over the entire island; it could join forces with the wind from the North only if someone recognized its inherent dignity.

An outside observer of these early post-war years – an American soldier, say, waiting on the ship which would take him home – saw a turbulent and ungovernable country. In that soldier's uncomplicated vision – like that of his commanders – the advance of the Communists was not simply part of the wind blowing from the North. The partisan brigades were insisting, in a defeated country, that they had won a victory over the Nazi-Fascists. And this victory had to have a political implication, it signified a right to govern the new Italy.

But the soldier would also have seen the growing demonstrations taking place in Sicily, as in Naples and Rome. The analysts in the intelligence services were trying to understand how far Italy could be left to itself or, alternatively, to what extent it might be necessary to keep the country "under observation". Left-wing politicians seemed determined not to turn their backs on the growing movements in the South, but to channel them towards gaining control over the entire country. But here an old historical obstacle once more emerged to prevent the development of a single popular national movement in Italy. The uprisings in Sicily, whether their cause was hunger or objections to military service, were seen with distrust and, occasionally, with contempt. The partisans from the North gradually came to dominate the entire historical picture of the time; the uprising in Naples against the Germans, known as the "Four Days", became, as time went by, increasingly similar to other rebellions which the monarchically spirited populace of the city had been involved in. Battles like the one in Barletta, or like the ferocious and dramatic struggle on Cefalonia, where the Italian army fought against the Germans, were sidelined and forgotten. This was done in order to leave the space for a narrative of the war in Italy in which only the "wind from the North" had any right to claim victory.

Any event which didn't fit in with this ideological scheme was at first ignored, then regarded with contempt, and then rejected: while the heroism involved was acknowledged, such events did not represent the pure socialist ideals which were on the other hand embodied by the events in the North. As long as the workers in the South marched under the red flag, then their movements were accepted and recognized, but when they went on unplanned and frequently disorderly demonstrations, then they were rejected as "vestiges of reaction" or "hidden forces" linked to "a repressive system of ownership". In the streets of Naples left-wing demonstrations occasionally met one organized by the monarchists: they would hurl abuse and then blows at each other. The city was divided in two halves which refused to communicate. Even the obvious and documented fact that monarchists had also played a role in the resistance was concealed.

In Sicily the mothers who had protested, even at the risk of physical blows, to prevent the obligatory call-up of their sons had been marginalized and harshly criticized. No one thought that those women could be tired of the war; they were seen as defeatists, and their protests were a blot on the country's liberation.

The Communist party was a member of the temporary government along with other anti-Fascist parties. It aimed at reinforcing its own position with an electoral victory as part of a united left-wing grouping. But the Americans decided the Communists had to be stopped at all costs.

If the Italian State as a whole was weak, in Sicily it was once more non-existent. So little was it present in the island and so distant did it seem, that the Sicilians' enthusiasm for the Americans transformed itself into the dream of making their land part of the United States. Although geographically quite absurd, the project won many adherents. A separatist movement sprang up, propelled forwards by those who wanted regional autonomy for the island, those who wished to see it become an independent State, and those who were already sewing another star onto the United States flag in their imaginations. For their part, the Americans were planning to reoccupy Sicily with their armed forces in the event of a Communist victory in the general election. A triumvirate of men led the separatists; Lucio Tasca, the head of the great estate owners, Finocchiaro Aprile, a leading Freemason and, last but not least, the Mafia godfather Don Calogero Vizzini.[40]

From Trapani to Catania, the separatist movement rapidly grew in numbers. You could find almost everything in it: from those who truly hoped for the moral renewal of Sicilian society, to mafiosi who were planning their future business affairs in a Sicily where everything had changed so that everything would stay the same. The workers continued waving their red flags on demonstrations in the estates; the men who organized them made sure they stayed far away from the separatists' processions. The word "separatism" rather than "autonomy" made the leaders of the Left shudder. While all this was happening, the situation of the island was little short of disastrous. Social injustice was frequent and widespread; the inhabitants were still dependent on American handouts for their food.

---

40 "The historical reality doesn't match the popular belief that Calogero Vizzini did a lot of good for many of the people in his town. It's true that when he handed out jobs, took an interest in agricultural reforms and tried to bring improvements to the town, he was a great man. But when he wasn't obeyed he turned to crime. His life was a singular one. He never married; his only real interest was giving orders and being obeyed. But that's one of the defining characteristics of a godfather. A godfather is powerful because he succeeds in exercising his authority. It's said that Vizzini used to stake a personal claim to public contracts, saying 'this one's for me', and no one else would then apply. This is the defining trait, the ability to command everyone and everything, to be the father and the boss over everything." General Angiolo Pellegrini.

During one distribution of flour there was one injustice too many: a young man became angry and killed a *carabiniere*. His name was Salvatore Giuliano. He went into hiding as the leader of a gang of bandits. Young men from many different villages and towns abandoned their families to join him. In their eyes the Italian State had died long ago. With foreign troops occupying their land and a restricted sovereignty based on the secret articles in the "long" armistice of surrender, they knew nothing of the new State now being born from the ashes.

Without even bothering to try to work out what was causing such disturbance in Sicily, the weak Italian State sent in the *carabinieri* to hunt the young bandit down in the mountains he had known since his boyhood. But the forces of law and order were not up against some street delinquent who'd been forced to go into hiding: Giuliano showed an immediate talent for guerrilla warfare. It's difficult to say when and how he developed this; perhaps native instinct guided him or perhaps he was just very good at turning his terrain into a trap for his enemies.

Giuliano was able to avoid the troops which encircled him – he was as well informed as if he had a network of military spies – and whenever he came into open conflict with them, he won every skirmish, even when the government finally acknowledged the seriousness of the situation and the number of deaths and sent – for the hundredth time – the army in.

He was able to establish control over the area where he and his gang moved about freely enough to be able to receive journalists and cameramen. He went in and out of residential centres. He was contacted by mafiosi, freemasons and secret service agents, such as the American journalist Mike Stern, a reporter and an officer of the OSS, the forerunner of the CIA, who did a photographic feature on him.

In the midst of all the comings and goings and the armed skirmishes, someone convinced Giuliano that he was leading what would turn out to be the nucleus of a future revolutionary army to back the separatist movement. He dreamt of becoming one of history's protagonists. From being a rebellious young man who committed a murder by mistake, he'd turned into a feared bandit, and then a victorious guerrilla fighter. Now he could become the military leader who would succeed in making Sicily the forty-ninth State of the United States. He was so convinced by this that he even sat down to write directly to the American President.

A dense web of interests between the Mafia and American and Italian spies grew up round the figure of Giuliano and undermined him. He was in direct contact with the godfather Vito Genovese while the latter was working for the military government. They can't have been too secret about it, since they had a photograph taken of themselves together, kept in the FBI archives and now widely available on a number of specialist Internet sites, where the image is described simply as "Salvatore Giuliano and Vito Genovese", just like one of the many photographs available of the bandit. It shows the stout ugly Mafia boss standing next to the handsome guerrilla fighter, tall and glamorous, just like the pin-up he became for many women. Further inquiry has revealed that the photograph was recorded in the archives sometime in 1946. The archivist who catalogued and duplicated the image can't have known at that time who Vito Genovese was. He or she simply transcribed the photographer's note scribbled on the back on the image. The quality of the photograph is poorer than those taken by Stern for his feature on Giuliano, which show the bandit on his own and in the pose of a romantic warrior. Historians and researchers have been puzzled by the true identity of the smiling man standing next to Giuliano. The possibility that the man is Mike Stern himself has been ruled out. The fact that no photographs of Vito Genovese in this period when he was working for AMGOT exist makes a certain identification very difficult, even though it's acknowledged that the man in the image closely resembles him. All the archives which hold a copy of this photograph, including the FBI's, continue to insist that the other man is Genovese. Could he have been a namesake of the Mafia boss, someone belonging to the Genovese Family who owned an estate where Giuliano had frequently gone into hiding? But this would not explain why the man is wearing military uniform.

Vito Genovese was working for himself, for the Commission of Cosa Nostra, for the Allied military government, for the American secret services and for several Masonic lodges. Being photographed with Giuliano was not in his interests. If the man shown is Genovese, then Giuliano himself must have asked for the photograph to be taken as a sign of "friendship", a proof of confidence in his role as a guerrilla leader. It would be a kind of seal of approval of his wish to come out of hiding, no longer a delinquent, but the heroic leader of the cause of Sicilian independence. In 1946 it was a photograph which Genovese couldn't refuse, especially as it was Giuliano who wanted it taken. If one accepts the description of the photograph found in all the archives, then it is a document which provides direct evidence of the contacts between Salvatore Giuliano and Vito Genovese and opens up a new path of inquiry into the underhand dealings of the secret services in a country which still had restricted sovereignty. If one rejects the description, then an identification remains to be found for the man who seems pleased to be photographed standing next to the most dangerous outlaw of the period.

It was also made clear to Giuliano what the priority was: if Sicily were to join the United States, then the Communists had to be stopped first.

Giuliano's gang had been infiltrated by common criminals, aimless young men alongside killers who'd been sent by their Mafia Families. Someone took the decision to use these men to fire on the workers – the Communists – who were occupying the estates. The American Department of State saw no problems in hiring criminals of various nationalities from Italy to Japan to stop the Red advance in different parts of the world. But the way in which this was put into practice can't have been agreed in detail with Giuliano himself, since he wasn't present at the meeting to decide these issues, which was held at Portella della Ginestra.

On 1st May 1947, the symbolic day for labour, his gang started shooting at the workers who were demonstrating against the estates. A massacre occurred. The dirty hands behind the incident were rapidly covered up. In the following year, on

18th April 1948, the general elections was held. People with rags on their feet were induced to cast their votes with the promise of a pair of shoes, or a packet of pasta, or a suit, or a hoe and a spell as a farm labourer. The campaign had been interminable, but the actual vote passed in a flash. The united front of Communists and Socialists lost. Salvatore Giuliano realized that was the beginning of the end for him.

During his restless nights on the run, he'd been joined by various women, one of them an attractive journalist. Between sudden escapes and shoot-outs he'd fallen in love with her. They'd had a child called Salvatore. With the Mafia's help Giuliano made sure the boy was sent out of harm's way before circumstances deteriorated even further. Forty years later, the adult Salvatore junior denied the godfathers had had anything to do with his rescue.[41]

So the guerrilla bandit sent his son away, started to avoid making fresh contacts, even with women, tried to renew his contacts with the Americans, even threatened the Mafia: he knew he was no use after the Communist defeat at the polls. In fact he was worse than useless: his gang overran the countryside and attracted the attention of the police, making it difficult to conduct criminal business, since it disturbed the silence and calm which the Mafia needed in order to work. There were too many armed skirmishes, too many police around, too many *carabinieri* and soldiers killed. And there was no possibility that Giuliano could start a new law-abiding career in the normal world.[42]

Sicily had been made Italy's first autonomous region. The separatist movement of which Giuliano was convinced he was the leader had fizzled out. The government in Rome was firmly in the hands of conservatives who supported the American line.

---

41 "It's the Italian State that says they are *padrini*. That will have to be proved. Because if you say *padrini*, you mean mafiosi. Since the Mafia does not exist, they cannot be *padrini*." Salvatore Giuliano Jr, son of Salvatore Giuliano.

42 "Giuliano the bandit – as they still call him – was a criminal through and through, charismatic, cunning, with excellent organizational skills. There's no evidence that he was a 'member' of the Mafia in Montelepre, his birthplace. He was a tool in the hands of the Mafia, and his legend was exploited by the Mafia for their own ends at a time of political crisis." Colonel Mauro Obinu.

All his former "friends" had gone. Giuliano roamed around for a further two years trying to find a way out, another role to play, but he always remained a bandit, isolated and dangerous. The godfathers duly pronounced the sentence of death: his corpse was offered up to the State in the courtyard of a house in Castelvetrano on 5th July 1950. In the press it was reported that he had been shot by *carabinieri*, but no one believed it. For many Sicilians the guerrilla bandit became a myth.[43]

A Medal for Luciano

This was the period when America was seized by a fit of hysteria and started to see Communists everywhere. Hoover launched his FBI on a Communist witch-hunt and threw all his resources into it, making sure it all got reported and filmed.

Meanwhile the Mafia continued not to exist. No one was concerned with it, and the godfathers could work on undisturbed, weaving their webs around the business interests of the post-war and Cold-War world. Luciano's thirty-year sentence vanished into thin air, as provided for in the secret agreements of Operation Underworld. There was even a proposal to award him a Congress medal, as if he were a war hero, for services rendered to the American Navy; the country woke up in time to stop it going through and causing a scandal.[44] He was released from prison and shipped off to Italy, with a dinner in his honour onboard organized by the Commission the day before his departure. In February 1946, the boss found himself in exile back in his old homeland, accompanied by his loyal companion Igea Lissoni.

He was in exile, but he was a free man. The police merely asked him to keep a low profile and avoid getting noticed, but this proved difficult. His arrival was filmed as a leading

---

43 "Bandits become legends only a long time after the crimes they've committed are forgotten." General Angiolo Pellegrini.

44 "Anyone that considers someone a hero that commits homicide, deals drugs and commits continued criminal acts, I think they need their head examined. This man was not a hero, he was a very bad man, a criminal, and criminals deserve to be off the streets. They shouldn't be roaming the streets of this city, or any city for that matter." Bernard B. Kerik.

news item for the newsreels shown in cinemas all over the country. Weekly magazines and daily papers carried features about his life, or at least what was publicly known about it. Luciano was the master of the low profile, had invented the theory that godfathers should be invisible, had set an example of understatement for the whole criminal fraternity. Now he was recognized in bars and restaurants, American sailors and young Italian men asked him for his autograph, droves of reporters pleaded for an interview with him. Some time was needed for a period of calm to re-establish itself. While Giuliano was attracting press attention, Lucky Luciano gradually disappeared. Working in silence, he made contact with Don Calogero, the one Sicilian godfather he trusted. He started to fit the new pieces of Cosa Nostra together and put into action the plan on which he'd been working for years.

Preoccupied by fears of Communism, America thought it could get rid of the Mafia without having to name it, simply by sending various godfathers back to Italy. The forces of law and order did not merely underestimate the level of international organization which the Commission had attained, they were completely unaware of it.

Sam Carolla was one such godfather who was sent into exile in Sicily in April 1947. There he became one of Luciano's men, and managed to get a transfer to Acapulco to take charge of local business. Once in Mexico he couldn't resist the temptation to re-enter the United States secretly, but the federal agents tracked him down again in 1950, and once more shipped him off to Sicily as if he were simply an illegal immigrant rather than a ruthless Mafia boss.

Joe Adonis ended up in Milan with his luxury wardrobe and his capital intact. With his elegant air of being a successful businessman, he had no problems getting his money into Switzerland and depositing it in a secret bank account. Somewhat later he joined the legal practice of Michele Sindona – a tax lawyer known to the Mafia bosses for his dexterity in transferring money to avoid taxation – to help administer part of the work. The police did nothing more than record the frequent trips he made into Switzerland.

It's Better to Command

Under the direct influence of Luciano,[45] the Sicilian Mafia was changing rapidly. The agrarian reforms which the government had introduced were beginning to dismantle the great estates; as its traditional sources of profiteering disappeared – agricultural produce, control of the water supply, exploitation of sulphur-mining, cattle-rustling – so too did the honoured society. The new types of business which the American cousins brought with them made such things as the exploitation of men and children employed as slaves in the sulphur mines, and the kickbacks from the supply of pipes to carry water to citrus plantations, seem like small beer. Confronted by the secret alliance between Lucky Luciano and Don Calogero Vizzini, the old world of tenant farmers, caretakers and share-croppers who tyrannized the labourers had to make way for new generations, to the young mafiosi who had learnt their trade in the new school.

Luciano introduced the new organizational model and knowledge of criminal activity developed in the United States with the flood of immigration into the country: criminal activity which was alert to all the social and economic effects of advanced capitalism. And with this he also brought the new rules he had devised based on the model of time-honoured Mafia traditions: invisibility, Families and the connections between Families, the capacity to become a parasitic state corrupting the legal State.

The secret of the Mafia's exceptional longevity as a secret society lies precisely in its capacity to absorb the new, to change the framework within which it operates, and to transmit its culture to younger generations. Those historians who imagine they understand its concealed structure because it's been described by the *pentiti*, by Valachi, Buscetta, Contorno and Brusca and their ilk, haven't grasped this. Everything the *pentiti* said referred to the years before they were arrested; faced with their confessions the

---

45 "Lucky Luciano was undoubtedly a highly intelligent and effective criminal who changed the ways in which Cosa Nostra operated by introducing a 'managerial' structure which finally put paid to outmoded methods and interests. He also had the foresight to build connections between the two Mafias and their shared business interests by coordinating and unifying, much to the subsequent advantage of the present-day Mafia." Colonel Mauro Obinu.

Mafia immediately closed ranks. It changed its structure, dissolved the Commission, closed down the more obvious communication channels, did away with the men it could not be certain of. The danger is therefore that at the point when we think we understand the Mafia, it has already changed the way it operates within civil society. Investigators into the way the Mafia operates are among the first to use their historical knowledge of the organization to try to identify the genetic elements which enable it to regenerate itself whenever the social conditions change.

Vizzini didn't need lessons in how to reorganize the Sicilian Mafia; for years he'd been its head of State, a significant figure in its historical development. He'd built up a consensus round him which enabled him to take up political roles in normal society; the debacle of the separatist movement had left his authority not merely unscathed but strengthened. He resigned from his post as mayor of Villalba in order to spend more time on his business interests in greater secrecy and circumspection. He was the Mafia's leading authority on the island, but you could come across him in the local coffee bar; his business interests were worth millions of dollars, but he lived unostentatiously at home, looked after by his devoted sister. He had no mistresses and never married. He never did anything which might attract people's attention: no gleaming car to drive around the town in, no expensive clothes to distinguish him from his fellow citizens. No personal vices, no wild parties, no bullying or one-upmanship. He led an almost Spartan life among people who got up before dawn to work in the fields. His only interest, the only activity which appeared to give him pleasure, was giving orders – sometimes terse, sometimes whispered, sometimes entirely wordless.

The two godfathers thus provided a new school for the younger generations, who were trained up in silence and complete security,[46] but not everyone, in the complex world of the Mafia, felt

---

46 "It's essential for the Mafia to hand down the lessons of the past to new generations. Without constant monitoring of the possible candidates for 'affiliation' and for subsequent membership, Cosa Nostra could not go on thriving. The selection process is formal and rigorous, because the wrong choices would damage the unity and secrecy of the organization. The men who are allowed to join Cosa Nostra must be highly reliable – they'll only leave the organization with their death." Colonel Mauro Obinu.

they had to follow their family line. In Corleone the control of organized crime ended up in the hands of a disturbing figure, a godfather who was a practising doctor, quite capable of killing a child with his bare hands and then looking after a sick old man for free, or tending some young mafioso who had not even been recommended to him by friends of friends. Dr Navarra, Don Michele Navarra, was the undisputed ruler of Corleone; he'd attained this position, his authority over life and death, with a chilling combination of favours and terror. Being a doctor and being a Mafia boss made him diabolical; under his command there emerged a generation of killers who were among the most ferocious and barbaric ever known, and all the while he continued to practise medicine in a town completely subjugated to his authority. Like Vizzini, Navarra didn't seem to have much inclination for worldly pleasures – apart from giving orders. As the old Mafia saying puts it, "*Cumannari è megghiu ca fùttiri*" ("Commanding is better than fucking").

Written in Sicilian dialect it seems less vulgar; certainly if you translated "*fùttiri*" as "making love", you wouldn't understand a thing. The twentieth century tended to reinforce the identification of love with marriage, and to see sex taking place only within marriage, but in earlier times matrimony was much closer to the concept of patrimony. If women didn't possess their own patrimony or dowry, then marriage was merely a contract for a way of life which often resembled slavery. Love existed outside marriage, was opposed to marriage and, at times, to the whole social order – like Romeo and Juliet, Tristan and Isolde, Lancelot and Guinevere. Despite the modern identification of love with marriage, it's still difficult today to say how many marriages are based on love and how many on power. And when, in a particular society, we see men whose family life is based entirely on their authority, and who derive their right to sex from their power to command, no one criticizes. It's not even regarded as a venial sin.

A corollary of the law of "*cumannari*" stipulates that the power to command allows one to demand sex as and when one wishes. It took centuries for the chain of command which leads from the exercise of authority to the supply of sex on demand to be broken, although godfathers like Vizzini didn't go down this path, preferring instead the pure pleasure of commanding.

But it's also true that however powerful a mafioso may be, this does not prevent him from becoming genuinely fond of his own family, so that he loves his offspring, and grows to love his wife too, after a manner of speaking. In this, mafiosi are no different from ordinary folk. Some have taken their families with them when they've had to go on the run, like Totò Riina. Giovanni Brusca went into hiding in the basement of a villa together with his wife and his five-year-old son Davide. He'd got rid of the corpse of another mafioso's little boy in an acid bath, but he loved his own son and didn't want to be separated from him even when the situation was desperate. In his hideout boxes of toys were found – pieces of Lego scattered over the kitchen floor, on the bed the plastic models of dinosaurs which kids go wild about, a child's mountain bike, a Super Nintendo and a video recorder with a supply of cartoon videos. Just like in any other nice family.

While he was in hiding, the Mafia boss Antonino Giuffré sent affectionate letters to his family via the organization's own secret postman. Here's a passage from a letter to his son at university about his fiancée: "Dear Salvatore, I'm glad you can tell your father about your personal feelings for your girlfriend so that I can appreciate what you feel for her and find a place in my heart for her too". And to his wife he writes: "My dear Gioia, I hope and pray you are not in any difficulty. I send you all my love and kisses".

Once the principle of "*cumannari*" has been established, the women who have helped to build the blood family have a precisely defined role to play in the system. They're responsible for reproduction, for making sure there will be a new generation of mafiosi; they give an air of social respectability and of honourableness which also serves as a proof to fellow mafiosi that her husband is a decent man who abides by the organization's traditional rules and customs. "*Cumannari è megghiu ca futtiri*" in this context is far from being some obscenity uttered by a Hollywood gangster: it's a kind of guarantee that the man you're dealing with is worthy of respect, serious, trustworthy, someone you can do business with. Because doing business is ultimately what it all comes down to.

In Don Navarra's Corleone, the only law was the rule of violence, but in other places in Sicily a new and distinct type of Mafia godfather was emerging, more in line with the modern system. It was then a common belief that certain areas of the island were unaffected by Mafia power. The word "Mafia" there was just a synonym for vigour or courage. If a striking young woman who held herself well walked by on the other side of the street, the men who looked at her would say, "What a mafiosa!" The word *"babba"* on the other hand denoted something or someone who was feeble, possessing no Mafia qualities. The area round Catania or Messina and a few others were all described as *babba*. So deeply held was this conviction that it took a quarter of a century to see the truth of the matter, that there wasn't a single part of the island free from the Mafia's control.

It is in the undisturbed tranquillity of a backwater like Messina, quintessentially *babba*, that Michele Sindona began his career. He started out by dealing with the occupying American troops, but once this was over, he worked hard to acquire a sophisticated knowledge of banking, and learn how to move huge sums of money around in the global financial market. It hardly mattered whether the money came from Mafia racketeering or church charities: money is colourless. At least that's what Sindona believed as he worked away in the shadows: money was money, and the rules of the market applied wherever it came from. It was all a question of knowing how to move it around the world, getting the most out of different legal and regulatory systems.

He opened a studio in Milan, came and went as he pleased in the Vatican, and was familiar with leading politicians in Rome. He worked in close contact with the most hidden levels of the Mafia, the same type of men who had brought down Notarbartolo, who worked behind the scenes in the leading banks where money moves and is recycled rapidly.

Sindona moved so much money so fast that he ended up in control of the Franklin National Bank in the United States, saw ministers regularly and had cardinals to dinner. No one ever thought of asking the small clerk from Messina where all his money came from; the fact that he came from a city regarded as *babba* protected him for a long time. Decades passed before Sindona was forced to come out into the open, hunted down by the killers sent by the Mafia, who wanted the money back which had disappeared in the twists and turns of his financial manoeuvring.

The Paradise of the Mafia

Luciano kept a base in New York: it was run by Meyer Lansky, his right-hand man, his childhood friend, practically his alter ego, a kind of virtual image of the exiled boss. The Commission continued to manage Cosa Nostra in complete invisibility; the years passed by and the Mafia went on not existing. Various Families did well out of the way business was going: the Bonanno, the Gambino, the Genovese, whose godfather, Don Vito, had managed to re-enter the United States without difficulty. Whenever a favour was needed, you only had to ask and a "zip" arrived from Sicily. Those who were marked out to die had to die, and if possible their corpses had to disappear too – death itself had to become invisible.

In the absence of Luciano's direct authority and leadership, however, the various bosses regarded each other with surly suspicion, ready to attack if anyone poached on their territory or got his hands on a piece of business which was rightfully theirs. Only those who'd taken Luciano's lesson to heart, like Carlo Gambino, were circumspect about running such risks.

In Mario Puzo's novel *The Godfather*, and in the film made from it, the fictional protagonist who dominates the story is called Don Vito Corleone, like the Sicilian town. The demands of the Hollywood star system meant that Marlon Brando was asked to play the role, with his burly physique and an imposing jaw made even more prominent by make-up and padding. Various godfathers, all from Luciano's school, lie behind the inspiration for the character, but the style of his authority is taken from Gambino. Gambino's style was muted: the others thought he was a weakling and a coward. He kept to the sidelines, never responded in kind, never issued threats or uttered verbal abuse. He stayed out of the fray and didn't listen to the false rumours about him which went the rounds – they may even have pleased him. He let such things take their course and he let people say what they want; the wizened little man would only show a thin smile. He'd followed Luciano's example and was set to become his finest disciple. His real weapon was his intelligence,[47] but he didn't want others to realize this. The Mafia was once more undergoing a period of upheaval, and it was necessary to focus on the coming changes.

In his exile in Italy, far from New York and from his former companions among the "Young Turks", Luciano felt uneasy. His birthplace in Sicily, Lercara Friddi, had organized a big party to celebrate his return. The sugar-almond cakes and the sweet local wine couldn't really replace the champagne he'd swigged in the New York nightclubs; he couldn't forget the glamorous world of the American Mafia where he moved around in casinos and luxury restaurants. American mafiosi might be invisible, but they were determined to live it up as much as they could. Luciano had managed to get out of prison, where the testimonies in court of various ladies of the night had put him. He'd made a big mistake, even though he was familiar with the old Mafia warning about steering clear of prostitution as a business. And his mistake meant that he was barred from ever going back to the United States.

But he could try and go to what was considered to be the Mafia's paradise: the island of Cuba. So he packed his cases and left Italy like an ordinary tourist and arrived unnoticed in Havana in 1947. On the island he met Meyer Lansky and many

---

47 "I think that the role typified in the movie *The Godfather* has never existed. It was a highly romantic view of what many people say was modelled after Carlo Gambino. But every Mafia Family in Sicily and the United States are vicious criminals, vicious murderers, they're not the romantic family individuals portrayed in the movie." Thomas V. Fuentes.

other bosses; they all had the air of middle-aged men enjoying a holiday, spending their time by the pool or on the gaming tables or in local nightclubs. But Luciano had summoned them for what is now called the Havana Conference.

Cuba was not a casual choice for their meeting. It was near the United States coastline, it was at the centre of every kind of trade, there was gambling, and prostitution and drugs were freely available. Fulgencio Batista, the dictator who ruled the island, was a personal friend of Meyer Lansky's; his regime guaranteed the utmost privacy for the bosses' conference.

Frank Sinatra was also a guest at Luciano's hotel. When news of the Mafia conference became public, he told the police that he'd gone there only for a singing engagement. "It seems like Sinatra will only ever sing for the Mafia," wrote some American newspapers. The "Voice" was photographed embracing Luciano. Urged on by the FBI, the Italian Police searched Luciano's house in Naples and found a gold cigarette case inscribed with a dedication from Sinatra to his great friend Lucky. In the Westchester Premier Theatre in New York, Sinatra was photographed with Carlo Gambino, Big Paul Castellano and various other bosses. The photo was published, but had little effect: Sinatra was the most popular singer in America, his concerts and discs and films were among the biggest money-spinners in show business. He was called to testify in front of commissions of inquiry on several occasions, and always managed to get off the hook by making some joke which then got reported in the papers, as for example when, accused of having helped to carry millions of illegal dollars, he quipped that he'd never have been able to lift the cases. His son was kidnapped when he was trying to make a name as a singer, and then mysteriously freed after only a couple of days. The two idiots who'd carried out the job hadn't the faintest idea of what they'd got themselves into. They weren't aware of his many powerful friends. The only certain thing known about Sinatra is that he was never charged for his links to the Mafia bosses.

In undisturbed Cuba, between a visit to the casino and a concert by Sinatra, Luciano explained his plans to the others.

The project consisted of setting a true global market before the concept had even been thought of, creating a worldwide organization for trade in the first merchandise which would reach everywhere: drugs.

The bosses needed to be able to buy and sell consignments of drugs rapidly, and they had to be confident that they were supported by an efficient system which took care of every stage of the process, from cultivation to selling. The business would be done by verbal agreement, with subsequent payment guaranteed, just like the selling of stocks and shares.[48] In Luciano's view, cultivation should move progressively eastwards from Turkey to the Far Eastern countries, whose governments would turn a blind eye to the vast plantations, and whose armies would be happy to take an agreed share of the profits. The refining needed to produce pure heroin could be done in France under the control of the Marseilles gangs, or – and here Luciano suggested an optional alternative – in Sicily, which would be a secure enough place to set up some refineries. The centre for distribution would be Cuba, although Luciano sensed it was no longer as secure a place as it used to be. Alternatives needed to be readily available.

The channels already employed for cigarette-smuggling were to be adapted to the requirements of the new business. In this field, too, Sicily – and Italy as a whole, thanks to emigrants scattered all over the world – appeared to provide excellent opportunities for the distribution of drugs by the so-called "raindrop method".[49]

---

48 "The Mafia has its own kind of Stock Exchange. For the major consignments of drugs there are agreements whereby a group of bosses make verbal promises to buy a large lot, which will then be distributed among all those taking part. They then undertake to pay for the quantity they have agreed to buy. This is how the whole system of the Mafia narcotics trade works – by verbal agreement. There's someone who guarantees the arrival of the goods and someone who guarantees the payment of the consignment." General Angiolo Pellegrini.

49 "The so-called 'raindrop method' consists of a series of disguised journeys. The elderly lady off to visit her relatives in the United States who manages to conceal a couple of kilos of heroin on her person, or shopkeepers who manage to disguise small amounts among their usual products – compared to huge quantities of refined heroin, this is an easy method to get drugs through customs controls." Colonel Mauro Obinu.

Luciano's hunch about Cuba was confirmed a few years later, when violent disorders, the first signs of an emerging revolutionary movement, erupted throughout the island.

Heroin started to travel in the trunks of emigrants who were more or less unaware of what they were carrying. It was added to sweets and cakes bound all over the world. The quantities of refined heroin began to need a larger-scale commercial system. Luciano got Vito Genovese to open a factory making sweets and toffees in Sicily for export. Frank Coppola set up a business producing tinned vegetable soup; judging from the quantities which were exported, it seemed as if enthusiasm for the product had swept the world. Carlos Marcello established a factory for tinned food in Tunis and built up a huge market. Gaetano Badalamenti, based in Hamburg, started to trade in tinned food and citrus fruits. Nick Gentile organized a chain of sardine-canning factories. The godfathers found that with these methods the drugs were so well concealed business was easy. Only on rare occasions did a consignment get searched by the police. There'd be astonished reports in the press on the tricks used by organized crime to disguise the import of heroin, while the police would put the curious receptacles on display.[50]

Other godfathers occupied themselves with managing the import side of the business all over the world. In New York Joseph Profaci was confident enough to open the Mamma Mia Import Company to receive the disguised heroin. He and many others, like Joe Bonanno and Vito Vitale, became the entrepreneurs of the first truly global market.

In 1949 a journalist working for *Avanti* discovered the confectionary factory which was owned by Vito Genovese. He denounced it in an article, but on the very same night that the piece was being printed for the following day's edition the factory closed down and vanished. No one had yet really understood how good Cosa Nostra's organizational capacities

---

50 "The scale of the business was at first completely underestimated. No one thought that the export trade was being used to smuggle drugs or that Sicily was actively involved." General Angiolo Pellegrini.

were.[51] Only small incidents or the discovery of some consignments got reported. The trade in heroin started when the Mafia still officially did not exist.

Luciano was able to think at twice the speed of his fellow bosses and could see much further ahead. In Cuba he tried to force the hands of the other bosses in an attempt to put an end to his humiliating Italian exile, so that he could return to the United States. 1948 was a presidential-election year; Luciano proposed a slowdown in the drug trade while the campaign was on. The bosses looked at each other in puzzlement. They held their breath. If Luciano was pushing for it, then the Commission would certainly agree to a halt in the drug trade in America. In silence each godfather ruminated on how he might go it alone.[52]

Thomas Dewey was the Republican candidate that year. Luciano hoped he would be elected and wanted to give him a hand. His great accuser, the man who'd got him sent to prison and then, for impelling military reasons, had secured his release, had run unsuccessfully in 1944, and was making another attempt with the united support of all the conservatives in America. In helping his campaign, Luciano hoped to gain some credit for himself which the future President would acknowledge by allowing him to return from exile.

On the night of polling day the godfather drank a celebratory toast, since it looked as if Dewey had won. Some newspapers hurried to print the morning's edition with headlines announcing his victory. But Luciano's hopes were dashed after only

---

51 "Up to at least the 1970s Cosa Nostra regarded the narcotics trade as secondary to its main interests and comparatively risky, because it involved non-Mafia criminals who couldn't always be relied on and were vulnerable to being infiltrated by the police. But over time, thanks to strengthening ties with the American Mafia and using the previous organization of tobacco-smuggling as a model, Cosa Nostra has developed a high degree of efficiency, and become a world leader in the field. Many Mafia Families, either working independently or as part of a coordinated plan, have set up large channels for the import of narcotics into Europe, with operative cells in numerous countries of North and South America and in Europe itself." Colonel Mauro Obinu.

52 "What's interesting is that La Cosa Nostra did not attempt to control the distribution or activity of the Sicilians in the US, but attempted to share in the proceeds, and some parts of the US Families did jointly engage in the activity. They weren't allowed to do so officially by the Commission, but unofficially some of them did, because there was so much money to be made." Thomas V. Fuentes.

a few hours when the counting of votes proved him wrong. The real winner was Harry S. Truman, who took an amused pleasure in being photographed reading the morning's daily papers announcing his rival's victory.

Despite all his precautions, Luciano's presence in Cuba was discovered. But before he was sent back to Italy and to exile, the conference had one more piece of business to decide: a sentence of death.

It was an important decision, and only the Commission could take it, since it didn't involve a mere foot soldier but one of the most prominent members of the organization. Meyer Lansky also voted for the death sentence. The condemned man was his right-hand man, Bugsy Siegel. When the leading bosses make a decision, there is no right of appeal, nor is the victim informed in advance of his impending execution.

The Flamingo

Only the rich could go to Cuba to visit the casinos and bordellos. For the godfathers the island was "cosa nostra", but it didn't fulfil maximum business potential. The Mafia wanted a place where they could profit not just from the rich, but from the average American citizen indulging his private vices. They needed a place where any ordinary person could go and spend a year's savings on gambling, find a prostitute at reasonable prices and waste the remainder of his money on getting high, and all without disturbing the public State and its concerns for public morals.

"Casino ships" permanently anchored offshore had been invented as a solution to the problem. But they were inconvenient: motorboats were needed to ferry clients continually back and forth, they couldn't be evacuated quickly if federal agents or the coastguards came to inspect them, and they were affected by bad weather. No floating casino had ever been successful. An easier place was needed where everyone could find satisfaction for the personal vices which Luciano had described.

The desert. Bugsy Siegel had come up with the idea, which got to Lansky, and then went from Lansky to Luciano. The Commission gave the plan its approval, and the godfathers invested a part of their capital. While the bosses were holding their conference in Cuba, a dusty unknown town in Nevada was being transformed into a dazzling city: Las Vegas.

With several million illegal dollars Bugsy had begun to build the Flamingo Hotel. "Flamingo" was the nickname of his new mistress, Virginia Hill, a woman known for her long legs and fiery character. Lansky's right-hand man was of the opinion that Las Vegas had to be glittering with luxury if it was going to attract masses of clients, and he was right. The city would dazzle and decoy all those punters who wanted to spend a few days indulging in illicit enjoyments, even if it were just once in a lifetime.

But Bugsy got behind in pursuing his grandiose projects, and the godfathers began to lose patience. Luciano and the others couldn't make out what was happening in the Nevada desert, nor why, with all the money they'd poured into it, the business hadn't yet started up. Their spies informed them that a part of the money had probably ended up in a secret account in Switzerland, placed there by Virginia Hill. They asked Bugsy what had happened to the money they'd invested; he already knew from the question that he was in deep trouble. So although the Flamingo Hotel wasn't yet ready for guests who wanted a room to rest in during the intervals between a game of poker and an evening at the roulette tables, he decided to open the casino. The money started to pour in as people came from all over the United States. But the Commission's executioners were already on their way.

It was a traditional ritual of Mafia killings that the victims had the right to see their murderers as they were dying. You could never shoot a man in the back. But killers also superstitiously believed that the last image a murdered man saw – in other words, their faces – remained impressed on his retina, like a photographic image, so carrying a portrait of the killers into the afterlife. When the police found Bugsy's corpse, one of the eyes was discovered several yards away from the body.

Virginia Hill was questioned several times by the magistrates in the case. She obviously couldn't deny knowing Bugsy and the other bosses, but she maintained she'd known nothing about any criminal activities. Bugsy might have been a gangster, but she was simply his girlfriend. She waited a long time before making a move. She knew about the Mafia, and knew they were capable of waiting a long time for the right moment to arrive. So she waited – until she thought the godfathers had forgotten about her. She left for the mountains on the border between Austria and Switzerland. She told everyone she'd found a new lover, a strong young skiing instructor. Virginia "Flamingo" Hill knew the Mafia, but she didn't know it well enough. She didn't manage to draw the money in time. She was found dead: the official verdict was suicide.

The Mafia Boss of Tokyo

The creation of Las Vegas was just one of Cosa Nostra's businesses all over the world. The war had opened up many opportunities, and the criminal underworld of the only country to have come out of it really victorious didn't let a single one escape them.

The occupation of Japan was dated officially from 2nd September 1945, when the act of unconditional surrender was signed onboard the battleship *Missouri*. Nicola Zappetti was a young man in the US army; on the day the Japanese surrendered, he'd been on sentry duty for a short while at Omura airport near Nagasaki. He was a navy sergeant and had been among the first American troops to land in the country; he didn't seem to have been affected by the terrible consequences of the dropping of the two atomic bombs on Japan. The streets were full of the dead and the cities razed flat, as in all the countries where the war had taken its toll. The scientists hadn't yet had time to study the effect of nuclear explosions and of radiation on humans, animals, plants, water and soil, but for the generals it was only the explosions which mattered. They knew that the Japanese army would have fought, soldier by soldier, to the death, never retreating, as resolute as the kamikaze pilots in the air after their last drink of sake. The dropping of the bombs would prevent all this and bring the war to an end and deliver the country into the hands of the conquerors.

But Sergeant Zappetti left others to go into the centre of Nagasaki, and instead followed the business instincts he'd first developed among the Mafia clans in East Harlem. In 1946 his naval division was sent home, he was released from military service, and the good times began to roll for him. The army had advertised no fewer than six thousand posts for jobs to support the occupying forces; as an ex-marine, Zappetti had the right to obtain one, and as a citizen of the victorious and occupying country he enjoyed a lot of other privileges too, large and small – he was allowed, for example, to bring his own car over from America to Japan on the Navy's ships.

Nicola explained the business opportunities there were in Japan to the East Harlem Families. On a brief visit back to New York, he bought a second-hand Ford for a few dollars, filled it completely with small bags, each containing twenty thousand flints for cigarette lighters, and made his way back to Japan. Not a single soldier stopped him to carry out a check. Zappetti had found there was an almost complete lack of flints in Japan. He sold them all quickly on the black market and became rich. Shortly afterwards he married a Japanese dentist who spoke good English; their wedding was filmed by a cameraman working for the army, who was producing a documentary on the relations between the Americans and the Japanese. Now he was in a position to make his first contacts with the Japanese criminal underworld; he knew his back was covered in New York.

The local criminal organization was called Yakuza. It was made up of different gangs, which in their structure closely resembled the Mafia Families in America. They controlled the black market: if Zappetti wanted to do business in Japan, then it was essential to come to an agreement with them. But this was easier said than done. Zappetti's advantage as a citizen of the winning and occupying power diminished with every year that passed. His plan was to set himself up as the Japanese branch of the American Mafia (an organization which still didn't officially "exist") – an excellent career move for a junior mafioso who'd been brought up on the streets of New York.

Finding a Yakuza boss he could talk to wasn't by any means straightforward. The older bosses insisted the organization was different from the Mafia, and worked to defend the poor and the oppressed. They were murderers and delinquents, but they claimed they took their inspiration from the old Samurai traditions – humility, a sense of duty, loyalty to their leader, stoical endurance of imprisonment and physical pain. Not so different from the Mafia code, but it was impossible to get the Yakuza bosses to see this. "A strong man doesn't die on the tatami," they kept repeating to the ex-marine as he tried to negotiate business with them. He himself thought that the tatami, the traditional reed mat found in Japanese homes, was rather uncomfortable, but he didn't pursue the issue.

Zappetti had an agreement with a colonel who worked in the Occupation Finance Office, through whom he was able to obtain a supply of otherwise unfindable items for the black market – the famous Zippo brand of cigarette lighters, nylon stockings, sugar and tobacco. The Japanese gangs would take care of the distribution and sale of the items. An undercover military detective managed to infiltrate the organization, with the result that the colonel was imprisoned and Zappetti arrested and sent back to the United States on bail. The only precaution the authorities took was to confiscate his passport. It could have spelt the end of all his ambitions, but Zappetti didn't lose heart. The most powerful Mafia boss he could manage to contact in New York lived on 110th Street. Zappetti asked to see him and was allowed to call. He calmly explained the situation in Japan – the role of the Americans, the revival in the economy, the Yakuza gangsters – exactly as it was; the boss listened to what he was saying and agreed to help him. A few days later Zappetti got his passport back and was able to return to Japan.

Once there he found a situation which was changing rapidly. Democracy was being introduced for the first time, but Communist propaganda was spreading among the workers. Zappetti managed to track down an authentic Communist – or so at least he and everyone else thought him – by the name of Leo

Yuskoff. He was a Russian, an accredited member of the Soviet Communist Party and also a gangster who liked to get drunk and drive smart cars. Together they set up a company which would, in the traditional Mafia way, combine legal and illegal business in order to ensure maximum profit with maximum security. They even invented a fictional Bank of Texas, with no offices and no capital, in order to put the name on headed writing paper and impress their business partners.

The American occupation of Japan lasted six years, seven months and twenty-six days. Zappetti exploited every minute to his own advantage. When the Americans finally withdrew, Zappetti's privileges finished too, and he had to get used to dealing on equal terms with the Yakuza bosses. Being an American was still an advantage, but Zappetti's name was now on the wanted lists of both the FBI and the Japanese Police. He was arrested a second time and once again had to ask the American Families to get him released, but the episode didn't set him back. Between spells inside and being bailed out with Mafia help he managed to get a number of initiatives going – among those which were above board, there was Nicola's Pizza, the largest pizzeria in Japan, where all the Hollywood stars who were in the country to promote their films – Liz Taylor, John Wayne, Harry Belafonte and, naturally, Frank Sinatra – went to eat.

The Communist witch-hunt in the United States also caused Zappetti a few problems. The authorities summoned him for interrogation as a possible Communist supporter, given his business partnership with Yuskoff. The police weren't interested in the fact that he was an Italian mafioso or that his partner was a Soviet mobster. Their orders were to stop Communism; that was all that counted. The Reds had to be stopped all over the world, country by country. American political strategists believed in the so-called "domino theory", which held that it only took one country to fall into the hands of the Communists for all the others to follow suit. In the struggle, the American Department of State made no bones about drawing on the resources of the criminal underworld, even in Japan. When an official visit from President Eisenhower to Japan was being planned, the Interior Ministry realized that there were only 15,000 policemen to protect the event; so an agreement was reached with Yakuza, who provided thirty thousand gangsters to ensure security throughout the visit of the American head of State. Sporting events were also part of a precise political strategy. In 1964 the Olympic Games were held in Tokyo, four years after they'd taken place in Italy, another country which had been defeated in the war and was full of Reds. Another agreement was reached with Yakuza, with the result that there was a noticeable reduction in the amount of crime during the period of the games.

Zappetti's business affairs were booming. A reporter from the New York *Daily Mirror* asked for an interview. When the article came out, the former junior mafioso was described in the headline as the "Mafia boss of Tokyo". But Zappetti made a mistake. Instead of lying low in order to reacquire some invisibility, he was puffed up with pride at the thought of being a Mafia boss, and believed it would give him greater prestige and authority. He even agreed to be interviewed for an American documentary film on relations between America and Japan, as a former marine who'd stayed in the country. Zappetti was allied to Yakuza, but at the same time under their control. The Tokyo police made him "Public enemy No. 1" and put him at the head of their list of foreign gangsters operating in Japan. Zappetti's frequent trips back to New York were also under FBI observation. He tried to improve the situation by becoming a Japanese citizen in 1983. At that time the country's law obliged foreigners applying for citizenship to change their names to a Japanese one. Zappetti adopted the surname of his fourth wife, Koizumi, but it didn't do him any good. He was forced to employ two killers from East Harlem as bodyguards.

Yakuza preferred to manage its own affairs; it wasn't in their interests to have a mafioso working in Tokyo, even less so when he was so visible and known to the police in Japan and in New York. The Japanese Families were capable of controlling a large part of the production of drugs, and they also had huge financial resources which they could launder and recycle in places like Las Vegas and Los Angeles. Zappetti was not included in this new line of business – the FBI and Japanese Police were keeping him under close observation, and he would attract too much attention to the trade in huge consignments of drugs. No one wanted to involve the man who'd become known as the "Mafia boss of Tokyo".

Mafia Meeting

The godfather in East Harlem who'd helped Zappetti out on various occasions also belonged to the Commission which Luciano had set up, and of which he was the leading and most respected member. The organization's business was spreading to various countries; keeping the balance among all the different clans across the world in the last analysis depended on Luciano's intelligence. But Luciano was forced to stay in exile in Italy. When he'd been sent back from Cuba, the Italian Police had made him transfer his place of residence to Naples. The situation in Italy was changing. The massacre at Portella della Ginestra and other events like it had roused people's consciences. For the authorities the Mafia continued not to exist, but a minority started to protest, loudly, against the organization.

One day, as he was walking along the street, dressed modestly, bespectacled, with the air of a retired mathematics teacher, absorbed in his own thoughts, a passer-by approached and slapped him resoundingly on the cheek. The godfather didn't react, didn't say a word, went on his way. No one was ever able to explain why the passer-by had done such an outrageous thing to the boss of bosses. Perhaps he wanted to show off, or thought he could punish an old boss who was unarmed. But he'd made a big mistake. The Mafia waited as usual for the right moment; after many years had passed, Gaetano Badalamenti sent his killers to murder the man like a dog. His corpse was displayed as a sign that he'd paid with his life for insulting Luciano.

But apart from this episode something was genuinely changing in the country. Luciano had to resign himself to remaining there and trying to manage his business from the Mediterranean.

The Italian government passed a law which abolished the great estates in Sicily. With their disappearance the honoured society lost its traditional raison d'être. The new godfathers looked on in silence, busy with the affairs of Cosa Nostra and well-camouflaged in civil society. They knew they had to look ahead. No one put up a fight to keep the old restricted sources of income; it was only worth fighting, with shoot-outs and the risk of death, to carve out more territory in the new global market and its main merchandise.

But managing the global market for drugs was not straightforward. The godfathers had to work on the business organization like the board of directors of a multinational company. It was necessary to protect the cultivation, pushing it further eastwards, and to check at source the harvesting done by the producers. Relations with the gangs in Marseilles who were responsible for refining the heroin were strained. Men had to be sent out continually all over the world to check up on business or to start up new enterprises. Expert chemists were needed to work in the refineries. Those involved had to make sure that the garages and cellars full of phials and stoves could be cleared in minutes, or that the equipment was "disposable" and could be left behind if a quick getaway was needed. Transportation required ships, trucks and commercial insurance. There was a very high number of fulltime "employees" involved in the business, and they needed to be paid. Recycling money could be tricky; men with sophisticated banking expertise were needed to avoid the risk of losing most of the profits from the sale. Cosa Nostra's market was in continual expansion, and the new organizational levels which emerged from the drugs trade had to be ratified and new agreements had to be reached between the leading Mafia bosses.

While Sicily slumbered on, in 1957 Lucky Luciano held a summit of American and Italian godfathers at the Hotel delle Palme in Palermo.[53] The meeting seemed like the reunion of old friends who had emigrated – lots of drinking, eating and hearty laughter. The Mafia, that secret and parasitical state, does not much care for archives. It doesn't keep minutes of its meetings or lists of

---

53 "The meeting which took place at the Hotel delle Palme in October 1957 is a very significant event in the history of organized crime. It was an opportunity to bring together the leading personalities of the American Mafia with their peers from Palermo and other towns in Sicily in order to reach agreements on the narcotics trade which would dominate transatlantic business for the next forty years." Colonel Mauro Obinu.

those present; it doesn't issue documents or press communiqués. In Palermo there wasn't a chairman or a secretary, and no one declared the meetings open or closed – in fact in the hotel there didn't seem to be any obvious meetings. Like all underworld conferences, the bosses met, perhaps in small groups, and talked; then they parted, perhaps to talk a bit more in pairs, and then everyone would get together at mealtimes.

It was just like the social reunion of any group of people – veterans, former comrades or anyone else. Investigators couldn't even establish how many people were attending. The arrival from the United States was recorded of Joe Bonanno, Camillo Carmine Galante, Giovanni Bonventre, Joe Di Bella, Vito Vitale, Charles Orlando, John Priziola and Santo Sorge. Although Luciano didn't like the Sicilian godfathers, some of the leading members of the new generation were allowed to take part. Giuseppe Genco Russo, Vincenzo Rimi, Cesare Manzella, Domenico La Fata and Calcedonio Di Pisa were all seen entering the doors of the Hotel delle Palme.

Once agreement had been reached over the issues to be discussed, and once the series of dinners was over, they all returned to getting on with their own affairs.[54] A further conference would be needed in the United States to extend the agreements decided in Sicily to everyone over there. But Vito Genovese took everyone by surprise with an initiative of his own. A few months after the Palermo summit, he summoned the American bosses to a meeting in the mountains near New York, known as the Apalachin Conference.[55] Lucky Luciano and Meyer Lansky immediately realized what was afoot: Don Vito was resentful about Palermo, where once again the exiled Luciano's huge influence over the Commission had been confirmed; now he wanted to take advantage of the godfather's absence from the United States. Probably he also wanted to

---

54 "The significance of the meeting can be summed up in the following way: Cosa Nostra borrows a suit from its American cousins, but that doesn't mean it gives up its own independence and identity. In doing so it laid the foundation for a flourishing narcotics trade." Colonel Mauro Obinu.

55 "We believe that the main purpose was for the bosses of the American Families to decide whether or not they would engage jointly in heroin-trafficking with their Sicilian 'cousins'." Thomas V. Fuentes.

revive the old idea of the "boss of bosses", with himself or one of his allies in the role. If Genovese had his way it would be a retrograde step for the whole organization, threatening the well-oiled machine which worked on a global scale.

The Apalachin Conference was disguised as a plenary session of the Mafia. They ostensibly discussed new business opportunities, but behind the scenes a challenge was being mounted to the new organization which Luciano, Lansky and their allies had worked so hard to create. Luciano stopped his men from attending (except for the shrewd Carlo Gambino, as a fifth column) and decided to do something which was almost unheard of in the world of the Mafia: a tip-off.[56] The news that a large meeting of mobsters was taking place at Apalachin was passed not to federal agents but to the New York Police. For the first time there was a raid on one of the meetings of organized crime. Hoover and the FBI were caught on the back foot. All the press started to talk about the Mafia, the Apalachin Conference, who the godfathers were and what their business interests were. The police raid showed that not only did the Mafia exist, but a central authority – the Commission – also existed.[57] Hoover decided to move fast in an attempt to recover lost ground. He brazenly and cynically declared that his agents knew all about Cosa Nostra and had been keeping it under observation. Naturally – Hoover asserted – this secret and nameless organization which the bosses called Cosa Nostra had been well known to the FBI for some time.

Hoover was a past master at relations with the media. His brazen declarations allowed him to gain time while newspapers

---

56 "Our opinion is that Luciano was out in Italy at the time, and he was sort of jealous about what was going on. At that conference, a number of his associates didn't show up, so the automatic perception was that since his associates weren't there, they couldn't be endangered, so he was the one that gave out the information." Bernard B. Kerik.

57 "They'd meet in different places: in back of restaurants, in social clubs, in homes. They never would meet in any one place, because they didn't want to be detected. Then occasionally there would be national meetings involving the Families from all over the country, and that's what was interrupted and discovered in Apalachin, NY in the late 1950s. They were having a national meeting of all the Families. That was rare. Those kinds of meetings took place infrequently, because they were too dangerous." Rudolph Giuliani.

and magazines kept printing stories about the Mafia. In the American way, to avoid excessive repetition an acronym was coined: LCN, short for "La Cosa Nostra". Luciano had never wanted the organization to be given a name, and now, thanks to Hoover, the American Mafia had been given its definitive label.

In the mean time the FBI's finest agents passed their nights reading books and articles in an attempt to acquire all the information accumulated over time by those journalists and writers who believed the Mafia existed and had spent time and effort investigating it. All the articles and features, the news items from the crime pages and the brief cuttings which had appeared in previous years were collected and catalogued so that the FBI could start to repair their ignorance about the Mafia. It wasn't easy to pull the wool over the eyes of sharp-witted American journalists. If they were to be given even merely adequate replies to their questions in press conferences or when they crowded round on the steps of the law courts, then hundreds of books and thousands of articles had to be read and digested.

Luciano had caught the FBI on the back foot, but Cosa Nostra had lost its invisibility, and the man responsible, Vito Genovese, had to pay the price, despite being a leading American godfather, the boss of one of the Mafia's most powerful Families. The world of organized crime blamed him for what had occurred. At Apalachin huge risks had been taken: many junior mafiosi had given themselves up and been arrested to enable the bosses to make their escape. The federal agents were opening up investigation dossiers by the dozen. Business was suffering.

Vito Genovese knew the Mafia. He became anxious and insecure, he saw spies and traitors everywhere, even among the foot soldiers of his own gang. He tried to work out which way the wind was blowing from the Commission. The due amount of time was allowed to elapse. Then a tip-off delivered Genovese into the hands of the FBI. He was charged with drugs trafficking and the prison doors closed on him for the rest of his life.

Enrico Mattei

The potential pros and cons of the most significant crimes had to be discussed and approved by the Commission. Cosa Nostra never killed people recklessly, especially when important business interests were at stake.[58]

There was a man in Italy who was pursuing the biggest business interest in the world and had ended up getting in the way of the seven leading oil companies, known in the press as the "seven sisters". Enrico Mattei had discovered and continued to discover gas and oil everywhere, including in Sicily. As became clear in the 1990s in the confessions of the boss Tommaso Buscetta, the *pentito* Gaetano Iannì and other mafiosi, Mattei was becoming a nuisance and was upsetting the global trade in "black gold". According to the information provided by Buscetta, someone asked Cosa Nostra to help. Once more the Mafia stepped in to play a significant role in events.

Enrico Mattei had been one of the greatest of the partisan commanders during the Second World War. Throughout the conflict he kept in contact with leading industrialists; his political allegiances were Christian Democrat. He had succeeded with the utmost difficulty in saving the industrial plants of northern Italy from devastation by moving authoritatively between all the different parties involved. As a member of the innermost committee which controlled the operations of the Resistance, he knew from the inside all the secrets of the Italian civil war, which had been fought within the wider conflict between the Allies and the Germans. He'd helped to make all the important decisions, working always in hiding in Nazi-occupied territory. He'd also been among the most important partisan leaders who took the decision to send commandos to capture Mussolini. Their aim was to get hold of the dictator and make a final reckoning with him before the Allies claimed him. The commandos captured Mussolini a few hours before the Allied secret service squadrons arrived;

---

58 "The Mafia kills in order to eliminate a potential enemy who could harm their interests. It also kills as a warning to others – to tell them they'll meet the same fate if they go down the same road." General Angiolo Pellegrini.

they shot him and hung him up by the feet in piazzale Loreto in Milan to display him to the crowd. During the operation the gold and the papers the dictator had taken with him as he fled disappeared. In this traumatic episode in modern Italian history Mattei positioned himself with great ability, managing to limit any public notoriety while at the same time holding on to his authority with the support of the country's industrialists and the Catholic forces working for the Resistance.

An inquiry was later held by the Italian authorities on what happened in Dongo and Giulino di Mezzegra, the places on Lake Como where Mussolini was captured and shot and where the gold and papers were thought to have disappeared. Mattei was called as a witness. A sequence of murders and bizarre suicides had removed several of those who'd played a leading part in the events. The lack of witnesses and documentation meant that the episode has become not only the subject of serious study by historians, but also of fantastic speculation on the part of those whom Renzo De Felice calls "tuppenny-ha'penny historians". Mattei told the judges that he knew nothing about the gold or the papers which had disappeared. He was already concentrating on rebuilding the country, together with those of his former partisan comrades who remained loyal to him during all the years of hiding.

When the war ended, Mattei could have taken his pick of any of the most eminent political positions but, to everyone's amazement, he asked to be made the director of Agip, an oil company no one thought had any future in an Italy which would have to resign itself to depending on Marshall Aid to get back on its feet. Mattei found oil everywhere. After only a few years, his company, together with Italy, had become one of the leading players in the world oil market. Such an outcome was completely unexpected, especially to those who controlled the interests in the market. The plans of the leading American oil companies risked being derailed by Mattei.

Mattei had no scruples about pressurizing and on occasion hiring politicians to support his initiatives. At the height of the Cold War, he went to the Soviet Union and signed an agreement with the Soviet authorities giving him access to

Russian oil wells. As the head of Agip he managed to create a much larger and more powerful company, Eni, and launched it into signing contracts with Arab countries and establishing research programmes in various parts of the globe.

If you examine Eni's business fifty years after Mattei, at the beginning of the twenty-first century, it will be seen that Italy still enjoys notable advantages in having access to the oil wells of the former Soviet Union, one of the richest oil-producing areas in the world. Communism has fallen, the Cold War has been forgotten, but the influence of Mattei's original agreement with the Russians can still be felt.

Mattei laid the foundations and provided the resources for Italy's unexpected economic boom in the 1960s. He got the agreement he had signed with Soviet Russia, the mortal enemy of the Americans, into practice. In Italy, allied so closely to the United States, he moved with complete independence. Civilians were dying in parts of the world where the Cold War brought tensions, soldiers were getting killed in Korea, Vietnam was increasingly under pressure and nationalist movements were sweeping North Africa.

Mattei started to become a problem for the large oil companies, a problem which even heavy political pressure on a country with restricted sovereignty failed to solve. With an unscrupulous lobbying campaign in Parliament and within the government, the founder of Eni had managed to build up a protective wall round his interests. He'd become the most powerful Italian in the world. He surrounded himself with his trusted ex-partisan comrades, men who'd fought by his side during the war and whom he'd brought in to the companies he controlled. Mattei felt secure with them to the point that he turned down an offer of help from the Soviet intelligence services.[59] The KGB sensed

59 "The Mafia tries to kill as efficiently and cleanly as possible. I don't know if it's proverbial, but the idea is certainly of Mafia origin: 'The perfect murder is one which doesn't leave a body and doesn't leave a memory'. Cosa Nostra kills only when it concerns their interests and to defend their control of their territory. Leaving a stone in the victim's mouth is a superseded piece of symbolism – not because there's no longer any need to send out a message by murdering someone – but because the practice belongs to a rural world where the killer could waste two minutes putting the stone in the mouth." Colonel Mauro Obinu.

he was in imminent danger: they invited him to spend a holiday in a Crimean dacha while they solved the situation.

According to Buscetta, the President of Eni couldn't have had the slightest suspicion that one of the ex-partisans was in contact with the Mafia. Mattei was in an aeroplane which crashed at Bascapè near Milan on 27th October 1962. It had left from Catania, where it had been sabotaged by Giuseppe Di Cristina, the son of the Riesi boss, Don Francesco, who'd been trained in the school of Vizzini. Evidence was tampered with, the scene of the crime was chaotic, since it wasn't sealed off, even the recording of a television news feature which had been filmed live by an eyewitness was wiped while it was in the RAI archives and rendered unusable. The possibility of sabotage was acknowledged, but the inquiry had to be closed since it was impossible to identify the perpetrators. Only in 1994, after Buscetta's disclosures and those of other *pentiti*, did the magistrature decide to reopen investigations. They concluded that the plane was definitely brought down by sabotage, but they still couldn't identify the men responsible.

The same year that Mattei was killed, Lucky Luciano died of a heart attack in Naples airport. He had gone to meet a Hollywood producer who wanted to acquire the rights to make a film about his life, which never got made. It wasn't the way he thought he'd die.

Kennedy, Cuba and the Mafia

A few months after Mattei's death, in January 1963, the new Italian Prime Minister Amintore Fanfani flew to the United States to ratify Italy's membership of NATO. Three months later President Kennedy came to Rome on an official visit.

This was a difficult time for the President – that is to say, even more difficult than usual. De Gaulle had refused to join the nuclear-protection alliance which the United States had offered its allies. Berlin, which Kennedy had visited before going on to Rome, was divided in two and the East German guards shot dead anyone who tried to get over the wall into the west.

When his visit was first planned, Kennedy, America's first Catholic President, had asked for an audience with the Pope, John XXIII, known in Italy as the "Good Pope". But John died on 3rd June and Kennedy saw his successor instead, Paul VI, whose election, after a third round of voting in the conclave, had been announced with the traditional white smoke on 21st June.

The new men in power in Italy were in the welcoming party for Kennedy as he stepped off the plane. In front of the cheering crowds who'd gathered to see this popular President, there was the strongly pro-American Antonio Segni, who'd been elected President just a year earlier thanks to a political consensus which Aldo Moro had helped to create. And Giulio Andreotti, who was then the Defence Minister and one of the Italian politicians most trusted by the Americans, could also be seen walking quickly in the group which escorted Kennedy from the steps of the plane. The crowds in the city under the hot sun waited for the President's cavalcade to pass. It was also being broadcast live on television to ensure maximum publicity. The message was that Italy was a stable and secure ally of the United States and would remain within its sphere of influence.

Kennedy had come without his wife Jacqueline, who was pregnant. Their son, Patrick, was born in August, but survived only a few hours. Events seemed to be against the handsome young President; his brief period in office had been full of problems. The Cuban crisis which had threatened to destroy him was only just over. When Cuba fell into the hands of pro-Communist guerrillas, the Americans felt threatened.

The American Mafia were also displeased to see their "paradise" disappear. The island's dictator, Fulgencio Batista, a personal friend of Meyer Lansky's, had sent Fidel Castro to prison in 1953, but after a popular uprising he'd been forced to free him. Castro had gone into the mountains, where Ernesto Che Guevara had joined him together with a dozen other men; they organized the revolution which would bring Batista's dictatorship down in 1959. Castro had managed to convince the American press that instead of a small group of supporters he had almost an entire army under his command. The press publicity had increased his fame and the number of men who joined up to fight for him. With a series of skirmishes, retreats and ambushes, the by now thickly bearded revolutionary guerrilla fighter had won – and a large part of the business interests of several Mafia Families had gone up in smoke.

An attempt to retake the island by exiles opposed to Castro had failed miserably: on 17th April 1961 he'd prevented their planned invasion in the Bay of Pigs. The various attempts to get rid of Castro were all unsuccessful: the one which lasted longest and was most talked about – because news of it got into the newspapers – was code-named Operation Mongoose, after the small animal used to hunt reptiles. The mongoose set to kill the Communist snake was the CIA and the Mafia working in conjunction: Mafia killers would be used to eliminate Castro. Nothing came of the plan. Some time later, in another undercover operation, the two godfathers who'd been involved, Sam Giamcana and Johnny Rosselli, were themselves murdered as they'd become too troublesome.

Luciano had been right in his predictions about Cuba. The crisis in the island led to a revaluation of Sicily as the golden island for Mafia business.

But Kennedy's failure to retake Cuba was not the only way the President had disappointed the Mafia. He'd been elected in 1960 thanks to a mere handful of votes more than his Republican challenger Nixon. According to some political observers, a part of these votes for Kennedy might have come from the unions, not surprisingly given that during the campaign he had spent endless mornings shaking the hands of workers outside their factory gates, so many that every evening he had to immerse his swollen right hand in iced water. Several godfathers might have exerted influence through the unions, especially in Chicago, where Sam Giamcana was one of the bosses. No one had asked them for this favour, but as usual they were hoping to elect a president who'd see things their way. But Kennedy didn't. There were two Kennedys in the White House, since John, in the face of general criticism, had appointed his younger brother Robert, despite his comparative youth, to the important post of Attorney General. Bob Kennedy might have been young, but he immediately showed he was born to govern. Under his tutelage, anti-Mafia operations really took off. If his full frontal attack continued, the bosses risked losing not only their reputations and their business interests; they stood to lose their freedom.

These thoughts and many others no doubt weighed on the mind of the President who stepped alone off his plane in Rome in the hot summer of 1963. Five months later he would meet his death in an open-top car, as he smiled and waved at the crowd of onlookers in the sun – just as he was doing as he drove through Rome, again in an open-top vehicle so that the crowds could get a good look, with the austere Antonio Segni sitting by his side.

Nowadays the Mafia bosses' ability to influence the course of historical events is well known, so it comes as no surprise that one of the theories about Kennedy's assassination attributes it to Cosa Nostra. Hundreds of books have been written on Kennedy and the Mafia, together with inquiries, documentaries and films, to support the idea that the Mafia played a role in what has gone down in history as the "assassination of the century".[60] In the absence of clear-cut evidence or a trustworthy witness, it must remain only a theory.

Kennedy's death brought everything to a shuddering halt, particularly the campaign for his re-election in the following year, which his staff were already working on. The anti-Mafia investigations might have started up again with a new impetus when Robert Kennedy entered the race to become president, but he too lost his life to an assassin's bullet. Sam Giamcana was eliminated in 1975, and with him disappeared one possible source of information on some of the secrets of the Kennedy administration.

---

60 Political assassination has been fairly common in the United States. The list of presidents who have either been assassinated or been the targets of unsuccessful attempts is a long one: Andrew Jackson, Abraham Lincoln, James Garfield, William McKinley, Theodore Roosevelt, Franklin Roosevelt, Harry Truman, John F. Kennedy, Richard Nixon, Gerald Ford, Ronald Reagan. To these we can add the assassinations of leading politicians: Martin Luther King, George Wallace, Robert Kennedy. Many so-called "minor" incidents have also been recorded, when armed men have been arrested in the grounds of the White House or near the route taken by a visiting president or leading politician.

The Foot Soldier Valachi

Joe Valachi was scared of death, not of a natural death, but of being killed by the boss of his Mafia Family, Vito Genovese, who regarded him as a traitor. Genovese had made many mistakes, but he wasn't stupid; he realized he'd been "shelved" – the Commission had turned their backs on him after what had happened in Apalachin. Now forced to work on his own, he went on making mistakes. He became suspicious especially of Valachi, one of his foot soldiers, but didn't see that Valachi had noticed his suspicions and was terrified – a bad move which an expert godfather would never have made, since it's a golden rule that you never let your intended victim see what he's in for, partly so he can't defend himself and partly so you can go on plotting in silence to make a lethal surprise move.

Valachi saw that he was being targeted by Genovese and started to look for a way to rescue himself. The signs that he was sentenced to death were only too obvious, even going by the traditional Mafia rule book. He looked around and saw that in the ordinary world significant changes were under way. The Commission was no longer headed by Luciano, and it was certainly far from being invisible any more. The United States government had made the struggle against the Mafia one of its priorities. The police in other countries, including Italy, were devising new forms of cooperating with one another. Men like Robert Kennedy had left their mark, and there was a new generation of anti-Mafia investigators and lawyers. The FBI was heavily involved, spurred on by the constant coverage given to Cosa Nostra in the press. There was a new climate which encouraged mafiosi to break the oaths of silence they had sworn with their blood when they'd first been initiated into their Families.

Valachi summoned up his courage and took on the awkward role of a "protected witness". In sessions which were broadcast live on television,[61] in front of millions of viewers, he told

---

61 "The greatest teacher in the history of the planet up to this point is the television... Young people spend much more time watching TV than watching their teacher in the classroom. It was television that first impressed the image of the Mafia on the American psyche." Mario Cuomo.

everything he knew about Cosa Nostra, and became the most famous *pentito* in the Mafia, though what he said didn't cause them too much damage – he was after all only a junior mafioso in the Genovese Family. But he set an example for others of his kind and he showed that collaborating with the authorities was a way of saving your skin. He'd had no contact with the upper echelons of the organization, but he was still able to provide a lot of information on the structure, the hierarchy and the initiation rituals of the Commission.

Peppino Impastato

The new social climate which the 1960s brought with them led to a kind of youthful rebellion and spelt the end of the indifference which had cloaked and supported the Mafia until then.[62] A generation of middle-class youngsters who'd been brought up in the increasing affluence of the west came out of high schools and universities to march in multi-coloured protests on the streets, sometimes peaceful, sometimes erupting into violence. Some were just dreamers and wanted a taste of freedom, others were urging the need for greater social awareness. In most countries the phenomenon lasted a year or two, but in Italy it went on longer. Many young people seemed to be infected with the mistaken belief that wanting to do good and holding noble ideals was enough to win the battle against the huge cynical edifice of the political establishment. Few understood the reality of their situation: not only that they'd been abandoned

62 "Many people's attitude towards the Mafia has changed. They used to be indifferent, but they're much less so now. They've understood that the Mafia is a criminal phenomenon, a parasitic organization which lives off the State: this change in attitude might spell the end of the Mafia. It's no longer possible to argue like those shopkeepers in the past, who used to say that if they'd had to pay two thousand lire in extortion money to the Mafia they could at least sell their products for ten thousand lire. Now they won't pay the Mafia and they'll sell their products for five hundred lire. This submerged economy can distort people's thinking. The Mafia only produces wealth for a few – for example the shops or services patronized by the bosses. For the others it produces poverty, because the Mafia demands payment from those who only earn five hundred. People need to understand that the Mafia is a criminal phenomenon which prevents a society from becoming prosperous." General Angiolo Pellegrini.

by all the political parties, both Left and Right, but also that they were regarded with scorn, as just the cosseted offspring of well-to-do families. From 1968 to 1977, each year brought a new influx of young "rebels" to go marching, to hold political meetings, to join in demonstrations. They were deluded, as some people said even at the time, but perhaps their delusion was inevitable.

In Sicily there was a young man by the name of Peppino Impastato who belonged to the movement. He decided to dedicate all his energies to one of the measures the movement advocated – opposing the Mafia. He was the son of a man of honour who belonged to the Family which controlled Cinisi, the town where he lived, and its district – not just a matter of olive groves, citrus plantations and orchards, since the territory included the land where the construction of the new airport of Palermo was planned.

With a mixture of courage and recklessness, Peppino Impastato started down a very dangerous path. It took courage because he attacked the boss of the Family to which his own father belonged. It was reckless because he went on even when he realized he was on his own. He set up a small private radio station and broadcast attacks on Gaetano Badalamenti, Don Tano. He was little more than a boy and he was attacking the honour of one of the leading men in the honoured society. Listeners tuning in could hear Peppino making fun of "Tano Seduto" or "Sitting Bully". He poured insults on him and demolished his authority; he described him as in decline, the exponent of a superseded world which Sicily would reject, a toothless Mafia boss whom it was time to get rid of. Badalamenti was indeed at a low point in his career, isolated and abandoned by the other bosses, but he must have realized that people, his people, might be listening, even with the volume turned down in the privacy of their own homes, to the young man's outspoken broadcasts.

Peppino's father was the link between his own family and the Mafia Family; as he tried to save his son's life, he was torn between his honour as a father and his honour as a mafioso. But the traditional rules don't allow real families to win: Tano

Seduto ordered the young man to be killed. And then he ordered all traces of the murder to be removed. The body was found on railway lines in Cinisi; the young man was immediately described as a terrorist who'd met his death trying to place a bomb for an attack on a passing train. The description of an extremist who'd been blown up by the explosive device he was carrying would have seemed especially plausible on the day it occurred, since it was 9th May 1978 and another dead body, Aldo Moro's, had just been found inside the boot of a red Renault 4 in via Caetani in Rome, where it had been placed by the Red Brigades who had kidnapped and killed him. The newspapers only had space for the story of Moro's discovery; Peppino Impastato was relegated to a brief mention on the pages covering regional crime stories. Years were to pass before the truth came to light, with his mother's determination, the investigations carried out by his friends and the support of a national anti-Mafia movement: the young man had been blown up by Mafia killers acting on the orders of Gaetano Badalamenti. Peppino had made a choice: he rejected all compromise, and with passionate civil commitment made his denunciations.

"Australian Grass"

All over the western world, in every city, there was a flood of "white powder". The global market had truly arrived; thanks to the godfathers' efforts, heroin was everywhere. Drug-pushers could be found at the entrances to schools, near park benches, around stations or simply in the streets – wherever there was a nearby wall against which the addicts could inject themselves and enjoy the "rush". And it wasn't only heroin on supply – there was "grass", "hash", "coke", amphetamine tablets, drugs of various types and varying strengths to induce youngsters to try them.

A young man keeping a pot of marijuana under his bed could be arrested, but in faraway countries vast fields of cannabis or opium poppies eluded discovery, or were even under government protection.

Crops were grown in plantations in the vast uninhabited spaces of Australia. The Black Hand had arrived, along with the first influx of immigrants into the new continent, at the end of the nineteenth century. Just as in America, where criminal gangs had set up a protection racket with workers on the sugar-cane plantations,[63] the immigrant labourers, isolated as they were in the vast Australian spaces, had no choice but to pay up.[64]

The historical development of the Mafia in Australia seems to resemble that of the American underworld. In time the first local godfathers appeared, the bosses who built up their own Families and the secret world of organized crime, with the aim of entering the business of the global drugs market. They could exploit the capacities of the Calabrian peasants who had emigrated to Australia in their thousands. It hardly matters whether the peasants were willing or were coerced; they were isolated and defenceless in the vast open land, and they had no choice. The way they organized their work in the fields, and their network for transporting the fruit and vegetables they harvested, proved invaluable for bosses like Robert Trimboli. By means of his control over this labour force – or forced labour – vast fields for the cultivation of marijuana were planted, which grew quickly and abundantly in the rich soil under the hot Australian sun.[65] But the Families who made up the country's underworld retained a countrified air; the "sophisticated" American godfathers

63 "In the old Sicilian way of thinking, the trade in drugs was allowed, but only if your children and the friends of your children weren't involved. Young Sicilians weren't allowed to get involved. The expanding drugs trade in the United States and in Europe and on the Italian mainland left Sicily unscathed – and this has confused many people. It's meant that dozens of organizations to do with the drugs trade have been set up in the island, but they're kept firmly away from other areas of life." General Angiolo Pellegrini.

64 "Many Sicilians emigrated from Sicily – and there were some men of honour among them, who have gone on to set up new Mafia Families – in Canada, in the United States, in Latin America, they start criminal activities based on the rules and methods of Cosa Nostra in Italy." Francesco Gratteri.

65 "The first Mafia murders and crimes date back to the 1920s. The businesses of the Australian Families spread into diverse fields, such as the backstreet abortion racket and illegal betting. Melbourne was hit by a Mafia war over the control of the vegetable market. In their first raid against the cultivation of marijuana in 1974, the police discovered two twelve-acre plantations, well-hidden among vineyards and cornfields." From the Australian Police's report *Project Alpha*.

found these new gangs from the new continent too coarse and backward.

American bosses like Vinnie Teresa are recorded as making several visits to Australia looking for new business and maintaining contacts with the Families back in the United States. This was the same Vinnie Teresa who would later become a *pentito* and tell the investigators the truth about the Sacco and Vanzetti affair. The messages he brought with him to Australia were for the gangsters of Anglo-Saxon rather than Italian origin. The American Cosa Nostra wanted nothing to do directly with men who worked in the fields. The kinds of business which Teresa wished to propose involved gambling, prostitution, racketeering and an exchange of killers and wanted men between the two continents.

Jimmy Fariano, another American *pentito* who had been over to Australia on several occasions, told Peter Lamb, head of the National Crime Authority, that Cosa Nostra didn't do business with Italian-Australians because "they were all peasants".

But even if they'd been snubbed by their American cousins, the Italian-Australian bosses quickly adopted not only the weapons but also the culture of the American Mafia, including its ability to infiltrate the world of politics. In the town of Griffith, thanks to a uniform vote from the immigrant community, regardless of ethnic origin, in 1968, and again in 1972, Albert Grassby, of Irish descent, was elected. The majority of the inhabitants were Italian, almost all agricultural labourers from southern Italy. Grassby became the Minister for Immigration, and one of the first things he did was to allow a large number of Italians back into Australia who had previously been expelled by the government. Whether he chose or was obliged to introduce the measure, one of the consequences was to let several criminals back in, mafiosi disguised as immigrants – Domenico Barbaro, for example, who shortly after he returned was arrested once more for attempting to launder the proceeds from a kidnapping.

The Italian-Australian mafiosi might have been peasants, but they knew when a historic opportunity turned up on their doorstep. Supplying the soldiers fighting in Vietnam with reefers and "hash" became their biggest money-spinner, made easier because Australia had sent troops to the war and also took in American combatants during periods of leave. In addition to marijuana and hashish, there was heroin, cocaine, amphetamines and all the other drugs which many soldiers took to enable them to face the violence of an all-out conflict – the century's longest war, in which American planes dropped three times the number of bombs they'd used in the Second World War, and in which there were no fixed battle fronts, and the enemy could burst out on you from any side. It was colossal business for the drug merchants. Consignments of drugs could be sold with impunity, with only the occasional inconvenience of a check by the military police.

An active Liberal Party politician in Griffith by the name of Donald Bruce MacKay decided to join the battle with the Mafia, and told the police where they could find certain plantations under the control of the boss Antonio Sergi, one of Trimboli's men. The police raided the plantations and sprayed herbicidal chemicals in an attempt to kill off the plants. They discovered other fields and ploughed them up with tractors or cut them down. And when aerial reconnaissance photographs revealed that huge areas of cultivated land were involved, they set fire to them and burned the crops. A lot of Mafia business as well as the plants went up in smoke. Robert Trimboli had Donald MacKay killed on 15th July 1977, and got rid of the body according to the time-honoured rules of the Mafia.

He thought that getting rid of MacKay would mean his business could start up again, and he felt confident enough to extend his dealings to include the production of heroin. By carrying out a political murder he thought he'd acquired the prestige and the authority to become part of big Mafia business, the kind controlled by Cosa Nostra in the United States, who looked down their noses at Italian-Australian organized crime. But as it turned out, Trimboli was destined to remain on the sidelines: the global market in heroin already had its preferred channels, and there was no room for Trimboli and his gang to muscle in, despite his acquisition of several consignments.

The war in Vietnam lasted for ten years and brought in enormous sums for the Italian-Australian peasant mobsters – money which once it had been laundered could be reinvested in the construction industry. The Vietnam war detonated a rebellion among young Americans, who took to burning their draft cards in public. The rebellion spread all over the world with huge peace demonstrations and protests in which young men like Peppino Impastato took part. When the war was over, the protests began to die down, but something had changed permanently, both in civil society and in the criminal underworld.

The Perfect Lobby

The new climate, a State which gave the first signs of moving against Cosa Nostra, as well as international cooperation between police forces, encouraged the formation in Italy of special anti-Mafia investigative teams, who often paid for their determination with their lives. Policemen like Boris Giuliano and Ninni Cassarà, *carabinieri* such as Emanuele Basile and Carlo Alberto Dalla Chiesa, magistrates like Gaetano Costa, Cesare Terranova, Rocco Chinnici, Giovanni Falcone, Paolo Borsellino – they form part of a roll call of the Mafia's victims, together with politicians, trade unionists and priests. The list is long, very long, and it's far from exhaustive, given that it also includes children, women and the elderly, who were just getting on with their lives, but found themselves in the killers' field of aim. They were citizens who didn't belong to any clan, or any lobby, or any Mafia Family, and they were killed because they were just accompanying or standing near the defenders of the State, those men who wouldn't hesitate for a second if asked to reply to the question: are you a citizen or do you "belong"?

There's a fairly common reply to the question: a bit of both, as far as numerous venial daily sins are concerned. In effect, both being a citizen and "belonging". As citizens, we want public transport which works efficiently and on time, but we also try to join some clan – better if it's not too well known

– which might help us to jump the queue or get a seat ahead of others. Citizens wish to feel safe from the threat of petty or large-scale crime, but it only takes a moment for us to choose instead to "belong", even if only to groups like the headlight-flashers. On roads in Sardinia and parts of southern Italy, when a driver sees a police patrol in the opposite lane – one of those patrols that station themselves to identify speeding motorists – he'll begin to flash his headlights to warn approaching cars what might be waiting for them just round the corner. It's an easily understood code; the drivers slow down and get ready to be stopped.

When it comes to the Mafia, it is determined to be the ulti-mate group, the perfect lobby, and it demands that its members belong to it totally.

The stories of the men who defended the State against the Mafia and of their fates share one characteristic: they were all alone, each of them was abandoned more or less unwittingly by the very State whose interests they were trying to protect at all costs. They thought they belonged to the State, and yet they were alone. They were working to bridge the gap which had widened ever further with the passage of time between the forces of law and order and the criminal underworld. The Mafia understood this. There were some among them who were intent on piecing together one by one all the parts of the jigsaw of Cosa Nostra's worldwide network. Giovanni Falcone, for example, who went to Australia several times between the late 1980s and early 1990s, in an attempt to build up a unified and coherent picture of the phenomenon he was fighting. And the Mafia knew this too.

Only the "Dishonourable" Talk

The sense of civil society which showed signs of developing in the 1970s made it possible to begin to break down the conspiracy of silence which surrounded the Mafia, and to encourage its members to become "collaborators of justice". For their fellow mafiosi they had dishonoured themselves, and were condemned to die for betraying their oath of loyalty and revealing the secrets of their Families.[66] For the second time in its history – the first had been with the emergence of Fascism – the Mafia found itself unprepared for a counter-offensive, which on this occasion arose from the slow but steady development of a collective social conscience.

Two of the pillars on which Mafia power rested started to crack. The social and political consensus which had supported various godfathers – and which they had been so skilful in building up – began to collapse. In order to protect themselves from the "dishonourable" who'd decided to collaborate with the police forces, other bosses were obliged to raise the level of violence and so break one of Luciano's most important principles: men working for the State were never to be attacked. But it had become a question of life or death for some Mafia Families: these policemen and investigating magistrates now had free access to the *pentiti* and collaborators, and with this new information they could inflict damage on the godfathers' business interests.

Serafina Battaglia was a "Mafia woman". She didn't belong to Cosa Nostra, because only men could be initiated as members, but she had her own definite role to play, and knew what the men in her family were up to when they were not at home. As a wife and mother she was the link between the real family and the Mafia Family; her irreproachable home life and her silence served as a cover for the activities of the mafiosi. She ensured that the formal appearances were respected and maintained, an essential task if the men in her family were to preserve their invisibility. Keeping up appearances: regular mealtimes, the floors swept and cleaned, religious traditions respected, pasta sauce bubbling away on the cooker and the washing hung up

66 "It must always be remembered that a *pentito*, even though he's collaborating with justice, is still a criminal. A high degree of professionalism is needed to deal with these collaborators. When you first speak to a *pentito*, he has many misgivings. Once one of them said to me: 'Until yesterday I was a criminal. I haven't become a saint overnight. I'll carry on with this criminal chromosome inside me for a while, and even though one day I'll try to free myself of it because I genuinely regret what I've done, I won't be able to destroy my past, because I've been a criminal for over forty years.' A *pentito* puts his own honour at stake and his own family in danger." General Angiolo Pellegrini.

to dry. A mafioso's family life had to hide his other Family. With her daily routine, a woman like Serafina Battaglia formed part of the honour of the men in her family.

When other mafiosi – men of honour who also had wives and mothers who ensured they were respected – killed her husband, Serafina did not say a word. She went into mourning and dressed in black and prepared herself to wait, just as a woman should in those circumstances. When the time was right, the Mafia Family would wipe out the memory of that murder with further bloodshed. The vendetta was inevitable. Serafina waited humbly as everyone expected her to do.

Omertà, or the conspiracy of silence which surrounds the Mafia, may be regarded as a sign of underdevelopment or of ignorance. It's a Mafia rule, but the Mafia itself cannot be described as "underdeveloped" – on the contrary, it thrives best in societies which are economically and culturally prosperous. *Omertà* equals confidentiality: the confidentiality of those who never speak out. "*A megghiu parola è chidda ca 'un si dici*" ("The best word is the one not spoken"). The secret firm which is the Mafia requires its employees to keep the rule of absolute confidentiality. It is "Our Thing" and it is never to be spoken about.

But "Our Thing" then murdered Serafina's son as well. When she saw the corpse of the son to whom she'd given birth, all her maternal instincts overwhelmed the rules of the Mafia culture she'd absorbed. She started to cry out, to threaten, to accuse the men of Cosa Nostra, the killers of the rival Family who'd murdered her husband and her son. She became the first woman to collaborate with the Law. What she did was entirely new and difficult to understand: she continued using the jargon of the Mafia world in which she'd been brought up, she was aggressive, what she said always seemed to have a double meaning which only men of honour could grasp.[67]

67 "I've broken the conspiracy of silence because they took my only son. I need-ed to speak out to the authorities because the Mafia have acted like real cow-ards. I've done my duty as a mother, I've acted honestly. I've got a gun, but I've never used it. Journalists say I've used it, but then they've got to make a living. I've got a licence to carry arms, but I've never fired a gun. My weapon is justice." Serafina Battaglia.

It still wasn't obvious – as later it would be – that the closer a collaborator is to the inner workings of Cosa Nostra, and the higher his position in the hierarchy, the more valuable his information is to the investigating magistrates.

Thanks to Serafina Battaglia's testimony, three Mafia bosses were given life sentences at a court in Perugia. The court of appeal leant the other way – an inclination which would lead to some extraordinary judgements in the years to come – and acquitted the three men. The godfathers were past masters at the art of ensuring trials went their way, but the sudden attack made their defensive strategy more than usually complex. Even those whose affiliation to the organization was cloaked in secrecy and who seemed totally beyond suspicion were in danger of ending up in prison along with the junior members.

Joe Bonanno and Carlo Gambino

From the very beginnings of the Mafia, several of the nobility had been involved in the organization in order to protect their own parasitic income and exercise control over the labourers on their estates through the power structures of a secret society. Both noblemen and godfathers were given the title "Don". They remained very much in the shadows, hidden and protected behind the lower ranks in the hierarchy.

An invitation from Sicily made its way through diplomatic channels to arrive in the offices which ran the Court in Buckingham Palace. Someone must have given it official approval, since the Queen accepted the invitation and added a stopover in Palermo to the programme for her State visit to Italy. With her husband, the Duke of Edinburgh, and accompanied by an escort of Italian Police and British intelligence agents, she walked through the streets of Palermo between two rows of onlookers until she reached the door of Palazzo Ganci. The *carabinieri* on guard duty saluted as she crossed the threshold. The Prince of San Vincenzo guided his illustrious visitor through the rooms which for months he had been preparing for the occasion. Much later the Prince was arrested and sentenced in two consecutive trials to eight and five years' imprisonment respectively.

Joseph Bonanno also claimed to be from noble stock.[68] The criminal fraternity in America called him Joe Bananas. He considered himself superior to everyone else, and boasted that he descended from an ancient Pisan family now in decline. The master craftsman Bonanno – who made the bronze doors for the cathedrals in Palermo and Pisa, now destroyed, and might have had a hand in the design of the leaning tower – was, he made out, one of his more famous ancestors.

By the time of his parents' generation though, the family must have fallen on hard times, since they had to emigrate from Sicily to America. That he made the journey to Ellis Island is at least one certain fact about Bonanno. Another is that he was one of Lucky Luciano's best pupils. He was more cultivated than the other bosses, something which was evident in the way he managed his affairs, and also in the autobiography he published with success in his old age. As a godfather he refused to be called "Don", even though – if you believed what he said – he had a double right to the title as a Mafia boss and as a nobleman. He preferred to be called the "Father". And he was indeed the father of a new Mafia Family which was among the most powerful in America.

Thanks to his innate capacities and his training, his cultivated intelligence and his criminal talents, he became in 1931, at the age of only twenty-six, the youngest godfather in the United States, respected and feared by his juniors and the other bosses. He made his money in all the usual ways, from the control of the Italian lottery in New York to the sale of narcotics. He was among the first godfathers to extend his business to Sicily, and was received with all honours when he attended the Palermo conference organized by Luciano. He had no misgivings about presenting himself in public as a

---

68 "He's one of those people about whom you would say, 'if he had gone in an-other direction, he could have been very successful'. Unfortunately he sought the direction of crime. But then he tried to insulate himself from facing what it was all about with pretensions of 'this is like a government', 'I'm like a head of State' and 'I'm a deposed head of State' when he retired." Rudolph Giuliani.

man of honour – he even called his autobiography *A Man of Honor*. The image of himself which he managed to convey was of a father devoted to looking after his family and to helping his friends – and, since he was willing, to helping the friends of his friends, including some trade unionists and politicians. His style was different from most of the Italian-American bosses, almost as if he really were the product of a high-class education. When his Mafia Family was involved in a turf war in the 1960s – known as the "Banana War" among criminals – there was a series of armed skirmishes and killings, until at a certain point he vanished. Both the police and the bosses thought it was a set-up, but whatever it was, it wasn't the move of an amateur. Bonanno remained out of circulation for all the time that was needed. He felt himself to be threatened, and so decided to adopt a drastic solution which would enable him to escape the situation and at the same time preserve a part of his business. His disappearance removed the principal target his rival's killers were looking for, but also left him free to reach a secret agreement with the enemy bosses without their having to lose face with their juniors.

It was a plot straight out of a thriller, which only Bonanno could have devised, and put into action while a turf war was raging. He emerged alive and well; the war had ended when he made his reappearance. But he made the decision to retire from the fray; he knew the peace agreement between the bosses was fragile, and he was also aware that a determined public prosecutor – Rudolph Giuliani – was investigating his affairs. He gave up direct control of his Family and spent his remaining energies on escaping his fellow bosses and Giuliani. He was the first to realize that the age of the great godfathers was over. He managed, as planned, to enjoy a long retirement in his country villa. This model was that of the godfather as pensioner – or like a former head of State, as Bonanno liked to call himself, albeit of the criminal underworld.

Carlo Gambino made a different choice and didn't go into retirement. Right up to the end he remained in charge of his Family. As he aged, his body became even thinner, his nose sharper, his eyes smaller and more evasive. It almost seemed as if nature wanted to help him make himself invisible. Indeed in the newspapers he was known as the "Invisible Don". There are some photographs of him, taken by reporters as he left an interrogation session in court, which show him with an inscrutable smile on his face, a kind of tension about the lips, which is the only sign of the spirit concealed behind such an unassuming appearance – the spirit of a powerful godfather who, after the death of Luciano, headed the most important Mafia Family in America. He was the authentic "boss of bosses", the model for the characters in dozens of films, from *The Godfather* to *Prizzi's Honor*.[69]

Men like Gambino and Bonanno succeeded in keeping alive for a long time the lessons which Luciano had taught them. After Luciano's death, there was no figure of authority strong enough to prevent turf wars breaking out between rival gangs, but thanks to Gambino and Bonanno, direct conflict with the State was avoided.

When Gambino died in 1976, his position was taken over by a rapid succession of men. The first was Big Paul Castellano, a surly bad-tempered man hated by his own *picciotti*. He wasn't cut out to be a godfather, and he didn't last long. He was murdered with a sudden burst of machine-gun fire in a New York restaurant. The Commission turned their backs on him, and left his dead body in a pool of blood for the federal agents to examine.

The Corleone Gang

While Carlo Gambino was building his empire in the United States, back in Sicily, in the town of Corleone, the godfather-doctor Don Michele Navarra regarded himself as powerful as a god. The inhabitants called him "*u patri nostru*" as in the Lord's Prayer, but were filled with the terror that only the fear of evil can bring.

---

69 "There have been plenty of Italian-American heroes in law enforcement. But they were not well known. They were not the subjects of series, of one block-buster movie after another, they were not four-hour spectaculars, they were not series like *The Sopranos*. What works in this country is blood dripping from a stiletto, rape, crushing a man's head with a golf club because your boss ordered you to do it, Italian-American thugs." Mario Cuomo.

The rituals and air of the sacred which Mafia culture has adopted in the service of evil, and the aura with which godfathers are careful to surround themselves, give rise to a kind of Mafia decalogue. The first commandment: "I am your godfather. You shall have no other godfathers apart from me", followed by "Honour your godfather and respect the members of your Family. They come before your own father and mother, your children and your brothers". Then there are the rules of how to behave in the Mafia: "Do not desire the woman of another man of honour, do not steal [men of honour do not need to steal], do not profit from prostitution". And, even though it may seem paradoxical, "Do not kill other men of honour. Do not kill unless your godfather or the Commission orders you to kill". Someone who is affiliated to the Mafia must learn to hold his tongue: "Do not speak to the forces of law and order, you must maintain a total silence about the Family. Never speak under any circumstances of Cosa Nostra." A mafioso must behave correctly and seriously. One very important rule states that he is never to tell a lie. A man of honour must always tell the truth; if he lies he will be killed on the orders of his own godfather. Or if he lies it is because he is about to kill someone, and therefore the person to whom he lies doesn't count, since it's as if they're already dead.

In his kingdom of Corleone, "*u patri nostru*" could condemn or save whomever he wanted, as and when he liked. He had trained up the most savage killers in the history of the Mafia. On his orders, Luciano Leggio, the most ruthless of his men, had murdered on 10th March 1948 the trade unionist Placido Rizzotto, who became a martyr of the peasant movement which was occupying the estates.

A young and outstanding *carabiniere* was sent to Corleone to investigate Rizzotto's murder in 1949. He was a native of Piedmont by the name of Carlo Alberto Dalla Chiesa. He knew that he was being sent to a place where no one would greet him, and where he'd be forced to spend public and religious holidays in his barracks among his colleagues and their close relatives. This was a period when the inhabitants of Corleone would never approach a *carabiniere*, even to give them seasonal greetings at Christmas or Easter, nor would law-abiding citizens who weren't involved in the Mafia dream of befriending a policeman, even in private. For the murder of Rizzotto, Dalla Chiesa immediately charged Navarra – who was arrested – as well as Leggio, who went into hiding.

Ten years passed by. Luciano Leggio, whom everyone called Liggio with an "i", now felt strong and bold enough to become independent. But life in the Mafia is not like life in ordinary families, where sons reach the age of majority and are free to get up and leave. If the godfather didn't want someone to leave, he had to stay. Navarra decided that his killer had to pay for his rebelliousness and ordered him to be shot on 28th June 1958. Liggio reacted violently. A kind of animal instinct enabled him to escape being killed. Shortly afterwards, on 2nd August 1958, he killed Navarra. The junior mafioso had murdered his father and was ready to take over his authority. Liggio was a new kind of mafioso in the criminal underworld of rural Sicily, with an almost military kind of daring. He enlisted a large number of *picciotti* to form a bloodthirsty gang which quickly became known as the Corleone gang.

Liggio was arrested in May 1964, but subsequently released. Investigators found new evidence against him, and he was re-arrested. Thanks to his lawyer and the Mafia network, he was freed once again. He managed to fix various trials and remained on the run for sixteen years. On one of the occasions when he was acquitted because of insufficient evidence, a team of television reporters went to Corleone to find out what ordinary people in the streets thought about it. The shots show people talking straight to camera and saying things like "Liggio's a good man", or "We're happy because he's coming home where he belongs". The best interpretation is probably that they didn't believe what they were saying, but knew they were obliged to live in a place where the Mafia was everywhere.[70] The interviewees seem to be saying to the reporters who questioned

---

70 "It must be said that huge steps forwards have been made in Corleone when you think of the almost complete conspiracy of silence which used to exist. Much has changed – there's a reawakening, a real sense of renewal." General Angiolo Pellegrini.

them then, and all the reporters since: "The State can't keep them in prison, the judges have set them free. We're just poor people who live in Corleone. What do you want us to say?"

Liggio was finally arrested and sentenced to life imprisonment in 1974. His successor as leader of the Corleone gang was Totò Riina, insultingly nicknamed "*Totò u curtu*" ("Totò the Shorty") by his enemies, but soon to show his considerable prowess as a criminal. His *picciotti* honoured him as if he were a real godfather by using the customary Mafia title of respect "Zu Totò", "Uncle Totò".

Riina continued the line set by Liggio. The other Mafia Families on the island tended to look on the Corleone mob as Sicily's own brand of "peasant gangsters". Riina and his men were determined to carve out a large slice of Cosa Nostra's business for themselves; the lesson they had learnt from the American model was one of pure criminal violence. Hadn't Lucky Luciano done away with Masseria and Maranzano when he wanted to assert his rule? Hadn't he planned and put into action the night of the "Sicilian Vespers" to eliminate all his opponents?

Overpowering the members of the Sicilian Commission, the Corleone gang took to killing foot soldiers belonging to other Families, and even began threatening the bosses themselves in order to make inroads into the drugs market. In an attempt to re-establish some kind of authority, a triumvirate was set up with Stefano Bontate, Gaetano Badalamenti and "Uncle Totò", but the arrangement didn't work and was powerless to stop the first Sicilian Mafia turf war from breaking out. The Corleone gang launched an attack of almost military intensity on the Families who refused to submit to them. On 30th June 1963, seven *carabinieri* were blown to bits as they were examining a car which had been stuffed with dynamite in Ciaculli. Just as in ordinary wars, bombs started to replace rifles and machine guns. Cosa Nostra employed increasingly more experienced bomb-makers. The principle established by Luciano that State officials were never to be targeted was abandoned once and for all. With all these developments, some of the local Corleone inhabitants came together to resist the total identification of their town with the Mafia.

Michele Sindona

The American Families began to demand an explanation for what was going on in Italy. They couldn't just stand by and watch this Mafia war, which was also damaging their own interests. Nor did they have any confidence in Michele Sindona, who'd recently arrived in the United States to keep track of his complex and frenetic system of money-laundering, and the strategy he was pursuing.

After being moved around from country to country and company to company, a large capital sum of sufficiently laundered dollars had finally got through the United States federal controls: Sindona could now use it to buy up the most prestigious private bank in the country, the Franklin National Bank, which duly fell under the control of the banker from Patti, a small town in the province of Messina.

But Sindona had come to the attention of American investigators; his career started to oscillate between successes and defeats. His most secret contacts were revealed, beginning with his relations with the Vatican. The Italian ambassador to the United States formally turned down invitations to receptions held in Sindona's honour because of his putative connections to the Mafia. In itself it was an unimportant and irrelevant matter – and yet it was a black mark against Sindona's name. The series of such incidents as these traced the route the financier's career had followed, on the borderline between civil society and the criminal underworld.

Political manoeuvring formed part of Sindona's DNA. He knew that politics must guide the *res publica*, the public weal as opposed to "cosa nostra". If society wanted more tolerance, fewer controls, more freedom of action, then it was up to politics to redraw the line between public virtue and private vice. Take prostitution for example: the State decides whether to manage the phenomenon or not, whether to allow brothels to be run as private businesses or to suppress them. Political debate guides society towards the demarcation between soft and hard drugs, decides if personal use can be condoned, and advocates the distribution of methadone as opposed to the public sale of heroin. Appropriate laws tell us where and how alcohol and tobacco can be sold, just as they fix in what ways and how freely capital can be moved around. Cosa Nostra negotiated the same issues.

For Cosa Nostra, it was essential to be able to influence the decisions of politicians on public policy. The progress of their business might depend on even the small shifts which a decision might cause. And political influence is easily acquired when the system works in such a way that there is no longer any direct contact between the electorate and the elected representatives who rule them. When there is a sense that direct public control has withdrawn, a gap or no man's land is created where Cosa Nostra can work.

"The public weal" against the "cosa nostra': some in politics have advanced the theory that one solution to this conflict would be to learn to co-exist with the Mafia. It would be a way of bringing the Mafia into the State, absorbing its capital and its members and transforming them into legal enterprises. This was what happened with the White Hand of organized Irish immigrant crime in the United States, where it was absorbed and ceased to exist.

But the Mafia is not just some super-gang of organized criminals: it is an entire culture, an alternative state. If it is not destroyed, if the series of contacts between civil society and the Mafia is extended, then there is the risk that it will succeed in swallowing up the legal State – while remaining invisible, of course, so that it can go about its normal business.

In Italy, Sindona had been rescued and had rescued others. A group of politicians had pulled him out of bankruptcy; he was also known as the "Saviour of the lira". He extended his affairs with new capital; he could transfer money around with such dexterity that the financial experts who were responsible for trying to track his moves were completely left behind. But as the pressure increased he was forced into increasingly riskier strategies, inventing and closing companies as "empty boxes" with the sole purpose of holding the money temporarily as he shifted it around. A few false steps began to gum up the frantic workings of Sindona's machine. Through his own FinBank he'd managed to get thirty-seven million dollars out of the country in the 1970s. He received the money from five hundred people who wished to remain completely anonymous.

However, he'd also had to flee from Italy, where a warrant for his arrest had been issued. Another warrant was issued in the United States which obliged him to pay out half a million dollars for bail. Somehow he managed to survive, with secret political contacts and operations in the world of high finance, until, once more with American investigators in pursuit, he ran up against someone who in his conduct and attitudes seemed to belong to a former age, like the old gentleman Emanuele Notarbartolo, the director of the Banco di Sicilia who'd been knifed to death on a train in the 1890s. He was a lawyer called Giorgio Ambrosoli, who in October 1974 had been given the task by a court in Milan of winding up one of Sindona's many fake companies, the Banca Privata Italiana. In June of the same year, Sindona had tried to bail out the bank with a hundred billion lira he'd obtained from the Banco di Roma, with the Banca d'Italia as guarantor. But now all Ambrosoli had to do was to put it into liquidation. He wasn't a policeman or a *carabiniere* or a financier. He would write a report, he would sign it off, and that would be that.

Ambrosoli worked on the job with his usual precision and honesty. All the circumstances surrounding Sindona's company were confused, but Ambrosoli perceived that there were some transfers of illicit capital. He took a piece of paper and drew some squares on it to indicate the "empty boxes" which kept appearing, and he gave each one a name and a location. Then he began to trace a flow diagram which depicted the routes the money had taken. Starting from a small point in the galaxy of corrupt finance, this young lawyer managed to reveal links between the money made by Cosa Nostra and the money handled by leading financial institutions. There was a layer of the Mafia behind these operations which worked in parallel with the bosses' Commission, but was much more obscure.

Ambrosoli showed his diagrams to journalists, pointing out the main stages through which the money had circulated. The American investigators realized that this was the key to understanding how Sindona had managed to take control of the Franklin

National Bank, and they asked if they could use Ambrosoli's discoveries as evidence in the case they were preparing against Sindona. On 11th July 1979, hardly a day after Ambrosoli had given his testimony on oath to the American investigating magistrates, he was murdered.[71] The identification of his killers led the police to the person who issued the order for his murder.

Sindona was sent to prison. He was intelligent and unscrupulous, and he believed he would have the means to survive even in this situation. He knew many of the most powerful people in the world, and he had done favours for many of them. He gave interviews to celebrated journalists. He never panicked even during his riskiest stratagems, as for example the time when he'd faked his own kidnapping by "revolutionary Communist cells" in order to escape the circle of investigators all over the world who were gradually closing in on him. He laundered the proceeds of the criminal underworld by transferring the money rapidly from company to company, never allowing it to stay in one place too long. But now in prison it was impossible to control the traffic: the game had come to an end. The flow of money which Ambrosoli had tracked lost the main motor; the elaborate mechanism of empty boxes started to seize up. The

---

71 From the grounds for the acquittal of Giulio Andreotti by the Court of Appeal in Palermo on 23rd October 1999: "On the basis of the evidence it can be proved that: 1) Senator Andreotti on repeated occasions took decisions which favoured the carrying out of Sindona's interests in the period after 1973; 2) among such decisions, particular importance should be given to those – even if they did not produce the intended result – which concerned the directors of the Banca d'Italia and the Commission established to oversee the liquidation of the Banca Privata Italiana, who opposed all attempts to 'accommodate' the issues. The role played by Giorgio Ambrosoli should be emphasized: if Sindona's interests did not in the end prevail, this is in large part due to Ambrosoli's sense of duty, honesty and courage. Sindona arranged to have Ambrosoli killed precisely because of his opposition to the efforts being made in the circles around Sindona to rescue the bank, efforts which had the full support of Senator Andreotti, some other politicians, leading members of the Mafia and representatives from the Masonic Lodge P2... There is however insufficient proof that Senator Andreotti, during the time when he was adopting measures designed to help Sindona, was aware of the links between the Sicilian financier and leading members of the Mafia... Nor is there any certain proof that when Senator Andreotti was acting to help Sindona in this way, he possessed enough information to enable him to become aware that the effects of his actions would have potential significance for the leading members of the Mafia on whose behalf Sindona was recycling money."

bosses wanted to know what had happened to their money. Sindona saw he was defeated and threatened to talk. He was sixty-five years old and should have known that threatening the godfathers is always an error, especially when millions of dollars are at stake. On 22nd March 1986, he was given a cup of coffee in his cell – it was laced with cyanide.

Another theory has it that he arranged for the coffee to be brought to him in order to stage a suicide attempt or fake an attack on his life with the purpose of gaining extra time, perhaps by being sent to a ward in a "supportive" hospital. He was certainly clever, unscrupulous and cynical enough to believe he could get away with it – he had after all successfully staged a similar incident on a previous occasion. But drinking that cup of coffee down to the dregs proved to be the last mistake of the banker from Patti in the province of Messina, which everyone knew was *babba* – the Mafia didn't exist there.

Stefano Bontate

One of the bosses who watched what was happening to Sindona but took care not to get dragged down with him was Stefano Bontate. He was a man of honour and the son of a man of honour, but he knew that in the Mafia you don't automatically inherit the title of "Don" from your father. It has to be earned anew in each generation. His surname was really Bontà ("goodness"), a rather appropriate surname for a Mafia boss who needs perfect camouflage. But Bontate didn't want to be invisible. He wanted to make his mark more authoritatively, make others feel respect whenever he was introduced or they mentioned his name. So he had his name officially changed; "Bontate" seemed a more appropriate name for a godfather who wanted to exercise authority and win acceptance into the wealthy circles of Palermo society.[72]

---

72 "The Mafia godfather is regarded as a second father... He would walk through the town square and everyone would stop to greet him respectfully. Such a figure no longer exists. Perhaps Stefano Bontate was the last example of the type." General Angiolo Pellegrini.

Bontate's passion for gambling in casinos and for living the high life, his multi-million-pound house and elegant wife, made him the exact opposite of the peasant mobsters in Corleone. Modesty was not one of Bontate's characteristics. He was in contact with various Masonic lodges. He offered to work for the intelligence services. With Giuseppe Di Cristina, a boss who was very loyal to him, acting as an intermediary, he played a role in the murder of Mattei. There was an immediate suspicion that he was involved in the murder in 1970 of Mauro De Mauro, a journalist on the Palermo newspaper *L'Ora* who'd been investigating the Mattei case. In true Mafia style, the body of the courageous journalist was never found.

Bontate became a business partner of Gaetano Badalamenti, before the latter declined into "Sitting Bully". He was on friendly terms with Tommaso Buscetta. He showed he was prepared to fight an all-out war against Totò Riina, even using tip-offs to the police as a weapon. But he was particularly determined to form a partnership with the Mafia cousins in the United States, and thus cut the Corleonesi off from any share in the big business.

At this point it occurred that several American Mafia Families received consignments of defective heroin which they couldn't sell. Millions of dollars had been invested. The Commission decided to find out what was behind it. Had Totò Riina sent the consignment in the hope that it would disadvantage his rival Bontate? Or was it a cynical ploy on the part of the Palermo boss to prove the peasant mobsters of Corleone were impossible to work with? The bosses in New York, Chicago and the other American cities which were affected wanted to reconstruct the itinerary of the consignment, find out how many chemists had worked on the heroin, and identify who was responsible for the error. The episode had something to do with the turf war in progress – a conflict of which the American bosses disapproved. For them it was out of the question to go around bombing magistrates, policemen, priests, women and children.[73] They preferred to deal with authoritative men like Bontate, who were closer in style and

---

73 "The Sicilians were told in very strong terms that if they came to the United States to conduct criminal operations, they were not allowed to use that type of terror." Thomas V. Fuentes.

make-up to the traditional mafioso type. At the same time they realized that Bontate was on the losing side. Several Families had seen well in advance where the "military escalation" started by the Corleone gang would end, and had begun to distance themselves by separating their business from that of their Sicilian cousins.

The agreements which had been made at the Hotel delle Palme meeting in Palermo were ignored in practice.[74] The increasing detachment of the Americans became evident just as Bontate was making an attempt to inherit the mantle of Lucky Luciano. The Corleonesi were determined to block him, and unleashed a second war with the aim of leaving the other Families rudderless. One of their first victims was Bontate, on 23rd April 1981.

"Old-fashioned" Godfathers

Riina's killers attacked the Italian State, and the State responded. The United States' government was also at war with Cosa Nostra, and had been for some time. In America the godfathers were up against the most powerful State apparatus in the world; they saw a drastic reduction in their room for manoeuvre and a corresponding increase in the cost of defending themselves against the attorneys. The heading "legal costs" became an increasingly significant item in their budgets, just as their diaries were filled with court hearings. None of the bosses in America wanted to have to deal with the problems the Sicilians were creating with their wars. Either the island functioned as the "Mafia paradise" it was intended to be, a place where business could be carried on in peace, or the Commission would look for alternative paradises, other islands.

---

74 "I don't believe there are any longer organizational or strategic links such as those which characterized the agreement reached between the two Mafias in 1957 in the Hotel delle Palme in Palermo. That said, it's also certainly the case that whenever there's a chance of increasing their profits by entering into a 'joint venture', the channels will always be open between the two organizations." Colonel Mauro Obinu.

The activities of investigators like Rudolph Giuliani were pushing the historic Mafia clans into crisis, notably the Bonanno clan, one of the oldest and most powerful Mafia Families. It had taken just one man, the Italian-American Joe Pistone, to create a lot of problems for many bosses in Cosa Nostra. Pistone was a federal agent who had managed to infiltrate the secret structure of the Mafia organization. He had adopted the pseudonym Donnie Brasco. After serving a long apprenticeship and patiently waiting in the organization's antechambers, he had finally been taken on in 1976, when he was thirty-six years old. He became part of an armed guard working together with professional killers, and he remained undercover inside the organization, taking part in various crimes, until he'd accumulated all the necessary evidence. When he gave up his undercover role, his testimony sent more than a hundred mafiosi to prison.

With this offensive in progress, the increasingly evident desire of the American Families to detach themselves started to cause concern to the bosses of the Sicilian Cosa Nostra. The number of *pentiti* or *infami* – what you called them depended on which side you belonged to – was also continually growing. The picture of the Mafia as a single entity began to emerge with increasing clarity from their testimonies. Sooner or later the investigators would be in possession of all the different pieces of the puzzle and target their attacks on the highest and most secret echelons of the Mafia. The police and the *carabinieri* realized that the war which was going on was not simply a battle between gangs for control of the territory.[75] In 1982 they'd compiled the "Greco Report", named after the first mafioso to be involved in their inquiry: in this they wrote that the conflict was about a clash of generations which had been brewing for decades and had finally culminated in a

---

75 "In the 1970s a Mafia Family in Palermo like the Santa Maria di Gesù comprised 130 to 150 men of honour – or so the *pentiti* tell us. It's certain that after the *pentiti* and the investigations which have revealed the inner workings of the Mafia the men who lead the organization prefer to avoid initiating other men of honour by means of the formal ritual ceremony of 'affiliation'. This has occurred in order to prevent the organization from becoming too 'leaky' and to keep the organization more tightly knit and more loyal." Colonel Mauro Obinu.

full-blown war between two different conceptions of the Mafia. There were the "old-fashioned" godfathers, those who thought they were inheriting the mantles of Lucky Luciano and Calogero Vizzini. And there were the gangsters who refused to play by the rule book, the Corleone gang and their allies.

Riina and his band of killers also belonged to a Mafia tradition which had developed in rural Sicily, quite outside the mechanisms of big business which the American Mafia had introduced. It was now ferociously determined to stage a comeback, and run roughshod over the rules which the Commission imposed. While the "old-fashioned" bosses continued to argue that any planned murder needed to be discussed beforehand, and that the organization should try for collaboration rather than confrontation with the State, the Corleone gang burst on the scene with bombs and massacres. It was total war, with every last soldier on active duty, showing no respect for the godfathers' authority or that of the Commission, and no hesitation about killing public officials and politicians.

The forces of law and order did not stay on the sidelines to watch. Five heroin refineries were discovered in Palermo. Retracing all the stages through which the Cosa Nostra's money had been laundered, it was revealed that the capital had re-emerged to finance the construction industry and the building of hundreds of apartment blocks in Palermo, which in just a few years had seen its population quadrupled, in what is known as the "Sack of Palermo". Thanks also to international collaboration, the police were able to draw up for the first time a global map which analysed the world of the Mafia and gave an overview of Cosa Nostra's activities – this they could use as a plan for the coming battle.

Meanwhile the Mafia war continued unabated. After the defeat of the old Families like the Bontate or the Inzerillo, the winning Corleone gang moved to make a direct assault on the State.[76]

---

76 "The stategy of the State against the Mafia has brought important results, thanks to more appropriate legislation and a more united political will. The expertise and methods of the investigators have also changed. All as a result of the same often dramatic and violent events." Francesco Gratteri.

The Mafia would have remained a banal form of delinquency if it hadn't been for its ability to build connections with the political world. For generations politics had been part of the organization's genetic inheritance. And even in an epoch-making war like the one which was being fought in Sicily, both sides maintained advantageous relations with politicians at all levels.

The Mafia's political skills had been acquired over many years, beginning back in the nineteenth century, with the godfathers who ruled in place of a distant and absent State. They would tell people what was right and what was wrong, how they should reply if a government official came to visit, the methods they should adopt to avoid paying unjust taxes. The next step involved telling the peasants who lived in the godfather's own "fiefdom" how they should vote whenever political elections were held. But political activity wasn't confined to dealing with institutions and election campaigns: the godfathers were always ready, especially in Sicily, to participate in popular mass movements – or to move against them.

Salvo Lima was "a friend of friends", and within Sicily was at the centre of a vast network of power. He became mayor of Palermo in 1958, and from there started to climb up the political ladder, leaving "safe" men, like Vito Ciancimino, in position behind him as he rose. It was while the Mafia were in control of the city that the capital used to finance the building of the apartment blocks in the "Sack of Palermo" came to light.[77] Lima, who was several times an MP and a member of the government, occasionally found himself in court, but was always acquitted. It's said that his motto was "I eat and I let others eat".

When it looked as if he was getting a bit too prominent and was turning into a liability in Sicilian politics, he was quick

---

[77] From the grounds for the acquittal of Giulio Andreotti by the Court of Appeal in Palermo on 23rd October 1999: "The Salvo cousins, deeply implicated in Cosa Nostra, were on several occasions asked by men linked to the illegal association to obtain favourable outcomes of trials then in progress; they told several men of honour about their close connections to the parliamentary deputy Salvatore Lima and, in conversations with many leading members of the Mafia, underlined their connections with Senator Andreotti."

to realize this, and moved slightly to the margins by getting himself elected to the European Parliament. Lima was the true heir of Don Vito Cascio Ferro's politician a century earlier, Palizzolo. Like Palizzolo, every time Lima was acquitted of the charges brought against him by those investigating his affairs, he was acclaimed by a crowd of enthusiastic supporters. Petitioners would crowd round him in his local bar, where he went each evening to receive the homage of his supporters, and where he would indicate to his secretary which favours were to be carried out.[78] The petitioner would kiss his hand; Lima would make a brief sign and the request would be duly noted down. All kinds of favours, large and small, were asked of him, and Lima, like the experienced godfather he was, took care to fulfil as many as possible so that the number of people indebted to him would be maximized.

Bosses like Bontate and Buscetta played an important role in the system Lima had created. Lima decided to channel the avalanche of votes which the system had brought him behind the wing of the Christian Democrats led by Giulio Andreotti, of which he himself was the undisputed leader in Sicily. This didn't involve selling votes: Mafia bosses didn't stoop to the kind of practices frequently found elsewhere in Italy, where canvassers offered a pair of shoes, some packets of sugar and an envelope containing banknotes in exchange for the votes of some poor wretch and the members of his family who were entitled to vote. The Mafia system was simpler and more perverse: politicians had no need to ask for votes. The godfathers decided who should get the votes on the basis of putting friends in local and national government from whom they could later ask for favours.

A politician was playing a very dangerous game if he thought he was in a strong enough position to take the Mafia votes and

---

78 From the grounds for the acquittal of Giulio Andreotti by the Court of Appeal in Palermo on 23rd October 1999: "The parliamentary deputy Lima, both before and after he became a member of Andreotti's wing of the Christian Democrat Party, was collaborating with Cosa Nostra. In conversation with the Parliamentary Deputy Evangelisti (a politician who was close to Andreotti) he spoke about his friendship with the leading Mafia member Tommaso Buscetta, and showed that he was clearly aware of Buscetta's power of influence."

then decide to do his own thing.[79] He was making a bad move if he assumed he could take his seat and then turn down the requests for favours from friends of friends. Salvo Lima was murdered by Mafia killers – the very man who, in the grounds given for the judgement in the Andreotti case, was described by the Palermo magistrates as the person who "both before and after his adherence to Andreotti's wing of the party was collaborating consistently with Cosa Nostra".

Andreotti too found himself undergoing a series of long and complicated trials. In the Court of First Instance, he was acquitted by the Palermo magistrates of Mafia connections, and in Perugia, again in a Court of First Instance, he was acquitted of involvement in the murder of the journalist Mino Pecorelli. But in the Second Instance Court, once more in Perugia, he was given a twenty-four year sentence as the instigator of the killing, although no evidence had come to light of who actually carried the murder out. Back in Palermo he was once more acquitted on appeal.

Buscetta, the Boss of Two Worlds

Tommaso Buscetta, known as Don Masino, tried to arouse the Families who'd been defeated by the Corleonesi. He seemed to be the right man to take over from Stefano Bontate and win back some of the old business. He wasn't the head of a Mafia Family, nor, apparently, did he belong to the upper echelons of the organization. He had travelled all over the world looking after the interests of numerous American and Italian bosses.

---

79 From the grounds for the acquittal of Giulio Andreotti by the Court of Appeal in Palermo on 23rd October 1999: "It is certainly not possible to identify conduct in support of the Mafia in Andreotti's attitudes towards organized crime while he was Prime Minister between 1989 and 1992. These three years are character-ized by a notable quantity of legislation concerning penal law, the regulation of police activities and the overall activity of the State against the Mafia... Yet these attitudes of the accused and the legislative measures introduced by the govern-ment he led did not prevent the Mafia from supporting candidates belonging to the Andreotti wing of the Christian Democrat Party in the regional elections held in June 1991. This proves that the electoral support offered by Cosa Nostra to the Andreotti wing of the party in Sicily was unconnected to any measures taken by the accused to favour the criminal association."

In São Paulo in Brazil, he went under the names of Tomas Felici or José Roberto Escobar. In the United States, he used the pseudonym Manuel Lopez Cadena, while in Canada, on the official passport he managed to obtain, he was registered as Adalberto Barbieri. He knew how the criminal underworlds in many countries operated. He was a figure of authority, a *capo*, but at the same time other men of honour, especially in Sicily, found him a bit of an anomaly.

He was notorious for his affairs with women, for his reputation as Cosa Nostra's Latin lover, and for his three marriages.[80] He had first married Melchiorra Cavallaro in 1944; his second marriage was with Vera Girotti in 1966. Finally he lived with a beautiful and fascinating Brazilian with whom he was deeply in love. She was called Maria Cristina De Almeida Guimarães; she came from a wealthy family and had no Mafia connections. These beautiful women were very much part of Buscetta's particular way of life; there was a kind of nonchalance in the way he crossed back and forth between the underworld and the surface, something in his attitude which was too "free thinking" for the men of honour, who preferred strict observance of the old dogmas. Yet the aura of prestige which surrounded Buscetta made him one of their own. Despite this, the plan to call him back to Palermo to take charge of reorganizing the Families who'd been defeated by Riina never worked out because of the continuing hostilities.[81]

Don Masino was forced to escape from Palermo in order to avoid being killed. He was arrested in Brazil and found that the police who work under a dictatorship don't necessarily respect

---

80 "In the rules of the Mafia you must be loyal to your own blood family. It used to be said that if you weren't loyal to your own family you would never get to the top in the Mafia hierarchy. Perhaps this is the reason why Buscetta, who was a great womanizer, never made it to the top, precisely because he was notorious for chasing after women. In the Mafia you must be secretive and never involve your own family. According to the Mafia, everything which is done in secret doesn't much affect the honourableness of the man who does it." General Angiolo Pellegrini.

81 "It is hard to say if Buscetta was asked to take over from Bontate, but it's clear that he was asked to return to Palermo and unite around him all the men who'd remained loyal to Bontate and Badalamenti in order to mount a response to the Corleonesi." General Angiolo Pellegrini.

the rules. The military regime which then governed the largest country in South America had no respect for human rights, and allowed Buscetta no possibility of legal defence.

The police seemed almost pleased to have an important Mafia boss in their clutches and decided to get a confession out of him and impress the rest of the world with their efficiency. Buscetta was subjected to various kinds of torture, including being suspended out of a plane during a flight. But he didn't talk, and was prepared to die. What would be the point of talking, how would he benefit by telling these madmen all he knew? And he knew in any case he wouldn't save his life. Better to die pushed headlong from an aeroplane in mid-air than end up the victim of a killer from Corleone.

When he finally made his decision to talk, it was because he found himself in front of a judge who spoke to him with the respect owed to a man of honour and who acknowledged his dignity as a Mafia *capo*. In prison in Brazil, he was weak from torture, depressed and close to suicide when, in June 1984, he was visited by Giovanni Falcone and the team of policemen and *carabinieri* who were working closely with him, including Gianni De Gennaro and Angiolo Pellegrini.

His new interlocutors managed to resolve the bureaucratic and political difficulties in getting Buscetta extradited to Italy. He felt he was in crisis, and during the return journey tried to take his own life. He arrived in Italy in a condition of extreme weakness, but managed to summon up enough pride to put a blanket round his shoulders and leave the plane on his own two feet in front of the TV cameras. It was 15th July 1984.

Buscetta was no mere *picciotto*, a Mafia foot soldier like Joe Valachi: he was a boss, Don Masino. He once denied being a *pentito* to Falcone: "I belong to the Mafia. I just don't agree with the man who's unleashed all this violence," he said, referring to the war being fought by the Corleone gang.

Don Masino knew enough about the Mafia to cause serious damage to the Families.[82] Since Falcone didn't trust anyone

---

82   "Buscetta's testimony enabled us to understand the way Cosa Nostra works and how it's structured. It also revealed the relationships between the different members." Francesco Gratteri.

else to do it, he himself transcribed by hand in hundreds of patiently written-out pages what Buscetta said during the extremely long interrogation sessions which followed.

The media attention round Buscetta's testimony created an atmosphere of tension in public opinion. The texts transcribed by Falcone were secret, and what could be learnt from the investigators' actions and declarations didn't give a clear picture of what Buscetta was saying. While Buscetta was talking to Falcone in a super-protected hideout, the police and the *carabinieri* were checking out everything he said in an effort to find objective evidence to corroborate it. Only when Buscetta testified in court did it start to become clear just how much he knew about the whole Mafia set-up.

Buscetta advised Falcone to delay the interrogation on the political aspects of the Mafia, because the significance of what he could reveal was such that it would risk bringing both of them down. It was best to proceed in order, starting with the military dimension of the organization. Buscetta warned Falcone that he too risked being killed by the Mafia because of the statements he was transcribing, but they both decided to go ahead.

In their war against Buscetta, the Corleonesi had killed his two sons, Antonio and Benedetto – their bodies were never found – then his brother Vincenzo and his nephew Benedetto, followed by his brother-in-law and two more nephews, Antonino and Orazio D'Amico. Riina and his men now started to close in on Falcone; police picked up the first threats from Riina's killers. But Falcone continued to interview and transcribe, and Buscetta went on with his own personal war against the Corleone gang. He had a lot to say.

Falcone resigned himself to living an armour-plated existence in which the greatest pleasure was sitting in a sun-filled room in the maximum-security prison in Asinara. A powerful explosive device had been found among rocks near his home, and this convinced him that Buscetta's predictions that the Mafia would also target him were right.

Don Masino started to paint a picture of an old-fashioned Mafia – an organization full of nobility almost, as he described it – which had been destroyed by the bad Mafia of the Corleone gang. His story was underpinned by a belief that he was not an *infame*, one of the "dishonourables", in short a traitor, but someone who had remained true to the good old principles which had been so beneficial. Falcone needed Buscetta to tell him everything he knew, so he let him talk on without interruption. He wanted him to feel at ease, free to reveal all his secrets, safe in the knowledge that he was entrusting them to someone who would not abandon him.

Buscetta considered himself a renowned boss. He would have liked to become a godfather of the same stature as Cascio Ferro, Luciano, Vizzini, Gambino and the others. He wished he had formed his own Family and become President of the Commission. In his version of events, Cosa Nostra had suddenly aged under the attack of the Corleone gang. They were the real "dishonourables" and traitors, because they'd reneged on the traditional rules which, to Buscetta at least, seemed tinged with a kind of romanticism.

He deliberately omitted describing his own crimes; he never referred to the fact that he'd spent his life as a leading member of a secret organization comprised of murderers and drug pushers.[83] But the "good" Mafia of Buscetta's version – as opposed to the bad Corleone Mafia – had never existed.

Buscetta's evidence enabled the investigators to begin to build up an overall picture of Cosa Nostra, and in 1986 led to the first Italian maxi-trial against the Mafia. Some years later Buscetta would come face to face with Riina in court, when,

---

83 "Buscetta was left free to say what he wanted, just as the mood took him, or to choose the topics which seemed to him important, the ones he preferred to talk about first – but whatever he told us was immediately checked and verified. It was clear that Buscetta wanted to appear as a gentleman, even to members of his own Family, making out that he'd had nothing to do with the narcotics trade or with killings. He wanted to appear above the fray, an authentic godfather. No godfather has ever accused himself of being a murderer. Buscetta wanted to make out he was better than he really was, a pure-bred mafioso of the old school who would never have participated in the drugs trade and had done his utmost to avoid the need for violence. It was a strategy his interrogators adopted to let him say whatever he wanted and then immediately verify what he said – as we did for everything he said – and then come back to him and question him about the discrepancies." General Angiolo Pellegrini.

after years in hiding, the latter was captured by *carabinieri* in January 1993. Buscetta launched a fierce attack on him not only in front of the presiding magistrates, but the Italian public as well. "Zu Totò" never lost his cold composure, and ignored Buscetta completely, as if he wasn't sitting in front of him in the maxi-security bunker which served as a courtroom, speaking into a microphone, as if he didn't even exist. It was the greatest contempt a Mafia *capo* could show towards one of the "dishonourables". So the war between the two conceptions of the Mafia was also played out in the courtroom. It was a battle between two determined heavyweights, two bosses who fought with words and silences, gestures and looks, knowing that everything they did and said would be interpreted correctly by all their fellow men of honour.

John Gotti, the "Teflon Don"

"My father is the last of the Mohicans. He doesn't care about making money." This was what Victoria Gotti shouted to the pursuing journalists who were shoving their microphones inside her car. She was a writer with a regular job in publishing, an ordinary job in the normal world, while her father, John Gotti, was beginning to have some problems in evading the American investigators. In 1992, as in previous years, many members of the Gambino Family, young and old, had gone to Sicily for the festival of St Rosalia. It was a kind of family tradition which had to be observed, even though they knew the Italian and American police would place closed-circuit cameras and micro-spies everywhere. But they did it every year – it wasn't a big deal. No business would be discussed – it wasn't the right time or place. In fact Sicily as a whole was no longer the right place for their kind of business. Buscetta's testimony and that of other *pentiti* had dealt severe blows to the Sicilian Cosa Nostra. The Mafia war discouraged contacts between the Families. The American cousins had enough problems of their own without running the risk of finding themselves landed with the Sicilian mess too.

No, if there was a subject worth discussing as they lined up in the procession to honour the saint, it was their own *capo*, John Gotti, known as the "Dapper Don", the last godfather of the Gambino Family, the most powerful in America. Journalists had also given him another name: the "Teflon Don", because whatever Gotti was accused of never seemed to stick. His lawyers would go on the attack, and he gave the impression that he could always wriggle out of every trap set for him by the American investigators. He was a "Teflon" Don in another sense too – he wasn't real, he was synthetic.

Gotti had no idea what it meant to be invisible. He drove around in a black limousine like a rock star. He wore flashy clothes. Seen on the tapes from the secret cameras planted by the FBI in Little Italy, he looked like some second-rate actor among the *picciotti*. The federal agents who were keeping him under observation outside his Ravenite Social Club at 247 Mulberry Street had two theories to choose from. The first was that Gotti knew he was being filmed, and the second was that he didn't have the slightest suspicion – but the result was still the same. The dapper man who went round slapping paunchy young men on the back seemed more like a parody of a godfather than the last of the Mohicans. He frequented the most expensive restaurants in New York in an attempt to revive Lucky Luciano's lifestyle in the 1930s, but he understood nothing of what Luciano had taught the Mafia. All he knew was that a real "Don" was surrounded by broad social support. During his trials, he asked his men to put on a display of such support. The result was a few clashes with the police, as dozens of hooligans broke windows and overturned cars under the lenses of the closed-circuit cameras – and as reported on TV news bulletins across the world for the next few days.

Gotti did a lot of people favours in order to keep his men loyal and to build up a clientele who would say he was the best and most generous man on earth – hyperbolic praises which cynical American journalists distributed to all the TV networks. A refusal to be invisible, a failure to appreciate the advantages of well-judged understatement, confrontation with the American State, an artificially created consensus – this summed up Gotti's situation, and it was about this, not their business interests, that the members of the Gambino Family were speaking as they moved among the candles and the flowers and the clouds of incense to celebrate St Rosalia, and as they waited for the festive fireworks to begin. And if they were talking about it, it was because they needed to find a solution.

On this occasion, the godfather hadn't come with them to Sicily for the festival, but this didn't mean he would be missing out on a firework display. Gotti would let off fireworks whenever an appropriate opportunity presented itself – to celebrate a trial where he'd been acquitted for example – beautiful displays full of colours and bangs. He would stand with a smile on his face, and watch the spectacle together with his underboss Sammy the Bull Gravano.[84] But the fireworks spelt the end of the figure of the Mafia godfather as history had known it. Metaphorically they dazzled John Gotti; among all the lights and explosions and parties and applause, amidst the flash of the cameras, he couldn't distinguish any more between what was real and what was false. The Teflon Don had been too near the fire for too long and had started to lose his power; the charges suddenly started to stick.

The Bull was his right-hand man and his favourite killer; Gravano would follow his boss round like a faithful dog as Gotti strolled the streets. But he betrayed him, and Gotti didn't realize in time; Gravano decided to talk, and so delivered the godfather over to the American justice system. Gravano had carried out an extraordinary number of murders for the Family, but as part of the witness-protection scheme he was never charged for any of them. His boss was put behind bars for life.

---

84 "The Gambino Family during the time of Gotti – during the late 1980s to early 1990s – was the most powerful La Cosa Nostra Family in the United States. It had over two hundred full members and ten times that number in criminal associates. So there was his underboss, his *consigliere*, soldiers, *capos* and as many criminal associates, which included business people, corrupt public officials, corrupt law-enforcement officers... That would be like trying to describe how many levels there are in a multinational corporation or a Fortune 500 corporation. This was an extensive criminal operation, and they conducted many types of criminal activities, ranging from labour-racketeering to entry into many related industries... with many things like gambling, loan-sharking, extortion, homicide, all in connection with their activities." Thomas V. Fuentes.

Though he was powerful and dangerous, Gotti ended up being a caricature of a godfather. His visibility and exhibitionism brought him to the attention of the investigators. Within the space of just two generations of godfathers, men led by the inscrutable and invisible Gambino were thrust into the limelight that Gotti liked so much. Profits were decreasing. Important men of honour were in prison. Many of the firms which had provided cover for illegal business had been flushed out. There was a storm in progress, a turbulent full tide was passing over their heads. It was a question of waiting, bending like the reeds, until it was over.[85]

The Murders of Falcone and Borsellino

In the same year that Gotti was given his life sentence, "Zu Totò" Riina and his Corleone gang embarked on a military escalation of what had now turned into a war against the Italian State.

On the road from the airport into Palermo, at the point where there's a turning for Capaci, along the stretch now marked out by blood-red guard rails, they detonated a bomb which blew Giovanni Falcone, his wife Francesca Morvillo and their armed escort to bits. The crater left by the explosion was comparable only to those caused by the heavy aerial bombardments of Palermo during the Second World War.

Two months later, as part of what was clearly a coordinated campaign of attack, a car filled with explosives went off, eliminating Paolo Borsellino and his bodyguards.

Giovanni Falcone was murdered on 23rd May 1992, ninety-nine years and three months after the murder of Emanuele Notarbartolo. Borsellino was murdered on 19th July 1992, ninety-nine years and five months after Notarbartolo. The century in between these two events had opened with the first important trial against the "honoured society", in which

---

85 "Many of them are in prison, many are getting older, and the newer generations of younger criminals in the Families are taking their places, but they're not as effective." Thomas V. Fuentes

Notarbartolo's son had openly accused the godfathers and revealed their connections with politicians, and it ended with the first maxi-trial which, building on Falcone and Borsellino's investigations, attempted for the first time to draw a complete picture of Cosa Nostra. Most of the years in between had been filled by a chorus of voices proclaiming that there was no such thing as the Mafia, although there was also a subdued refrain running through which said: "Yes, the Mafia exists, but there's a difference between the good Mafia and the bad Mafia."

Falcone and Borsellino were the leading proponents of the idea that a complete picture of the Mafia was needed, which would reconstruct the historical links between the different Families and provide an overall view of the underworld of Cosa Nostra. In blowing Falcone and Borsellino to pieces, their killers were trying to destroy not only the picture, but the very drive to assemble such a picture. They wanted to scatter the different pieces of the Mafia which had been put together, and keep them separated. It was an essential step in Cosa Nostra's new strategy of re-immersing its organization back into the shadows.[86]

Scenes from a Tragedy

The two attacks, coming so shortly after one another, were not just the climax of the offensive launched by the more militarized Mafia Families: they were also instrumental to their strategic rethinking. The aim was to destroy the map which the investigators were compiling by smashing it into pieces, so that they would become disoriented and lose their capacity and expertise in tracing the routes taken by Mafia business. Once more silence and invisibility would envelop the Families. For

---

86 "Cosa Nostra is emerging from a period of crisis caused by both internal organizational reasons and because the State is now better equipped to oppose the organization. Recent years have been stressful for the Mafia. In effect the tyranny of Riina and his henchmen and their opposition to the State has meant that the organization has been forced to become more democratic, so returning to the old view that the real essence of Cosa Nostra lay in the Families... This attitude forces the police to rely more on intelligence information." Colonel Mauro Obinu.

the *pentiti*, those who had had a crisis of loyalty and risked their lives by deciding to turn State's evidence, Falcone and Borsellino had been two such guides.

In fact Rita Atria regarded Paolo Borsellino as more than a guide, and more like a second father to her, while for his part the magistrate was as protective towards her as if she were his own daughter.[87] She was just eleven when she suffered her first heavy loss, and seventeen years old when she found herself at the centre of an unfolding tragedy. Though she was only a girl, she accepted the role she had to play and saw it through to the final act. The characters who moved around her seemed to be tragically driven by supernatural forces, the messengers of an ineluctable fate.

Rita's father, Don Vito, was what was known as a *paciere*, a peacemaker or mediator.[88] Anyone who had a problem would turn to him, and he would solve it by applying the rules he knew, the only rules which counted in Partanna, those of the Mafia. He was a man of honour, a godfather, a "leading member of the Mafia organization", in Rita's own words to the *carabinieri*. He was deeply attached to his youngest daughter, and would do anything for her; Rita too had a sincere affection for her father. She saw he was treated with respect by all around him, and she came to believe in the myth of her father.

Her mother Giovanna lived in the reflected light of her husband's prestige and respectability, and took care to do nothing which might lessen it. As a wife and a mother, she showed the inhabitants of Partanna she knew how to bring up her children by the traditional rules. Her husband's family was after all the foundation of his honourableness. Rita had a brother, Nicola, of whom she was very fond: at first he was her play-companion, but later, as her world started to collapse around her, he was a rock to which she could cling. His wife Piera, Rita's sister-in-law, had

---

87 "She grew up precociously, and she knew a lot more than the people around her. But what was it which made her so mature in her speech and in her actions, what was the event which gradually made her aware of what was surrounding her?" From the diary of Rita Atria, an autobiography written in the third person, in S. Rizza, *Una ragazza contro la Mafia*, Palermo 1993.

88 "My father did all this, as far as I could tell, not for money, but as a matter of principle and prestige in the circles which mattered in Partanna." Rita Atria, op. cit.

become her best friend, the kind of friend a seventeen-year-old girl shares her anxieties and dreams with. C. was Rita's childhood fiancé, her first love, the boy for whom she wanted to grow up quickly into womanhood. A little love-mate – and a disturbing little traitor. Finally there was the magistrate Borsellino. He might be described as the *deus ex machina* of the drama, if he were not at the same time its bravest hero. The tragedy unfolded act by act, sweeping Rita along with it. It is surprising to see how well-aware such a young woman was of what was happening.[89]

When still a child, living in an anonymous house, surrounded by the invisible forces of the Mafia, she started to keep a diary, reminiscent of the diary kept by another young girl in an anonymous house in Amsterdam, waiting for the violent hand of another State run by murderers. A war was going on around Rita too, a Mafia war in which her father was murdered, shot in the head at close range in November 1985. Nicola was just twenty-one; according to Mafia tradition he was expected to step into his father's shoes. No longer could he keep Rita company; he now had two families to attend to, his own family and his Mafia Family. It is said that standing hand in hand beside their father's coffin, brother and sister swore to take revenge, not realizing the forces which were in play.[90] Rita was only eleven and no one paid her any attention.

It's also said that someone in the circles which matter in Partanna tried to find out more about Nicola's oath to revenge his father. But in a world where the lawful State and the Mafia state border each other, where "to spy" is a synonym for "to ask", there's no need for espionage. Everyone knew the rules: sooner or later Nicola would do what he had to do. He would avenge his father's killing, unless he was killed first.

89 "Before you fight the Mafia you must examine your own conscience and then, after you've defeated the Mafia inside yourself, you can fight the Mafia among your friends, the Mafia in what we are and in the way we live." Rita Atria, op. cit.

90 "The only way of getting rid of the affliction that is the Mafia is to make the young people who are forced to live among the Mafia see there is another world, full of simple and beautiful objects, a pure world where people treat you for what you are, not because you're the child of a particular person or because you've paid a kickback to get a favour done. Perhaps an honest world will never exist, but that shouldn't stop us from dreaming of one. If all of us tried to change, perhaps we could achieve it." Rita Atria, op. cit.

The due amount of time elapsed. Nicola managed to survive an attack; his sister ran to be by his side. She was now sixteen, and had begun to understand what kind of organization her own family belonged to, who they were and what the other Families were like who were fighting among themselves. She knew that they wanted to kill her brother. But she still loved him.

On 24th June 1991, killers entered the pizzeria run by Nicola Atria. He'd only just started it as a business, but the time he'd been allowed by the Mafia was up. Their faces were uncovered: the rules state that it is a matter of honour to let the victim see who is about to kill him. He was shot with the classic Mafia weapon, a sawn-off shotgun.

In the following act, Piera Aiello, Nicola's beautiful young wife, enters on stage. She knew she had married a man of honour. Even though she was in love with him, she had tried to get out of the marriage, but Don Vito had intervened. He hadn't threatened her – he'd simply explained with patriarchal calm what the rules were which govern men of honour. She was free to do what she wanted. But a woman associated with a man of honour remained so for the rest of her life, whether she married him or not: she was branded.

Her husband's murder horrified Piera: she went to the magistrates and told them everything she'd learnt from him about the more recent dealings of the time-honoured and industrious organization. She was determined to save her only daughter. Borsellino descended to sweep Piera away to safety before her assassins arrived. She came under the programme for the protection of witnesses and continued to testify about what she knew.

Rita was not yet eighteen. She took the stage with a resolve which only she knew she possessed. Her childhood had not merely been passed in a Mafia environment: she'd been brought up within the Mafia, had been nurtured on it.[91] The shadows

---

91 "She tried desperately, from the time she was a little girl, to understand what was right and what was wrong, she tried for years to discover, to see what everyone had kept hidden from her, but what she discovered so hurt her that she could no longer distinguish between right and wrong. She'd always heard that each person's destiny is fixed three days before they are born, and that in the same way you are born you are destined to die." Rita Atria, op. cit.

of the Mafia had fallen across her carefree games with Nicola. More than thirty murders in Partanna occurred while Rita was growing up: the war between the Ingoglia Family, to which her father and her brother belonged, and the Accardo, more commonly known as the "Cannata", was being fought to the last man.

Behind Rita, C. shyly appears, her childhood sweetheart. He too had been brought up in a family saturated with the Mafia. He wasn't an affiliate, they hadn't pricked his finger for his blood and his soul. But he was familiar with the rules and knew it was best not to break them: "the Mafia Family takes precedence over your own family". When he was told that Rita was now an enemy he should destroy, he managed to muster enough courage at least to run away rather than harm her.[92]

Now the mother enters. So far she has not been given a single line to say. As far as the role she was supposed to play was concerned, she could have remained silent. But she decided to speak. Giovanna told her daughter that she would be the first person to ask for her to be killed if she continued to talk to the police.[93]

Once again the magistrate came like a *deus ex machina* to take Rita and put her under protection. She was concealed under a series of different names; she led a life under constant guard in anonymous houses in crowded residential areas. Borsellino

---

92 "The others in the clan told my fiancé he had to hurt me in order to threaten my sister-in-law, who was collaborating with the police. They also told him to leave me because I was dangerous. And C. did leave me, saying that he wanted to save his own skin. We listen and do what we're told to do, some for money, others out of fear, or because their father is a boss and you must follow in his footsteps." Rita Atria, op. cit.

93 "I'm starting to write again because one can never be too careful. After my death I want very few people to attend my funeral. My sister-in-law Piera Aiello and her family should come. My sister Annamaria and any of the *cara-binieri* who would like to be there can come – all the people who have helped me in my fight to see justice done for the deaths of my father and my brother. Under no circumstances should my mother come to the funeral, or try to see my body after my death. Among my uncles only Alessio Atria can come to my funeral, no one else. I should like there to be many flowers, but I don't want any white flowers. The coffin should be white or black, and only a single rose should be placed on it [...] I am certain that my life will not be a long one, either because I will be killed by the men I accuse during the trial or because it is willed by fate." Rita Atria, op. cit.

26. Nicola Zappetti
(1923–92)

27. Enrico Mattei
(1906–72)

28. Fidel Castro arriving at the MATS Terminal,
Washington, DC in 1959

29. Joe Valachi (1903–71) testifying
in front of the cameras

30. Giuseppe (Joe) Bonanno
(1905–2002)

31. Michele Sindona
(1920–86)

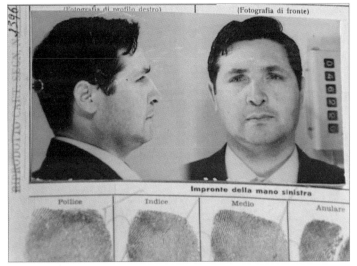

32. Mugshots and fingerprints of
Salvatore (Totò) "Shorty" Riina (b.1930)

33. Totò Riina
c.1960

34. The killing of
Michele Navarra

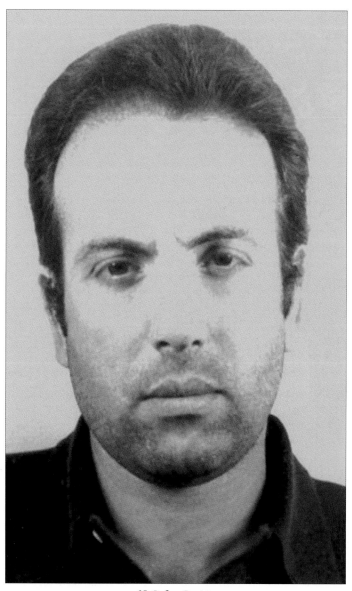

35. Stefano Bontate
(1939–81)

36. Bernardo Provenzano
(*b*.1933)

37. The arrest of Bernardo Provenzano
in April 2006

38. Giovanni Falcone (1939–92)
and Paolo Borsellino (1940–92)

39. The scene of Giovanni Falcone's
assassination

40. The scene of Paolo Borsellino's
assassination

41. Tommaso Buscetta (1928–2000)
interviewed by the police

42. Tommaso Buscetta
c.1990

thought that in this way her safety would be guaranteed. But then he himself became an actor in the drama, even though his role as magistrate meant that he shouldn't be in it at all: Rita started to look upon him as a second father and began to love him with real filial love – until his killing plunged her once more into anguish.[94]

The day after the event, at the exact time it occurred, Rita thought of the bomb: it exploded among her thoughts, wrecking them as it had destroyed the street, the Via D'Amelio, the magistrate and his bodyguard. Two more days and again, shortly after two in the afternoon, she saw and thought of the bomb. The security men told her she needed to change house; more than ever it was imperative to protect her from the killers of Cosa Nostra.[95] They transferred her to one of the most crowded parts of Rome, hiding her in another anonymous apartment, behind a bell tower named after a family of Egyptian immigrants. But even the name of the street where she'd been put was a reminder of the tragedy: viale Amelia, in the Tuscolano quarter of Rome. It hadn't occurred to anyone. At two o'clock, once again, Rita found her thoughts filled with the bomb which had caused the massacre in Via D'Amelio. And the day after, and the day after that. With Borsellino's death all her hopes in a new life had gone – the only life worth living, one without the Mafia.

According to the information in the inquest, on the seventh day after Borsellino's death, at two p.m, with the thought of the bomb again in her head, she checked the front door was

---

94 "Now Borsellino is dead, no one can understand the emptiness I feel in my life. Everyone is frightened, but what most frightens me is the thought that the Mafia will win and the poor fools fighting against the windmills will all be killed... Borsellino, you died for what you believed in, but I am dead without you." Rita Atria, op. cit.

95 "Judges, public prosecutors, those who decide to collaborate with the forces of justice are today more fearful than ever before, because they know inside that no one can protect them – no one, if they decided to speak, can save them from what they call the Mafia. But the truth is that they will really have to defend themselves from their friends: politicians, lawyers, magistrates, men and women of high social standing in the eyes of the world, whom no one will ever succeed in revealing for what they really are." From the secondary-school examination essay written by Rita Atria.

locked, and then threw herself out of the window. Her guards had protected her against Mafia killers, from external enemies, but they couldn't protect her against her own thoughts.

Her body was taken back to Partanna for the funeral. Her sister-in-law, Piera, commissioned a tombstone. Only women carried her coffin, their faces strained with the effort of finding the strength to carry it as far as the tomb. They had lost fathers, husbands, brothers and sons to the Mafia, and now, like a silent chorus of Erinyes, they lifted Rita's coffin in front of the stunned bystanders. To the townspeople who knew them they seemed to bear a message, like ancient divinities bent on revenge for the blood which had been spilled; all realized they were capable of transforming themselves into Furies. The message was clearly understood in a place where all meaning was coded according to the rules of the Mafia: these women had found the strength to overcome their fear. Women on their own against the Mafia. As Rita herself had requested, no one from her family attended the funeral.

On occasion dramatists insert a minor character into the play to act as a foil to the nobler figures in the action. The priest who presided at Rita's funeral decided to hold it in a small area outside the consecrated walls rather than inside the church in front of the altar. He was quick to explain that he hadn't allowed it to be held in the church because Rita had committed suicide and was therefore a sinner, and defended himself by saying that decisions had been taken "by the authorities responsible for public order". So the ceremony was held in the open air, under the hot Sicilian sun. The moment arrived for the sermon, and the priest began to read what he had prepared. A deep dissenting murmur rose from the crowd when he remarked that the reason for Rita's revelations had been her deep state of depression. He managed to make things even worse when he said that suicide was sinful. The chorus of women, who had remained silent until then, shouted out: "Rita didn't sin, she talked." Then the Mayor, by way of reply, declared that the town should not be "criminalized" and said that the results of the trials should be awaited before anyone was accused of belonging to the Mafia.

In November 1992 it was still warm in Partanna. The tragedy was not over yet. Rita's mother was left alone on the stage. Unspeaking. She entered the tranquil cemetery. She had nothing she wanted to say, no important phrase or memorable remark, but she carried a hammer. She broke the silence of the cemetery by hammering on her daughter's tombstone, so that the photograph of Rita attached to the marble relief of an open Bible fell off. The custodian heard the noise and ran over. The *carabinieri* came and charged her. This woman of the Mafia, who had no one left in her family, told the police in her statement she couldn't bear the thought that Piera Aiello had had Rita's photograph placed on the tombstone. For Giovanna, Piera was no longer her son's wife – she was the dishonourable woman who had carried him off, before his killers had carried him off. "I'm not a monster. I'm just a woman who's lost everything. I love my daughter Rita. Piera Aiello is to blame for everything" – these were the words which the newspapers reported.

Piera, the *pentita*, was the cause of all that had happened. It was her fault that the Atria Family had been destroyed in the Mafia world. And when the tragedy had played itself out, she in her wickedness had not allowed Giovanna to take away the bodies as was allowed even in wartime. Even now Giovanna's children were dead, they were to be taken from her. The tombstone she had broken was a symbol of her daughter's separation. It was for this reason, to break the marble barrier which that world had erected round the tomb of her daughter, that she had gone into the cemetery with a hammer in her hand.

When the tragedy was completely concluded, Giovanna did for one moment come out from the shadows. She went up and embraced the widow of Paolo Borsellino and thanked her.

Pax Mafiosa

In killing Falcone and Borsellino, the Mafia had not only killed two outstanding investigators: they had also murdered the best guides to the organization – in order that no one again would find the way between the world of daylight normality and the underworld. Cosa Nostra slowly started to change direction as if steered by some hidden helmsman. Gradually – over the long stretch of Mafia time – Families dropped out of view. Only the Corleone gang continued their war against the Italian State, still trying to attack while exposing itself to increasingly harsh countermeasures.

The Pope too spoke out during a visit to Sicily. In May 1993, John Paul II gave a speech in Agrigento in front of a vast crowd who had come to hear him. He was known for his physical strength, for his determination to exercise his authority, and even for his capacity to harangue those he regarded as the enemies of the Church and of humanity.[96] He pointed upwards with his index finger to remind the men of the Mafia of another judgement waiting for them after the one the world would pass on them – the judgement of God.

The bosses planned a new phase of the war, and their engineers put it into action. The Uffizi Gallery in Florence, two churches in Rome and the Pavilion of Contemporary Art in Milan were all bombed. There was nothing symbolic about the attacks: they were devastating explosions. A rapid restoration was undertaken of Italy's damaged artistic heritage, to avoid any lasting effects on public opinion. Shortly afterwards, father Pino Puglisi, a parish priest in Palermo, well-known for his anti-Mafia position, was murdered. But the war waged by the Corleone gang was nearing its end.

"Zu Totò" Riina was captured. He'd been a fugitive from justice longer than anyone else in the history of the Mafia. Giovanni Brusca, who had constructed bombs and killed and tortured in Riina's service – he was the man who had detonated the explosion which killed Falcone – was also arrested and decided to turn State's evidence. He was responsible for a long series of the most savage crimes, including dissolving the body of a child in acid, the son of a *pentito* – or in Brusca's eyes a

---

96 Speaking about the right to life, Pope John Paul II said in his speech at Agrigento on 9th May 1993: "The Mafia cannot ride roughshod over this holiest of God-given rights. The people of Sicily, so deeply attached to life, cannot live for ever under the pressure of the culture of death. To those who bear the responsibility I say: 'Change your lives! The time will come when the judgement of God will be upon you.'"

"dishonourable", who with his confessions was damaging the Corleone gang and their allies. Brusca's decision to collaborate had nothing to do with repentance: it was a straightforward business deal in which he would provide information and in return save his own skin. He had information which only one of Riina's closest bosses could provide, and he counted on it saving him from both official punishment and the killers the Mafia would send to get him. It was all a question of business, nothing else.

The higher up in the organization the informer was, the more valuable the information he provided. Faced by the new "dishonourable", Riina adopted an attitude of contemptuous detachment. He didn't respond, he didn't show any emotion at all, he hardly spoke. And this wasn't simply because he knew this was how an authentic godfather should behave, it was also to send a message to the underworld. The message was: silence. The war was over, and the *pax mafiosa* had taken its place. It was a unilateral decision, like all the decisions taken by Cosa Nostra, and Riina hoped to force the Italian State to accept it – or at least to be gradually sucked into it.

The police forces realized immediately what was up. They knew they had to keep on the attack, tightening the circle round the Mafia's capital and its assets. Mafiosi had learnt from their ancestors the art of keeping their heads down and their nerves under control as long as was needed.[97] Once again the reeds bent as the full tide swept over them. Riina's face remained motionless, not a flicker of expression passed over it, as the court confiscated the handful of properties they'd been able to trace back to him by removing the man of straw in whose

---

97 "There are various ways of attacking Cosa Nostra. First of all it's necessary to arrest those who are guilty of associating with the Mafia. Then it's important to target the Mafia's accumulated assets, confiscate them, work out how they recycle their money, what companies they use. All the time Cosa Nostra is trying to find new ways of escaping the net, we should be trying to devise new methods of targeting their assets. This is important, because when Cosa Nostra starts to lose money and becomes poor, it becomes more difficult to run the organization, to pay the wages, for example, of the men who are arrested. We have had some *pentiti* who've collaborated because they were hired as killers, only to be abandoned by the Mafia and left without support." General Angiolo Pellegrini.

name they were registered. They succeeded in expropriating a large modern building in Corleone and turning it into the new local agricultural college.

In order to manage the land which was confiscated from the Mafia, a consortium was formed by the local towns of Altofonte, Camporeale, Piana degli Albanesi, Corleone, Monreale, Rocca-mena, San Cipirello and San Giuseppe Jato. To work the land, some youngsters set up a co-operative in November 2001, named "Placido Rizzotto – Libera Terra" after the trade unionist from Corleone who'd been murdered by the Mafia. Even the graduates among them put on their overalls and worked as labourers in the fields, planting for the future harvest. The soil was good, and they worked like experienced farm labourers. But the local mafiosi sent flocks of sheep onto the fields to destroy everything they'd planted; no one was allowed to sow land belonging to the godfathers and make a profit from it. Eventually, in 2002, with the Mafia immersed in silence, the youngsters managed to thresh the wheat they'd grown, make flour from it, and then pasta, which they sold under the brand name "Libera Terra". "Legal" pasta, with the phrase "grown from proceeds confiscated from the Mafia" proudly displayed on each packet. Perhaps they should have sent a couple of packets to the German weekly magazine *Der Spiegel*, which had just published a feature on the Mafia with a cover which showed a plate of steaming spaghetti and a pistol above it.

The project was to identify what belonged to the Mafia bosses, sequester it and then use it to benefit society; from the production of pasta, olive oil and wine to setting up farm guest houses for tourists and even a riding school on land which once belonged to the local mafiosi from the towns which were part of the consortium.

Bernardo Provenzano, the last big boss left on the run after the arrest of Riina and his bandits, watched, from a series of unfindable hideaways, the activities of the youthful co-operatives. Even on estates which were once his property, they were producing "free" olive oil. Provenzano was old and in bad shape and being pursued by investigators. He let them think he might even be dead, while the other bosses continued to refer to him as a symbolic figure who would keep the peace among their Families. His right-hand man Antonino Giuffrè was very much alive and was responsible for transmitting Provenzano's orders to the Families. Later, when Giuffré decided to turn State's evidence, he explained how the Families had tried to use Provenzano with his prestige and authority as a centre or focus for the new strategy, and to ensure the more restive *picciotti* towed the line. There were to be no wars, no feuds, only silence.

Consensus and Violence

It was a silence which came from far back in history, and now returned to cloak the underworld in Italy and America and wherever else the Mafia did its business. The Families knew the strategies they had to adopt when they were on the defensive, and the price they had to pay as men of honour in order to become once more invisible. The process would probably require a very long time; the few men with brains left in the Mafia would not only have to reorganize the Families, but also nominate new bosses and even form a new Commission.[98] It was also a question of replacing the engine which made the Mafia function.

There was a time when the bosses of Cosa Nostra needed to be recognizable – as mafiosi they should be invisible, but they needed to be recognized as godfathers. They were to be respected, honoured and feared – not only by other men of honour, or by the friends of friends, but above all by the society in which they lived. But after the defeats inflicted on the Mafia no mafioso could fill such a role. It was too dangerous for a godfather to take a stroll round his town. Even if he gave up holding court at the local bar with petitioners kissing his hand and managed to distribute his favours in another less public way, he still ran the risk of being identified and targeted. The bosses who headed what remained of the Families were forced

---

98 "They're very reluctant to even publicly name a boss, much less to have the bosses meet and conduct meetings as an organization or as a Commission." Thomas V. Fuentes.

to camouflage themselves. They had to give up the need for something which was implanted in mafiosi from the very beginnings of the organization: they had to do without the support of a social consensus around them.

The Mafia as a secret organization originated in the world of the great estates and the barons, in a mysterious atmosphere of violence and fear. It was in such a world and in such an atmosphere that the bosses had acquired their powers of intimidation. But the intelligence of the Mafia lay in its recognition that it needed to create the consensus of others alongside the power to intimidate them. Consensus and violence. The behaviour of men of honour needed to embody, in the eyes of impoverished and illiterate peasants, the principles of a rudimentary justice which was typical of the backward regions of southern Italy. The kind of justice which offered to protect people from a distant but oppressive State; the kind of justice administered by a godfather who was on the spot, a "mediator" who would listen to a petitioner's problems, whether it was about rights over a stream or getting employment.

To these two elements of consensus and violence, Lucky Luciano had added a third: money. Money became an extraordinarily powerful tool in Cosa Nostra's activity – vast sums of illicit capital waiting to be reinvested in any number or kind of enterprises.

It was the gradual loss of the Mafia's invisibility which led to the constant erosion of the consensus which supported it, to the point where the organization's Achilles' heel was exposed: the traces left by the money as it was moved around. These traces were almost impossible to erase when the police in every country were working together, and when laws had been devised especially for the purpose of marking indelibly every movement of international capital.[99]

Under Provenzano's leadership a new kind of war developed between the State and the Mafia. It isn't easy to fight against

---

99 "Whatever problems arise which seem to force the anti-Mafia investigators to pause, they should in fact never pause; as soon as they do, the Mafia exploits the pause in activity to make itself even stronger. It wants to be left in peace." General Angiolo Pellegrini.

someone who's good at hiding, at standing still, at melting into the background. Sequestering Mafia property was only the first battle in the war: the real aim was to show everyone that crime didn't pay. But to accomplish this, the State not only had to return the assets which had been stolen by the Mafia back to society, it also had to make sure that those assets generated more work than they did when the Mafia owned them. The bosses knew they needed to intimidate the people who were involved in this process, so that everyone would see the State was incapable of managing the expropriated assets successfully. But arson and bombs and destruction are not appropriate behaviour for men intent on keeping their heads down like the reeds. One could wait, at least, for mistakes to be made – such as in the case of the sale of the Hotel San Paolo in Palermo, which saw its market value plummet after it was sequestered.

But the other front in the war was still active: money, the Mafia's capital. The houses, villas, factories and hotels which the Mafia owned were only the tip of the iceberg of their economic power, the assets which could be realized most easily. Below the visible assets ran the rivers of liquid cash, too quickly for it to be tracked and targeted by the State.

The Mafia became intent on transferring its wealth onto the stock market through electronic dealing, while the State fought back to protect the role of the financial markets as a function of democracy from the potentially lethal contamination of illicit money, in an effort to defend the public interest from the power of Mafia capital.

History shows us that the Mafia fears two things above all others: imprisonment with additional punishments, and the confiscation of their assets. A harsh prison regime means the bosses can no longer command. At a football match held in Palermo on 22nd December 2002, a large banner was held up in the crowd protesting against such a regime with the words: "We are united against 'Law 41 bis'" (which provides for tough incarceration policies against mafiosi), and "Berlusconi doesn't care about Sicily". The initiative was thought to come from the Brancaccio Family, and appears to have been carried out in the middle of the stadium crowd without anyone "noticing" anything. On 12th January 2003, a reply was hoisted on another banner in the stadium in Bologna: "Give us freedom of expression. Solidarity with the 'ultras' in Palermo".

The sequestering of their assets impoverishes the bosses. An impoverished Mafia no longer has the strength to maintain itself as an alternative state, and it can't win social support. Once it's lost the backing of a consensus, it can't generate new godfathers. And without godfathers to lead it, it can't reacquire the old essential habit of invisibility. In June 2003, while the Families were still maintaining their silence, an inquiry by the Public Prosecutor in Palermo into the connections between the Mafia and the political system led to several prominent politicians being arrested or granted bail on charges of associating with the Mafia.

This was the engine which no longer worked for the Families who had graduated from being street hoodlums a long time ago.[100] Even the renowned bosses of the past had realized their sons were better off becoming lawyers or accountants. To the men who were once again trying to change everything so that everything stayed the same, who were training up a new generation of mafiosi who'd know about new ways of doing business, the images shown on TV of John Gotti and his *picciotti* on the streets of New York must have seemed ridiculous.[101] Men who were capable of engineering the rise and fall of stocks and shares on electronic financial markets, while all the time keeping their eye on the drugs trade, were

---

[100] "At the present time Cosa Nostra is trying to reshape its activities, after a turbulent period of internal crisis caused by the organizational tensions of Riina's leadership and a series of defeats at the hands of the Italian State. Cosa Nostra is now trying to restart its business interests, its old activities, but discreetly, without creating a stir, so that the State and investigators won't notice the changes which are taking place." Colonel Mauro Obinu.

[101] "The Mafia is becoming more corporate in their nature. They're lowering their visibility because of the amount of public attention they attracted, particularly using high-profile bombings and assassinations, such as the killing of Judge Falcone in Italy. Now they realize that it only brings additional law-enforcement pressure on them when they commit those type of murders, so now they are becoming more secretive, and trying not to attract as much public attention as in the past." Thomas V. Fuentes.

put at risk by the possible repercussions of the Teflon Don's antics, which were damaging the interests of the entire Gambino Family. They were compromised by bloodthirsty thugs like Brusca, who'd armed himself with a missile in his war against the State. They were embarrassed by "Shorty" Totò Riina, who still thought he had the power to fix trials, and so had told several bosses who'd been released from prison because of some procedural hitch that they didn't have to go on the run – only the State didn't give way, the trial results weren't "fixed", and the bosses were led back to prison. Men like Gotti, Brusca and Riina no longer had a place in the underworld. Its own history suggested that the Mafia should start training new generations.

An example of this emerged in the revelations of the *pentito* Antonino Giuffré in March 2003. He mentioned that several American *picciotti*, mostly from the Bonanno Family, had taken to visiting Sicily to learn how to become men of honour according to the old rules. There was a school for the new cadres where they learnt to respect the force of tradition. The methods were effective – a kind of field research, at a time when the Mafia had withdrawn far back into the shadows.

If this is the case, then it's a plausible hypothesis that the new recruits were able to observe and admire Provenzano in action. The police took two years to discover that the boss, by now ageing, weary and still being hunted down, had visited Marseilles twice, in July and again in October 2003, to undergo an operation for prostate cancer at the Ciotat and Casamance clinics. His choice of Marseilles was probably significant: from the time of Lucky Luciano onwards, the French port had played a leading role in Cosa Nostra's global system for the refining, transportation and distribution of drugs. The contacts which the organization had built up over the years in the city must have been so secure and invisible that Provenzano could avail himself of them several decades later. Perhaps some of the new trainees were even invited to celebrate the godfather's return from France at a party held in the Hotel Jolly in Palermo on 22nd November 2003 – after which no doubt it was back to their "books".

But the Marseilles trips had an unforeseen consequence for Provenzano: the police were able to obtain samples of his DNA. From the biopsy sample which had been taken from the patient, Giuseppe Novelli from the Tor Vergata University in Rome was able to extract Provenzano's DNA, compare it to that of his brother, and conclude that the two had the same father and mother. The hospital files from Marseilles which the police had taken as evidence also showed that Provenzano had a scar on his neck, was 1.65 metres tall and weighed 68 kilos. One of the last quasi-mythical figures in the Mafia was no longer quite as invisible as he famously used to be. It had been a mistake not to have got rid of the biopsy material, and now there was a new problem to deal with. Provenzano had always been skilful in never leaving any electronic traces behind him: no computers, no mobile phones, no emails or credit cards. But now he had to be careful about even the smallest physical traces – no saliva on glasses he'd drunk out of, or on cutlery he'd used, no handkerchiefs he'd blown his nose in, no nail-parings or hair-cuttings or dirty clothes in the laundry bin.

When he'd gone to Marseilles, Provenzano had used the identity of Gaspare Troia, a seventy-three-year-old baker in Villabate near Palermo. Yet another *pentito*, Francesco Campanella, in addition to shedding new light on the local political contacts who were protecting Provenzano while he was in hiding, had explained to the investigators how the official stamp on the identity card which the boss had needed for his trip had been falsified with a genuine one obtained from the local births-and-deaths registry office. Campanella turning State's evidence was yet another price paid by Provenzano for the successful operation on his prostate. Following up Campanella's testimony, the police made dozens of arrests – engineers, architects, ordinary foot soldiers, and also a former mayor of Villabate, a curious character who moved with ease around the borderlands which should serve to protect the laws of democratic countries, but all too often let the barbarians cross over. As the mayor in Villabate he had even sponsored anti-Mafia activities, such as setting up a "Committee for the Respect of the Law", which had held a public ceremony to award a prize to the television actor who'd played the role of the so-called Captain "Ultimo", the code name of the *carabiniere* who had led the operation to arrest Totò Riina.

The Last Godfathers

Lucky Luciano had died of a heart attack in 1962: he fell to the ground dead in Naples Airport. The legend goes that he was waiting to meet a Hollywood producer who wanted to make a film about his life – so it was business to the very end for the boy from Lercara Friddi. He was only sixty-five. He would have told someone his story and then made a deal on the rights, perhaps securing a percentage of the film's takings. On the downside, the film would have meant interviews and publicity. But the man who was responsible for the Commission was certainly not short of an idea or two about how to manage this deal to his best advantage. Only that he wasn't expecting to die.

The Commission organized a grand funeral for him. Igea, his loyal companion who had accompanied him into exile in Italy, had died of cancer a few years earlier, a cause of great grief to Salvatore Lucania. Yet, at his funeral, reporters saw another woman crying at the door of the church where the ceremony had been held. Some *picciotti* tried to shield her from the cameramen and the photographers. She was a young Neapolitan who'd taken Igea's place in Luciano's house, if not in his heart.

Vito Cascio Ferro had died during the Second World War at the age of eighty. After the Iron Prefect had struck, he'd been moved between prisons until he'd ended up in a cell in Pozzuoli. Cesare Mori hadn't just arrested him and provided the court with enough evidence to sentence him; he'd made sure that Ferro was unable to communicate with his men. Isolated and deprived of all his power, he'd grown old in prison, until an American bombardment in 1943 flattened the prison and he was left buried under the ruins.

Al Capone's days, on the other hand, had come to an end under the Florida sun, in 1947. He was only forty-eight and had been sent to prison for tax evasion. He hadn't escaped from prison;

the United States government decided it was pointless spending public money to keep him inside. Scarface had turned imbecilic, rotten with syphilis. The FBI allowed him to return to his villa in Florida to sunbathe for the last time. He was no longer the slightest risk; his fellow mobsters avoided him like the plague.

His right-hand man Johnny Torrio, the "brain" he'd relied on, met a different end. After he'd managed to survive an astonishing quantity of bullets aimed at him in Chicago, he retired to private life and decided to enjoy his wealth with a two-year cruise of the Mediterranean. He was contacted by various bosses who, if they failed to persuade him to take part in their affairs, at least wanted to benefit from his advice. Johnny the Brain's opinion – on whether to buy a particular consignment or how to deal with an internal feud – was always held in high esteem. He returned to America, but not to the Mafia, although those who wanted something from him knew where to find him. He died of a heart attack in 1957, sitting in a barber's chair, watching the passers-by on the New York street outside.

Calogero Vizzini died in his bed in Villalba in 1954. He had never married, and it was his devoted sister who cared for him to the end. His clerical relatives arrived to give him the last rites and celebrate a sung mass for him. The mafiosi who had worked for him had a sacred image printed; to make sure the message they'd had printed on it was clear, they put the most important phrase in big letters on a black cloth hung over the door of the church: "His Mafia was love".[102] A crowd of people from all over Sicily followed the coffin; magistrates and police officers were seen standing in the street to the cemetery as the funeral procession passed by. An endless stream of people came

---

102 The sacred image distributed at Calogero Vizzini's funeral carried the following poem: "In vain hatred and envy threw their last ungenerous darts at his still-open coffin. In that final hour of lament, love proved stronger: its resounding voice spoke to all upright people of his kindly features and his noble and generous heart. In commerce and in industry his achievements were unequalled. He anticipated and began the agrarian reforms. He improved the lot of lowly mine-workers and won people's affection and esteem. He was an enemy of all injustice, he was humble with the humble, and great with the great. He showed with words and deeds that his Mafia had nothing to do with crime, but was respect for the law, the defence of rights, greatness of spirit. It was love".

to visit the small burial chapel belonging to the Vizzini Family, not only mafiosi or men who'd been part of his network, but also impudent journalists and the simply inquisitive could be found – can still be found – searching for the tomb while they look at all the quaint names on the gravestones. The custodians of the cemetery still point out where Vizzini's grave can be seen, adding eagerly: "There the great man rests who did only good for the people of Villalba. That's all we know about the matter."

Salvatore Giuliano wasn't a godfather, but the myth of the guerrilla bandit which surrounded him when he was alive has made his burial place a favourite destination for tourists who like the thrill of the Mafia. He was killed on 5th July 1950 at 3.30 in the morning while he was asleep, by his cousin, Gaspare Pisciotta. A rather mysterious sentence is displayed over the entrance to the cemetery at Montelepre: "We are as you were, you will be as we are". The tourists read it, enter, discover that Gaspare Pisciotta is buried only a few feet away from Giuliano and walk out, rereading the phrase over the entrance.

Joe Adonis, the vain Joseph Doto, died in 1972. After Lucky Luciano died, he realized that he'd lost his only mentor. According to some newspaper reports, he was seen in tears at the funeral mass for Luciano. He was living in exile in Milan, and had asked for special permission to attend the great boss's funeral. Not that he'd ever asked for special permission for his regular visits to Switzerland, where, on the advice of Sindona's studio in Milan, he kept the money he'd accumulated after years of Mafia activity. But his master was being buried, and he had to be officially present at the ceremony in Naples. He went to the church carrying a large wreath decorated with a ribbon carrying the words "So long, pal".

Frank Costello died on Long Island in 1973 at the age of eighty-two. He'd realized in time that godfathers of the type he had been no longer had a role to play. His widow arranged a modest, almost spartan funeral for him. She'd asked other Mafia bosses not to attend. A bare hearse was followed by a handful of his relatives; the coffin was lowered into the Costello Family tomb. An entirely ordinary ceremony, if it hadn't been for the FBI agents who were filming the entire event.

Carlo Gambino died of a heart attack at the age of seventy-four in 1976. The Family had organized a memorable funeral for him. From daybreak a crowd of friends of friends gathered at the door of Gambino's house, where they were held back by a threatening guard of *picciotti*. A long line of limousines passed by as all the bosses of the American underworld came to pay their last respects. Carrying Gambino's coffin was considered to be a great honour, fit only for Cosa Nostra's most important men, even if all of them knew an FBI camera from a hundred yards away was filming their faces and their every gesture, moment by moment. The *picciotti* escorting the coffin only moved into action when reporters tried to get too near – they were protecting their boss for the last time.

Stefano Bontate was killed in 1981. It was 23rd April, a rainy day, and he had just celebrated his forty-third birthday with a quiet drink in the company of a few friends. He felt safe, too much so, since he left the house and got into the driving seat of his silver-metallic Giulietta on his own. He'd forgotten how to act like a general in command of a war front. For a war was going on, only Bontate didn't realize it. He couldn't tell the difference any more between who was lying and who was telling him the truth. It was his birthday and he wanted to spend it in a villa he owned in Santa Maria di Gesù. He didn't know that his right-hand man, Pietro Lo Iacono, had passed over to the enemy, the Corleone gang. A burst of machine-gun fire, the convulsions of the nerves in his body for a few seconds, then he was slumped over the steering wheel.

Meyer Lansky died in New York in 1983. He was eighty-one, and succeeded in dying in bed. He felt himself getting old and wanted to retire to Israel. He decided to take some money with him just to help him settle down there; when the Israeli customs opened his bag, they found four hundred thousand dollars inside. In theory, as a Jew, he had the automatic right of entry. The Israeli Parliament had passed the "law of return", whereby any Jew, ascertained as such, from any country, had the right to become an Israeli citizen. The problem with Lansky was that he wasn't just "any Jew", but a Mafia mobster. He was sent back to the United States from Tel Aviv airport.

The Italian-Australian godfather Robert Trimboli died in 1991. His *picciotti* wanted to organize a funeral for him on the scale of Carlo Gambino's, but it turned out to be sadly lacking in Mafia style and tradition: once more the Australian underworld showed it couldn't really compete with the Americans. Everything appeared to have been well organized by the *cosca*, including the security guard made up of *picciotti*. At a certain point in the proceedings, as was inevitable, all the journalists and photographers and cameramen wanted to get closer, to get better pictures of the Family and the other bosses who were present. A scuffle broke out, with people hitting and kicking at each other, usually missing. It developed into an undignified punch-up in which some mafiosi ended up fighting on the ground or in the bushes with reporters, while the security guard, the *picciotti*, looking uncomfortable, like peasants dressed up in their Sunday best, started hitting out at whoever came within their range, oblivious to the fact that they were on camera. The Australian press had a field day, and the story ran for days.

Joe Bonanno wanted some tranquillity for what he thought were his final few years, and retired in voluntary exile to a country villa he owned in Tucson in Arizona. In 1968 he was sixty-three; he'd been the first to realize that the age of the great godfathers was over. Joe Bananas had prepared his departure with care. First he had managed to end the Mafia war which was tearing his Family apart. Then, in retirement, he settled down to write his memoirs, *A Man of Honor*. And then life went on, and on. At the beginning of the third millennium Joe Bonanno was left watching, from his wheelchair, how the world – the underworld and the normal world – turned. He died at the age of ninety-seven on Sunday 12th May 2002. The "Father" was no longer just old, he was one of the ancients. His funeral was shown live on the Internet. Four hundred people turned out to pay their last respects. There was a heart-shaped wreath and another one shaped like the island of Sicily, where he'd been born, in Castellammare del Golfo, in 1905. When the coffin had been placed in the crypt, his Family released forty white doves over the Holy Hope cemetery. Back in Sicily the celebrated godfather was still known as the "Dove".

John Gotti died from throat cancer on 10th June 2002, shortly after Bonanno's death. He was in the Springfield federal penitentiary, and was just sixty-one years old. No one ever dared to tell him he'd never been a real godfather. Even in death things didn't go well. His funeral was very much in the style of the man who'd been known as the Dapper Don. His son, John Junior – whom his father always openly referred to as the "Imbecile" – and his brothers, Peter and Gene, were not there to carry the huge gleaming bronze coffin. They were themselves in prison, and hadn't asked permission to go to their father's funeral because "the Gottis don't ask the State to do them favours". So the organization of the funeral was left to the two women in Gotti's Family; his wife and his daughter, both called Victoria. They wanted to have a funeral similar to Gambino's, but they don't seem to have kept a very precise recollection of it. They gave detailed instructions to the undertakers Papavero. The firm collected his body from the jail in Missouri and arranged for thirty-five limousines, draped with black, to escort the coffin to St John's Cemetery in Middle Village. The last boss of the Gambino Family was going to be buried in the same cemetery where the remains of Carlo Gambino, Lucky Luciano, Vito Genovese and several other godfathers had been laid to rest. When the funeral cortege made its way down 101st Avenue, some old women started to sing "We love you John, we do love you".

Without a blessing, the Family's foot soldiers placed the coffin in the neo-Gothic Gotti mausoleum. The Catholic Church in America had recently been rocked by accusations of paedophilia, and it had been careful to avoid any sign of sympathy for the Mafia, refusing to hold a religious ceremony for Gotti. But the two Victorias weren't downhearted. Given that they couldn't have a mass, in compensation they had huge floral wreaths made in the shape of poker cards with a running flush of hearts, a giant cigar, a glass of Martini with an olive inside and a race horse, all surrounded by a waving sea of Italian tricolour flags held by thousands of the Teflon Don's fans. They'd all been handed a sacred image with the words: "Do not weep for me at my grave, I am not there, I am not dead". The FBI agents photographed one by one the bosses who stepped out from their luxury cars and made their way, relieved and imperturbable, to pay their last respects. But at least in death Gotti made his mark in one way: there was an avalanche of articles in the American newspapers on his funeral and on the Mafia.

Then the women from the family took centre stage – Gotti's real family, obviously, since the part of his Mafia Family which had remained invisible had no intention of emerging from the shadows. In 2000, John Gotti Junior announced publicly that he had left Cosa Nostra, a declaration which would have horrified any genuine "man of honour", beginning with the members of Gotti's own Gambino clan itself. But, led by John Gotti Junior's mother Victoria, the family lined up to support him at his trial for kidnapping and extortion in early 2006: as well as his mother, there was his sister Victoria (Carmine Agnello's ex-wife), his niece, Victoria, and his younger sister Angela – all the women in the family, in fact, apart from his wife Kim, who had the reasonable excuse that she was pregnant with their sixth child. A courtroom was the perfect vehicle for the publishing and media ambitions of his sister Victoria, a blonde bombshell set on self-promotion. The extrovert daughter of the Dapper Don had a lot of business interests to pursue: she was a columnist for *The New York Post*, and had written various books about her father. But her main objective was to advance her television career after the success of the reality TV show *Growing up Gotti*, which had won an audience of three million viewers on the A&E cable network – about her day-to-day life bringing up three out-of-control teenage children, spiced with a hint of Cosa Nostra, even though the declared intent was to show the family had nothing to do with the American Mafia. With all the surrounding publicity, the trial also provided Gotti's niece Victoria, a law student, with an excellent opportunity to further her career ambitions to become a successful lawyer. Seen alongside these energetic women and the new business interests they were busy pursuing, the old Mafia culture and all its rules seemed to pale into insignificance. But the Gotti women did make one concession to the past, to great theatrical effect: on Ash Wednesday, like a group of young girls in rural Sicily – in a town like Corleone or Villabate – they got up early to go to church, where, in accordance with tradition, a cross was traced in ashes on their foreheads. The priests always used to warn the faithful not to touch the cross, as a sign of piety and penitence, but to let it fade out by itself. The three Victorias, together with Angela, went straight from church to the courtroom, where they sat as usual in the front row. The Catholic Church may have refused them permission to hold a requiem mass for Gotti, but they now scored a victory in compensation, since five out of the sixteen jury members also had a cross drawn on their foreheads. A large part of the American media would have liked to package all this as a new Mafia show, to replace the now declining fortunes of the long-running soap *The Sopranos*. But John Gotti Junior wasn't up to playing a godfather – however journalists might try to hype and spin it, no one could seriously compare him to the bosses of the past.

All of these godfathers, each in his own way, from Don Vito Cascio Ferro to John Gotti, had made the word "Mafia" one of the best-known words in the world. When journalists wrote about international organized crime they would talk about the Russian or the Colombian or the Chinese Mafia – and many others which were and are merely criminal organizations. They may be powerful, violent and secret, but they lack the ability to become, like the real Mafia, the old honoured organization in Sicily, or Cosa Nostra, a state within the State.

Nevertheless the real Mafia, at that delicate juncture in its history, as the last godfathers disappeared from the scene, needed to collaborate with those other organizations. As several arrests and many *pentiti* in their confessions had revealed, the Mafia had its men everywhere, from Latin America to Asia.[103] The strategists for the new phase which Cosa Nostra

---

103 "But what concerns us now is that they are very cunning, and they are recognizing that they are now able to conduct criminal operations all over the world, and that they are able to engage in partnerships with other organized-crime groups from Russia, Eastern Europe, Asia, Africa and South America. So the fact that organized crime is becoming more global is not just rhetoric from American or other law-enforcement agencies all over the world. We believe it is a very dangerous trend, because they are not fighting with each other. They are engaging in partnerships. We know that the only way we can address it is to have our own partnerships throughout the world. We want to carry on the legacy of Judge Falcone." Thomas V. Fuentes.

was entering immediately imposed a silence, under the cover of which they could broker deals all over the world on their business activities, both the familiar and the emerging ones – people-smuggling, drug-pushing, financial speculation and the rapid transfer of capital in the global round of the world's stock exchanges as each day they open and close. And yet, as the silence descended, the men investigating the Mafia in Italy, the United States and in other countries began to glimpse the possibility of winning their struggle against the organization. The distinguished historian of the Mafia, Francesco Renda, has written: "The Mafia is a historical phenomenon, and like all historical phenomena, it had a beginning and it will inevitably at some point come to an end." For the investigators it was as if the truth of Renda's dictum could finally be applied.

Giovanni Falcone took part in conferences and debates on the Mafia when he could, or followed them indirectly by reading the published proceedings when his job demanded that he didn't go about in public. He kept up with the historical research being done on the organization, using it to supplement his own investigations and his own ongoing work. He himself was at pains to reiterate Renda's idea by stressing that we should not resign ourselves to the Mafia, because it cannot exist for ever. It had a beginning and we can work to bring about its end.

In his book *Cose di Cosa Nostra*, Falcone reminded his readers of the story of Leonardo Vitale. He didn't write about it as a random case study or because Vitale was the first man to turn State's evidence against the Mafia in Italy. In his testimony Leonardo had described Cosa Nostra as a single entity; if the magistrates who listened to him had taken him seriously, ten years would have been gained in the struggle against the Mafia.[104] At the time even those who were inclined to believe him thought that he was really talking about a kind of subordinate level of criminality, prevalent in provincial towns and city

104 Rognoni-La Torre Law, art. 2: "Mafia-type criminal associations are defined as those associations whose members use the fact of belonging to intimidate and constrain others to obedience and silence in order to carry out crimes, to gain direct or indirect control over economic activities, franchises, permissions, private and public contracts, or to acquire, unjustly, profits or other benefits for themselves and others".

suburbs. Instead he had revealed for the first time the way the Mafia Families divided up the territory, confirmed that high-level meetings between the bosses took place to coordinate their strategy against the Italian State, and even predicted the dominant role and power Totò Riina and the Corleonesi would come to have in the organization as a whole.

When Falcone wrote about the Vitale case in his book, the story had sunk to the bottom of a mountain of facts about the Mafia. No one gave "crazy" Leonardo Vitale so much as a thought.

A Single Entity

After spending five years in various criminal asylums – the last in Bologna – Leonardo Vitale returned to Palermo in 1984. His mother and his sister – the only members of his family left – were waiting for him. They were glad to have a man about the house again, the last remaining man in their family, in a pitiful condition from the psychiatric treatments he'd had to undergo, and now also deeply devout. The religious crisis which had affected him ten years earlier had not been a ruse to deceive the authorities, not just a short-lived episode. He had changed his life. He spent his time praying and going to the local church run by the Capuchins; apart from the church, he almost never went out, staying at home in silence, lost in his own thoughts. He didn't seem to have any amusements, unless watching the television counts as an amusement. "I'm as mad as any normal person," he'd told the judges at his appeal trial. In the Court of First Instance he'd been sentenced to twenty-five years in prison. They'd also condemned his uncle Titto, Giovanbattista Vitale, the godfather of Leonardo's Mafia Family, and other men of honour, all of whom his testimony had helped to frame.

His trial had also caused big problems for many other Mafia Families. This "dishonourable" deserved to die. The Mafia could easily have killed him in prison. But what would be the point in that? That wouldn't have been a satisfactory way of settling accounts. Instead they'd tortured him, made his life impossible day in day out, forced him to eat excrement. His sexuality became deeply disturbed as a result. The violent religious crisis which had overwhelmed him also played into the hands of his torturers. The rumour started to circulate that Leonardo was a coprophage. The court decided that he was "suffering from schizophrenia and incapable of understanding or intending" – a madman, in other words. The appeal court sentenced him to five years in a criminal asylum.

The other men of honour who'd been brought before the court because of his testimony were acquitted, thanks to their clever lawyers and their ability to fix the results of trials. Only uncle Titta had had his sentence of twenty-one years' imprisonment upheld. But he never had to serve them, since the Mafia's own court had already passed sentence.

Giovanbattista Vitale, the godfather of the Altarello Family, and as such responsible for the chaos caused by his turncoat nephew, was judged guilty of having brought up a traitor – and a traitor twice over at that, because he'd betrayed both his Mafia Family and his own. The so-called *"lupara bianca"* or "white shotgun" method was used, where the victim simply "disappears" and leaves no trace. Leonardo never heard of his uncle again. His body was never found.

Staying at home, going to church, watching the television: Leonardo had plenty of time to reflect that 1984 was a very strange year. The Mafia was talked about all the time, and not only in Sicily. School children organized protest meetings and street demonstrations, politicians made statements, articles and manifestos appeared in print – all against the Mafia. But the *picciotti* weren't just looking on: they'd shot a journalist in Catania, Giuseppe Fava, precisely because he'd spoken out against the Mafia.

But in all this discussion no one bothered to connect facts about the Mafia together. Intelligent and sophisticated people spent their time debating the whys and wherefores of certain events, and never realized that these events formed part of a single context, an entire world, which was as extensive and ramified as the normal world in which these intelligent people lived. Leonardo didn't know Lorenzo B., whose arrest in Favara near Agrigento was reported as a curious incident, but he wouldn't have had any problem in identifying who he really was – this unemployed layabout who'd never filled in a tax declaration in his life, yet had millions stashed away in cash, owned various plots of land, two eight-storey apartment blocks and numerous cars including an Alfa Romeo 2000, a 162 and a powerful BMW.

Or the pensioner from Marsala who was found dead with his hands in his overcoat pockets? He was certainly a pensioner, probably in receipt of a pension from some institution or other. He didn't have a criminal record – some offences linked to gambling naturally didn't count. He'd been shot three times in the head at close range. His body had fallen to the ground where it was found, with his hands in his overcoat pockets, as if he were looking for something.

In Messina – where the Mafia supposedly didn't operate – tax officials had sequestered some clandestine stockpiles of liquid propane gas. Gas cylinders which hadn't been inspected – in effect potential bombs which could go off in people's homes – had been found in garages and cellars in the city centre, ready to be sold among the population.

All of this was just business as usual. As was the case in Canicattì, where the local beauty had been blown to bits when she opened the door of her Fiat 127 – it was stuffed with dynamite. Her name was Alfonsa B. The forensic experts managed to gather together pieces of her body, which had been scattered over a hundred-metre radius. On the third-floor balconies of a nearby apartment block, metal fragments from the chassis of her car were found. If she'd opened the door of her car at the time of day when the children were leaving school, there would have been a massacre. The first man the police took in on suspicion of the murder was a teacher who, rumour had it, was having a stormy affair with the woman. It took a whole day for the unfortunate man to explain to the *carabinieri* that they'd got the wrong end of the stick. It was true the woman was in love with him, although he didn't return her feelings. She was one of the wealthiest landowners in the area, a successful producer of a kind of grapes which were sold all over the country. Only four months before, Gina S., another producer of the same kind of grapes in the Canicattì region, had been murdered: she'd been shot three times in the head at close distance.

The beautiful businesswoman, the unemployed layabout, the pensioner. Another anti-Mafia student demonstration marching to Ciaculli. Leonardo switched the TV off and went to say his prayers, as he did every evening before going to bed. The following day, the same stuff, all over again. And the day after that, and on every subsequent day. Everyone was talking about the Mafia, but no one could really see it. It might be difficult to pick out the secret threads which lay beneath ordinary society, beyond the high walls of the villas where someone was ready to collect the dismantled rifles thrown over in a bag after a shooting. It might be difficult to trace the links between accountants' offices, hospital wards and courtrooms. But – Leonardo asked himself – the obvious and violent events which occurred every day, surely people could see the pattern behind these?

A baker was driving a delivery van full of freshly baked bread and biscuits to local customers. He was shot in the face from two feet away. His two brothers had been killed a few months before in the same way. The life of the Associate Director of the Palermo branch of the Banco di Sicilia had been spared, but his legs had been shot away by an unmasked gunman with a fully loaded 6.35 calibre pistol. Luigi C. was an unknown carpenter who made coffins in the village of San Cataldo. He'd been shot in the face three times. One of his cousins had been shot in the same way three years before while he'd been having a drink at the local working men's club. He too had made coffins for a living. The two had got some things wrong in the undertaking racket (there are kickbacks to be paid even in this line of work).

The result of an investigation came and went, hardly noticed in the news: in the space of a few years six thousand shops had changed ownership and ended up in the hands of the Mafia. Their owners thought that if they paid the protection money they'd be left alone to get on with running their business; they hadn't understood that the Mafia wanted the entire shop.

The union for construction-industry workers – bricklayers and unskilled labourers – was up in arms. They held a big meeting in the Isola delle Femmine cement works to protest, because for over a year no new construction work had been started in the capital Palermo. Leonardo realized immediately that the sack of the city was now over. His uncle Titta had been involved in all the property speculation, and Leonardo had helped to smooth his way whenever he needed it. Now that business too was finished – too many investigators buzzing around, too much attention. Not to mention the unfortunates who'd shelled out all their savings when they signed pre-contracts on apartments they were purchasing. Perhaps they didn't know the builder was a mafioso, or perhaps they did and thought it didn't matter – houses are built of bricks whoever builds them. When the builder was arrested and his assets seized, they lost their deposits, the houses they thought they were buying, as well as any chance of being in the position to buy another one soon. This was what had happened in the case of the Mafia boss D.F. and the eight construction firms which he owned.

It was clear that the focus of the Mafia's business interests was shifting. No more apartment blocks. Criminal proceeds were better hidden with the help of a combination of computer technology and high finance.

Leonardo asked a Capuchin monk about the six children in Yugoslavia who kept having visions of the Madonna. He was genuinely interested, and if it had been possible, he would have gone and joined the crowds of the faithful at Medjugorje. The Capuchin monk winced with irritation, and told Leonardo that he'd do better to occupy his thoughts with more serious matters, such as educating his soul and his mind, for example. At his age he had still not been confirmed. Confirmation classes were shortly due to begin; the monk told Leonardo to go to the parish office and enrol for them.

Leonardo could hardly believe what he'd heard. He got them to explain to him what preparing for confirmation meant and then told his mother and sister about his decision. They'd been unhappy with his obsessive interest in reports of killings, and thought that preparing for confirmation might take his mind off them. Leonardo had survived torture in prison and then years of detention in criminal asylums; from now on he would devote himself to his new spiritual life. But one thought kept haunting him, even when he was praying. He'd spoken out for nothing, absolutely nothing. He'd come out into the open and risked his life – for nothing. In the world outside, around him, a terrible Mafia war was being fought, but the magistrates who'd said he was a madman saw only isolated incidents. A killer had shot Rosario B., a butcher who belonged to the Mafia in San Giuseppe Jato. The customary pistol shots fired at close range to the head. Now it was the turn of Rosario B.'s relatives in America to be worried, starting with their son Francesco, who also worked as a butcher in New York, as well as his brother Giuseppe and two sisters, Rosa and Antonina, who all three owned pizzerias in the city. Their business must have clashed with that of an enemy Family – it didn't take much to understand what was going on, Leonardo thought. But the day Rosario B. was shot – 11th March – everyone's attention was distracted by another event – a new TV series, *La piovra* ("The Octopus" – "the murderer with tentacles dripping with blood") was about to be shown, with Florinda Bolkan and Michele Placido in the starring roles. He played Corrado Cattani, a detective who'd been transferred from Milan to Palermo. She was a businesswoman who was recycling money. Then the actress Barbara De Rossi appeared in the story as a young aristocratic drug addict, and Cattani is smitten by her beauty.

It was a strange year, 1984. While the episodes of *La piovra* were being broadcast, the extraordinary gathering of policemen and *carabinieri* for a top-secret meeting in the city's most luxurious hotel didn't escape Leonardo's attention. At the Villa Igea the Home Office minister Scalfaro held a meeting with forty magistrates from all over the country to discuss ways of protecting the *pentiti*. The minister and the magistates had been protected by an escort of more than a hundred men, whereas Leonardo Vitale, a genuine *pentito* – if he wanted to go to the Capuchins, his sister had to take him in her Fiat 500.

A detective in Palermo – a real one – had made a big mistake. His name was Cassarà. Leonardo knew who he was, and was familiar with his office in police headquarters. He also knew the Salvo cousins, whom Cassarà had just openly accused of Mafia activity. Not mincing his words, the detective had declared that the judge Rocco Chinnici, shortly before he'd been murdered, had been about to issue an arrest warrant for the Salvo cousins, the leading and very powerful Mafia "tax collectors" on the island. Cassarà had said that the Salvo Family had first been allied with the Bontate clan, but had later switched over to the Greco's. At last an investigator who was beginning to understand... Cassarà's statements had caused an uproar. Two judges immediately denied that Chinnici was intending to arrest the Salvos – it simply wasn't true, they said – but then, a little later, a captain in the *carabinieri*, Angiolo Pellegrini, swore on oath that what Cassarà had said was entirely accurate. Chinnici had told him – Pellegrini – that he was indeed intending to arrest the Salvo cousins.

Meanwhile the other detective – the one in *La piovra* – was forging ahead, week after week. Leonardo didn't care for the programme, but his mother and sister refused to miss a single episode. To Leonardo, as that strange year wore on, it seemed as if he was experiencing time like children do – the long days, the sunlit endless afternoons. The only difference was that there was the television. Everyone watched television. The Italian government, far away in Rome, headed by Bettino Craxi, had wrangled for months over how to divide up the directorships of the three State television channels. Then there was all the fuss about the phone-in chat-show hostess Raffaella Carrà, who'd signed a contract worth millions – no one would say exactly how much. "But after all she's Raffaella," Leonardo's mother and sister told him; like the studio audience, they would almost cry with emotion when Carrà got a good phone call. A parliamentary commission had set up an inquiry into the salaries paid to TV presenters, and the Prime Minister had demanded an explanation from the President of Italian State television. He'd been summoned to Craxi's office no less. Then once all the fuss about Carrà had died down, the spotlights turned on a young Sicilian from Sciacca, called Giuseppe Melluso, who lived in Milan and had joined – who'd introduced him isn't known – the Turatello gang. He had accused the celebrated TV presenter Enzo Tortora of drug-pushing. Drugs, television and Mafia. 1984 was certainly a very strange year.

While Tortora remained caught in Melluso's trap, with his health beginning to fail, over in the United States a certain Salvatore Farina had been arrested. He was a young Italian-American who'd just been on a flying visit to Italy. His father, Ambrogio Farina, had emigrated to America many years earlier from Castellammare del Golfo. He'd been caught carrying heroin worth millions of dollars, and was now in a New Jersey prison. But despite this, he'd still managed to do a favour for Cosa Nostra in Sicily. He got his son to go out to Sicily to kill the magistrate Ciaccio Montalto. In other words, his son was a "zip". He carried out his mission, although not as smoothly as he might have. The FBI agents arrested him while he was talking to his lawyer in his offices in New York.

Meanwhile in the fashionable circles of Palermo, people discussed *La piovra*, on which the general verdict seemed to be that it was sentimental and evasive. In April in Madrid they arrested someone who really counted for something in the Mafia: Gaetano Badalamenti. As the Interpol agents burst into his apartment armed with guns, Don Tano, now really transformed into Sitting Bully, merely said: "Careful with those guns. It's me. Don't you realize who I am?"

Watching the news bulletin on television one evening, Leonardo saw that the magistrate Falcone had had Giuseppe Provenzano arrested. Provenzano taught banking and finance at Palermo university, and was charged with recycling money for the Corleone gang. It was 26th April. The days seemed to pass by so slowly. Leonardo didn't bother to repeat to his mother how in Cosa Nostra you could find university professors, lawyers, doctors, engineers. She didn't like him talking about the Mafia.

In September, Michele Sindona was extradited from the United States and brought back to Italy in handcuffs. It made quite an impression on Leonardo to see him behind bars.

Then the 721 densely typed pages of Tommaso Buscetta's epic testimony burst onto the scene. Hundreds of arrests were made. Yes, that's what Leonardo had meant: that was the Mafia. Now it was his mother and sister who took to getting down on their knees to pray. And now someone recalled Leonardo Vitale, the Joe Valachi of the Palermo suburbs, as the newspapers had dubbed him. Buscetta's confession was compared to Leonardo's. Of course the comparison needed to be kept in proportion: Buscetta was known as the Boss of Two Worlds, the old and the new, while Vitale was only a *picciotto*, a local thug. But he too had described the Mafia as a single entity, a secret organization, centralized but ramified across the country, extending underneath and within civil society.

Every day the men who'd been denounced by Buscetta were led away in handcuffs. Leonardo began his confirmation classes. He had to learn certain prayers, and also train his mind and cultivate good thoughts. He thought it was the will of God that he should begin his new spiritual life in such an extraordinary year.

Even the Pope had gone to Calabria in October and had urged young people "never to give in to the temptation to become mafiosi". The Capuchins told Leonardo that these words had needed much prayer. It was the first time a Pope had spoken about the Mafia. He should pray too that the Pope would come to Sicily. Leonardo thought that if even the Pope condemned the Mafia, then perhaps a turning point had been reached. This seemed to him a good thought, which he should cultivate. He realized in the following days that the monks were right: prayer was needed, a lot of prayer.

A television journalist, Giuseppe Marrazzo, had done a documentary on the Mafia. It was scheduled for broadcast in the series Tg2 Dossier, but the transmission had been blocked. Yet another uproar broke out. The series editor said he wasn't to blame. The director who'd given the go-ahead to Marrazzo's project resigned in protest. The President of Italian State broadcasting, Zavoli, declared that State television was not trying to hide anything. The parliamentary commission of inquiry into the Mafia met to discuss the issue, while the parliamentary watchdog committee announced that it would take action. When, eventually, the programme was broadcast, one of the Salvo cousins accused Marrazzo of defamation and slander.

Leonardo's mother and sister seemed to be fascinated by everything they saw on and off screen about it. He only appeared to be interested in the daily news programmes – and often the news was shocking.

On 18th October in Palermo, a massacre took place beside which the St Valentine's Day murders in Chicago paled into insignificance. Eight men from the Quattrocchi Family were shot in a stable in open daylight. They no longer wanted to buy horses from a go-between who came from Catania (where the Mafia is supposed not to exist); someone had asked the town's main boss, Nitto Santapaola, to sort the matter out.

Tommaso Buscetta continued to talk, although many of his relatives had now been murdered – as usual, with three shots to the head. It was still all-out war.

On 25th October, a new *pentito* appeared: the boss Contorno. After his revelations, a leading orthopaedic consultant, Professor Andrea Vassallo, and a gynaecologist, Francesco Greco, the brother of a prominent boss, together with a series of other important men, were arrested. The most illustrious figure among the accused managed to make his getaway before the police arrived to arrest him: Prince Alessandro Vanni Calvello Mantegna of San Vincenzo, the descendant of an ancient family of Aragonese nobility. At some point in the family's history, they'd acquired the privilege of keeping their heads covered even in the presence of royalty, but the prince had had the good manners to have been bareheaded when he bowed and kissed the hand of Elizabeth II, who had been his unwitting guest only four years before.

And then another momentous event. A group of magistrates, working as a kind of team, moved into action. After long interrogation sessions, both the Salvo cousins were formally arrested on 12th November 1984. The warrant for their arrest had been signed by Caponnetto, Falcone and the Assistant Public Prosecutors Di Lello and Guarnotta.

Leonardo was absorbed in studying the catechism and in the spiritual exercises which the Capuchin friars had recommended to him. He began to lose interest in the television news and in all the incredible events of that interminable year. Now his thoughts were turned to Christmas; he wanted to prepare for the events in the liturgical calendar in a spirit of peace.

He wouldn't have watched the television any more, had it not been for the suicide on 18th November of Rosario Nicoletti, who threw himself out of a window on the eighth floor of an apartment block. Nicoletti had been the regional secretary of the Christian Democrats, and could no longer bear the atmosphere of suspicion and insinuation which surrounded him. The party in Sicily had been taken under the direct control of the party headquarters in Rome: the man responsible for it, Sergio Mattarella, had demanded that all current memberships should be cancelled and a clean start be made. How distant the days seemed when a Christian Democrat MP like Francesco Barbaccia could write to Palermo's police chief Jacovacci: "I should be grateful if you could arrange for the renewal of the passport held by Signor Tommaso Buscetta, a person whose interests are of close concern to me." The request was immediately granted: the Buscetta who got his passport renewed in this way was then still the dangerous Boss of Two Worlds. The idea of collaborating with the authorities against the Mafia hadn't even entered his head.

On 2nd December, Leonardo got ready to go out early. He had his confirmation class and, besides, he liked spending time with the Capuchins. When he was chatting to them, the days didn't seem so long, and he felt at peace. His mother and sister decided to accompany him in their Fiat 500. When the class and the prayers and the talking was over, they headed back home without rushing. Leonardo made his mother sit in front, while he curled up in the back seat of the small car. Cars didn't matter to him now; gone were the days when he liked to drive gleaming new models fast through the traffic lights of Palermo. When they arrived home, in via Siccherio, his sister got out to open the main gate to their house. It was an old plain low building – quite how it had remained standing with all the other big blocks which had sprung up around it was hard to understand. While his sister was walking back to the car, another 500 drew up alongside, almost touching theirs. As they looked, time suddenly froze.

The two women had the impression that something had exploded inside the car. They saw they were wounded and covered in blood, while Leonardo was slumped in the back seat.

Screams, sirens, police, ambulances. He was already in a coma when they rushed him to hospital.

He died on 7th December of that extraordinary year. The cause of death was given in the autopsy: the brain had been deeply traumatized with three large-calibre bullets aimed at the head, and fired at close range.

Interviews and Documents

Roberto Olla interviews Rudolph Giuliani, former Mayor of New York

RO: How did you hear about the Commission?

RG: I first learnt of the existence of the Commission as most Americans probably did back in the early 1960s, when Joe Valachi testified. I remember the testimony – I was a college student and a law student at the time. Then I read Peter Maas's book *The Valachi Papers*, which describes it. Long before I was a United States Attorney, I was an assistant to the United States Attorney, so I was involved in law enforcement for quite some time. So I always knew about the existence of the Commission from the time it was first revealed in the early 1960s. Of course as the United States Attorney I learnt a lot more about it in order to investigate and prosecute it.

RO: How would you describe the Commission? How did it work?

RG: The Commission really started in the 1930s. The idea was to have a governing body for the first of the five Families of New York, and then ultimately all of the Families all over the country. So with regard to New York, the heads of the five Families would meet on a regular basis and they would discuss their interrelationships, from things like who needed to be killed because they might be an informant, to how they were going to divide up territories for private carding, gambling, drug distribution – many different areas of criminal activity. Sometimes it would be more about legal activities, like dividing up the businesses they owned. The idea was to try to keep the peace, so that instead of resorting immediately to violence, they might be able to work out some of their disputes. Joe Bonanno described it in his book – and described it to me when I interviewed him and questioned him – as being like the United Nations, which is a rather exalted way to describe it. But he thought of it as the heads of State coming together and trying to create a peaceful environment in which they could make the maximum money.

RO: Where did they meet?

RG: They'd meet in different places: in back of restaurants, in social clubs, in homes. They would never meet in any one place, because they didn't want to be detected. Then occasionally there would be national meetings involving the Families from all over the country, and that's what was interrupted and discovered in Apalachin, NY in the late 1950s. They were having a national meeting of all the Families. That was rare. Those kinds of meetings took place infrequently, because they were too dangerous.

RO: Do you think there are bosses whom we know nothing about who are currently operating undercover?

RG: There always have been. Until Apalachin, which was in the 1950s, I think 1957 if I recall correctly – don't hold me to it exactly, but around that time – until then, many of them were largely unknown. Joe Bonanno, for example, operated in relative obscurity, until first the Keyfound hearings in the early 1950s, and then Apalachin in the later 1950s. And then even after that, a lot of them operated in obscurity. Many of them prefer not to be known as organized-crime figures, so they'll take on a legitimate business. With all of the FBI investigations and NYPD investigations and police work all over the country, most of them have now been revealed. But there probably are still some that operate below the surface.

RO: Mafioso bosses are also called "godfathers" because of several characteristics: their ability to build Families and to take control of the social life of the businesses in their environment. How would you define a *padrino*, a "godfather"?

RG: A boss, a person in charge of the organization. They call it a "Family", probably to soften it. It's not a Family, it's an illegal business organization in which a group of men pledge loyalty to each other, divide up different areas of business and divide up the profits they're making, with a large percentage going to the boss at the top. They all aid and assist each other's mostly illegal and sometimes legal enterprises: they'll own restaurants, garment businesses, whatever. It's like a cartel, except that the vast majority of what they're doing is illegal business. And that's why the racketeering statute, the Rico statute, was developed: to focus on exactly how they perpetuate and expand their criminality, so that it would be possible to prosecute it and do away with it.

RO: With the interviews you've had with many of the bosses, do you think that the descriptions of them in books and movies are very close to how they actually are?

RG: The descriptions in books and movies vary from very accurate to very inaccurate, but the reality is organized-crime figures are all different. They're human beings, and human beings have endless varieties of the way in which they act, and complexity. Some of the organized-crime figures are among the most vicious, horrible, awful human beings you'd ever meet – they have an almost animalistic quality to them. And some of them, except for the criminal part of their life, can be very nice people. They can be good friends, good fathers, good and loyal in other areas of business, and then they also have this other side of them in which they sell drugs, or kill, or whatever. So there's no one description of an organized-crime figure. The rest of their personality is not unlike society at large, which is very strange.

RO: Just for reference, could you describe Joe Bonanno?

RG: Joe Bonanno had pretensions of grandeur. He was obviously a very important boss, helped to develop his own Family, and at one time he exercised a great deal of control over all of the New York Families and the whole country. He was and is a man of substantial intellect. He's one of those people about whom you would say, "if he had gone in another direction, he could have been very successful". Unfortunately he sought the direction of crime. But then he tried to insulate himself from facing what it was all about with pretensions of "this is like a government", "I'm like a head of State" and "I'm a deposed head of State" when he retired. But that also describes some of the Mafia. There were pretensions of grandeur in the Mafia, they thought of themselves as recreating the Roman legions. Maybe that insulated them from the reality of the fact that they were pretty vicious criminals.

RO: Could you describe Joe Bonanno personally?

RG: I met him when he was an older man in his seventies, when he was held in contempt because he refused ultimately to back up his grand-jury testimony in court. He had testified in a deposition and then we were trying to get his testimony in court and he wouldn't do it. So we held a trial, or a hearing, and he was held in contempt and put in jail. Much of the time I dealt with him he was trying to pretend to be very sick. He would make himself appear like a very frail man. The interesting thing about that is he and some of his doctors were contending that if he testified he would die from the pressure of the testimony, and this was largely why they were trying to avoid the testimony. The judge didn't buy that, and put him in jail. Just think about it: that was back in 1985, and fifteen to sixteen years later he's still alive! He was getting out of jail claiming he was fatally ill even twenty-five to thirty years ago! He was getting doctors to put in affidavits saying that if he remained in jail he would die, and he has lived for twenty-five to thirty years after that. So you get a sense of the kind of games that they play.

RO: Could you describe how you were personally involved in the case of Joe Bonanno?

RG: I was personally involved because I investigated, and then ultimately was the United States Attorney that brought the indictment against the Commission of the Mafia, and I envisioned the case. I decided back in 1983 that we could put such a case together against the heads of the Five Families. I then worked with the FBI and my assistants in the United States Attorney's office and the Justice Department and the Police Department to build that case. Ultimately we convicted them all and sent them to jail for 100 years. That was one of the things, along with the Pizza Connection case and the large maxi-trial in Italy, that revealed so much about what the Mafia was, when so much was hidden before. Maybe people were going around claiming there was no Mafia, but the Commission trial established beyond any doubt that there was a Mafia, and put many of the heads in jail for 100 years.

Roberto Olla interviews Mario Cuomo, former Governor of the State of New York

RO: Your mother immigrated from Italy in the big wave of Italian immigration and arrived on Ellis Island. Have you ever asked her about the journey and arrival?

MC: The subject of my mother's immigrant status coming to the US and Ellis Island is a subject that I have dealt with all of my public career, because I wanted people to know. I wanted them to know that she was Italian, where she came from, that it was a legacy that I very much cherished and admired. So it's a popular discussion piece where I'm involved.

RO: Is there any episode that she told you about her arrival?

MC: There are two things about my mother's experience on Ellis Island specifically that are memorable to me. One of them is the following: unlike the common portrayal of Ellis Island as a glorious moment in the life of the immigrant, my mother despised the memories of Ellis Island, because it was such a harsh place to her. The way they were examined, the way people were sent back for the slightest defect. She wasn't happy about it. She was happy about making it to the United States, where my father had come before her, but she wasn't happy about the Ellis Island experience itself. The second thing about Ellis Island is the improbability. As a woman from Salerno – from Tramonti – if she had been interviewed by someone from RAI or someone from American television, the interview would have gone like this: "What do you want, what are you doing, Immacolata Giordano Cuomo?" She would have said: "Well, I'm going to meet my husband." "Do you have a baby?" "Yes, I do." "Did you bring anything else with you, any wealth?" "No, we have no money." "Do you have skills, are you a seamstress?" "No." "Did you go to school?" "No, I never went to school." "Did your husband go to school?" "No, we didn't have a school where we come from." "Do you have relatives?" "No, we have some remote *cugini*." "You know, times are hard in the United States [this was just before the Depression], so what do you expect from the United States?" "Oh, not much, a little job, my husband, we'll both work if we have to, a chance for my children to go to school, to be educated the way we weren't, the chance for them to work and have a family here, that's all. Oh, and one other thing, we would like one of our sons to be Governor of the State of New York three times." The very improbability of all of that is a part of the whole Ellis Island experience that is most significant to us.

RO: Do you think that is how it was for most groups, the improbability of the experience?

MC: I think that most Italian-Americans will tell you a story like the one I told. It might not be a political career, but there's Lee Iacocca, the captains of industry, the great actors and performers and entertainers, and professionals of all kinds. They were all a tremendous success. And they owe it to two things: to this marvellous engine of opportunity called the United States of America, and they owe it to their legacy, as Italians. There's something about the culture, about the values that these immigrants brought with them: their commitment to hard work, their commitment to family, their commitment to their own crude, simple religion, but a beautiful commitment. All those things helped them, and the success has been immense. You can't tell that from the way we've portrayed them on television – you'd think that the most successful Italians were the ones who got to be *capo di tutti i capi*, but that's not true. It was improbable, because one or two generations ago, the people who came here were very humble and modest of means.

RO: With regard to stereotypes, was there a strong racist feeling against Italian immigration into the US?

MC: When the Italians arrived and tried to work their way into the society, they were met by great hostility. They were called "guinea", "greaseball", "day-go", "wop". The best that they got was a kind of condescension, they were looked down upon. If it were the only immigrant group ever treated like that, you'd have to wonder about the US. You have to wonder even more, however, because every immigrant group has been treated that way. When the Irish came – even though they spoke the language, which we didn't – people put up signs saying "No Mick need apply for work" (since McDonald was such a common name). The Jews were harrassed here and oppressed the way they have been all over the world. Each wave of immigrants to the United States seems to settle in, achieve success, win the battle of survival, and then turn and say, "take up the gangplank, we don't need it any more." Each wave seems to resist the next wave that comes after it. That is selfish, egocentric, but it is a reality. So yes, Italians were treated roughly, but so was every other immigrant wave.

RO: So it wasn't specific?

MC: No.

RO: It has been said that in Little Italy there were only two choices: one was the Mafia and one was the Church. Would you agree?

MC: I wouldn't agree that the Church was much of an option! Obviously there were Italian-Americans who became priests, nuns etc... Mother Cabrini is an institution. But that's an exaggeration. The Mafia syndrome is tremendously exaggerated in the United States, because the US is particularly addicted to anything that is spectacular. Adolf Hitler is the most popular subject on the History Channel in the US – I think you can verify that. What is it about Adolf Hitler, other than the spectacular quality of his ugliness and his evil? So the Mafia is spectacular. It's extreme, colourful, romantic, in a negative way. That has occupied too much of the attention of the American people. It's disproportionate in its influence. So people will say, "On the lower East Side, where there were so many Italians, your only choice was to go into the Mafia." Incidentally, the program *The Sopranos*, which is so popular, said exactly that. In one scene that was of great interest to me personally, Gandolfini, who was Papa Soprano (I didn't see this, but it was reported to me), supposedly argues with his daughter and says, "we had to do it because they shunned us, they called us names, so we had to go into the Mafia." And his daughter says, "Really? What about Mario Cuomo?" There are five million, ten million Mario Cuomos who didn't go into the Mafia and still were able to make a living.

RO: So, what were the alternatives available to people in Little Italy and the lower East Side?

MC: The alternative that occurs to me immediately, beyond the obvious one of going to school, getting educated and doing all the things that educated people can do: being great captains of industry, doctors, lawyers, politicians – they've done all of that. If you look at the ranks of Italian-Americans in every field, we have a great deal of excellence coming out of the immigrant tradition. One thing that a lot of them tried, like my mother and father, who weren't able to get educated in this country, was small business. Entrepreneurial activities, opening up small shops, like the Koreans are now doing. This is very common to immigrant groups who don't have establishment help, who don't have a great deal of education, and therefore cannot get hired for a lot of work other than simple labour. So they open up their own business. That was very big on the lower East Side, in Jamaica, Queens, where I was born. My mother and father were taught how to run a grocery store by a Jewish couple, the Kesslers, who brought them in to Queens from Jersey City, where my father was just a labourer, and put them in a back room behind the grocery store. Mr Kessler had had a heart attack, so he couldn't do the physical work. My mother and father did the physical work for him, and gradually learnt the language, learnt the business. Seven years later, they owned their own grocery store without ever having been to school. You could tell that story over and over again about millions of immigrants, many of whom were Italians.

RO: Joe Petrosino, who fought the Mano Nera and the Mafia, was killed in Italy. Would you share a memory of Joe Petrosino? And what do you think is the memory of Joe Petrosino in the American mind?

MC: If you were to take a survey in the US right now, and I suspect somebody has done this, with the question, "What occurred more in our American experience: that most Italian-Americans became mafiosi, or that Italian-Americans became like Joe Petrosino and fought the Mafia?" they would laugh at that question. Eighty-nine to ninety per cent of Americans would say that they became mafiosi. They don't know Joe Petrosino. Most Italians wouldn't know his name. How many people know Di Pietro in Italy now? The sensational was not

Joe the policeman who did the right thing, and it wasn't even Serpico, who did it later for police corruption. Louis Freeh is Italian, he's head of the FBI. How many people know that in America? Great judge, great lawyer, he got into trouble politically, but everybody does in the United States, not because he did something wrong, but because he was trying to do something right. That part of story is not well told. When you write this book, people will read it, not because you are going to have Italian-Americans who raised a family and lived a decent life, but because you have the spectacular: the killers, the mob, the Mafia.

RO: What would you like to contribute to the memory of Joe Petrosino?

MC: The important thing about Petrosino is that he was quintessentially anti-mafia. If you did an analysis of the Italian-American experience, the children of those giants, the immigrants, the numbers would show that there is a great disproportion: there are many more Joe Petrosino types – not as policemen, but as legitimate, honest Italian-Americans – than there are Mafia types. It is just the opposite of the popular impression. If you keep watching television, most of the images of Italian-Americans depict Mafia figures or fools, big mouths, clumsy oaf types. Every once in a while there will be a benign figure, or even a respected figure.

RO: Who do you think is the heir of Joe Petrosino, of his legacy?

MC: No one. Serpico, Mafia-busting Attorney Generals... Benjamin Civiletti: if you ask people, they won't remember his name. I remember him. He was a great Attorney General of the United States. One of the judges in Watergate, Peter Rodino, the congressman. All those people were Italians. They were leaders in the move to clean up Watergate. So there have been plenty of Italian-American heroes in law enforcement. But they were not well known. They were not the subjects of series, of one blockbuster movie after another, they were not four-hour spectaculars, they were not series like *The Sopranos*. What works in this country is blood dripping from a stiletto, rape, crushing a man's head with a golf club because your boss ordered you to do it, Italian-American thugs. Even the Italians watch it. Why? I don't know – ask them, because I don't go.

RO: To what extent does the criminal activity of the Mafia influence the image of Italians?

MC: It is a tremendous burden on the Italian-American community. Many people are stereotyped in the US – it's a fun thing to do if you're an American, to make fun of particular ethnic groups, and much of it is pure entertainment and doesn't do any damage. But the disproportion in the way Italians are shown is so heavily negative because of the spectacular entertainment value of organized crime that it does psychological damage. If you are a child who grows up watching television, the reality is that five times out of ten an Italian will be portrayed as an organized-crime figure – it's bound to have an impression on you. Even if you seek to deny it, it's there in your brain.

RO: When you were a child, do you remember that feeling?

MC: God was very good to me. First of all, for giving me Immacolata Giordano and Andrea Cuomo. But then he allowed me to be born before television – which, you'll pardon me, was a great blessing. The images that were most vivid to me were Andrea and Immacolata in the back of the grocery store, not the television screen, not the movie screen, which we couldn't afford. So unless I went to the Queens Borough Library to ferret out books which were also disproportionately about ugly organized criminals, I could escape it. And I did. I didn't have the problem of the negative image of the Italians. Well, you did in the streets. But everybody in my neighbourhood did – the Blacks, the Portuguese – everybody was called something: "nigger", "day-go", "mick". And you got the general impression that we were all different, we had our disagreements. But I didn't understand what the Mafia meant until I was an adult.

RO: I think a lot of people may view it like you.

MC: Well, there aren't a whole lot of us left who escaped the television age growing up. Everybody who was born in the television age has been influenced by the Mafia. Some people are more intelligent than others. Some people will watch the Hitler films on the History Channel over and over again and be intelligent enough to say, "That wasn't all the German people – it might have been too many of them, but that wasn't all the German people." And some people are intelligent enough to watch shows on the Mafia and say, "That's not all the Italians, not even most of them, from my experience." There are some intelligent people who will discriminate, but there are a lot of other people who don't work hard at making the analysis, and they just allow the impressions to sink in. And the impressions are bad. And the impressions on the young are worse, because first impressions – as we all know – the earliest images are the most enduring and are the most effective, for good or for bad.

RO: For a long time the law-enforcement agencies denied the existence of organized crime and of the Commission. When was it that it was acknowledged?

MC: Television. When they started having hearings on television, with Joe Valachi. The greatest teacher in the history of the planet up to this point is the television. Television is the greatest teacher, there's no question about it, for better or for worse. A lot of it is for worse. We know that, with ugliness, the violence, the wild, bizarre sex being portrayed on the screen. Television is the greatest teacher because it has the greatest opportunity to teach young people. Young people spend much more time watching TV than watching their teacher in the classroom. It was television that first impressed the image of the Mafia on the American psyche.

RO: Were the newspapers strong before television in depicting the Mafia?

MC: The newspaper doesn't compare to the image on the screen. Sure, they wrote about Italian mobsters in Chicago, but that was a headline, once every six months. With television you get it every night, especially now when you have one hundred channels. It's there, just flip through the channels and you'll find a man with a scar on his face, swarthy complexion, speaks with an accent and wears his hat askew.

RO: Mafia bosses are called godfathers because of their characteristic of building Families, of having their rituals, and their ability to control the environment. Would you give us your definition of a *padrino*, a "godfather"?

MC: To me, a *padrino* is a priest! That's the image I prefer. If you tell me about a *padrino*, I'll say, "Wonderful, he's a little Neapolitan priest from Italy. He's a little bit heavy, because his greatest sin is pasta." And if you tell him, "Father, it's Lent," he'll say, "So?" What would *padrino* mean to a lot of people? The head of a group, either the biggest *padrino* of all, who has a Family of his own, or a smaller head of a subdivision. But why "godfather", why *padrino*? Because their authority is so complete. It's like a dictatorship. There's no legislature, no rule-making body, they don't consult, they don't go to the flock, to the voters. It's the Boss: the Boss tells people what's right, what's wrong, and people follow him. It's the ultimate Mussolini. It's a father figure as the Boss. That's what *padrino* means to someone who is oriented to law enforcement and crime.

RO: *Padrino* figures are now less strong than they used to be. Do you think there are still bosses like Lucky Luciano who live undercover and are as strong and powerful as Lucky Luciano was?

MC: I think the best authority on what the condition of the Mafia is, what the incidents of *padrini* and bosses are, and how it works now, is the FBI. They won't give you all the information, and they couldn't, but from what you can get from the FBI, or Interpol, they would tell you that the whole syndrome of the Mafia is withering with the culture, but there is plenty of organized crime going on. Remember that terrorism is organized crime, probably more lethal than anything else we have faced, but to a large extent it is more and more organized. Now it is done in sophisticated ways. It's not done bluntly by thugs who are sent out in a black limousine to beat people up with clubs. It's done with computers, business, huge investments. There's always a lot of that, but there's more now. But the FBI would tell you that the old Mafia is dying away gradually. And it's not all Italian-American any more, there are some African-Americans in some places, so the ethnic aspect of it is being dispersed as well.

RO: Are there neighbourhoods or markets or business sectors in which Italian-American people have been concentrated or marginalized?

MC: The old Mafia, when I was young, was able to maintain a consistent Italian-American population. There was always maybe one Polish guy, or a half-breed, like half-Italian half-Irish, and some of them even had Irish names. But that was the era of Italian neighbourhoods, with whole villages of Italians in Manhattan, like the lower East Side, in parts of Queens, the Bronx, Staten Island. All the Italians lived in one place, all the Irish lived in another place. That is changing rapidly in the city, it's fragmenting rapidly, people are being dispersed. When you lose that concentration of Italian-Americans, it gets harder to have a Mafia operation that's all Italian, because they're scattered.

RO: One of the characteristics of the Mafia has been dealing with politics, being able to corrupt politicians, but also to understand politics. What do you think about the connection between Mafia and politics, and their ability to deal with politics?

MC: Politics makes the rules for society, makes laws that will either help or retard your business. If we make an environmental law that says you can't use a certain type of coal, that may put you out of business. So politics is very important to anyone in business, and the Mafia is in business. Everybody who is in business, especially in the US, tries to corrupt politics, maybe not illegally, but by getting the politician to do what they want, whether or not the politician believes it's the best thing for most of the people. How do they corrupt you? With money. They give you money for your campaign, and in return you're supposed to forget about what's good for everybody and do what's good for them, because they give you money. A lot of that is done very successfully by big money in the US. So it should be no surprise that the Mafia, which has its own organized crime, its own desires for its business, should do the same. If the Mafia wants to reach a judge to make him more lenient in a case – that's pure corruption. Yes, of course, they will try to corrupt politicians, and always have. Not as much as they did in Italy. In Italy it seemed to be more of a cultural thing, and it didn't quite reach that level here. But yes, organized-crime figures have always tried to corrupt politicians.

Roberto Olla interviews Thomas V. Fuentes, former Chief of the Organized Crime Section, FBI

RO: In your opinion, what is the meaning of the statement "Today the Mafia is becoming invisible"? How is the Mafia changing?

TF: The Mafia is becoming more corporate in their nature. They're lowering their visibility because of the amount of public attention they attracted, particularly using high-profile bombings and assassinations, such as the killing of Judge Falcone in Italy. Now they realize that it only brings additional law-enforcement pressure on them when they commit those type of murders, so now they are becoming more secretive, and trying not to attract as much public attention as in the past.

RO: When do the mafiosi rely on straightforward crime, like homicide, and when do they resort to the investment of capital?

TF: I think their preference is to make money in any way they can, so their use of homicide is only a business tool when necessary in conducting other criminal operations. So they use homicide and terror merely to gain objectives and gain an advantage in order to make money.

RO: So they use homicide only for other criminal endeavours?

TF: Yes, to exact revenge, or to eliminate a rival, or to persuade others to cooperate with their criminal activities.

RO: Why at the moment aren't there any Mafia wars?

TF: At the moment they're making a great deal of money all over the world, and at the moment they appear to be cooperating with each other.

RO: Is that with all types of organized crime, not just Italian organized crime?

TF: Yes, we're seeing that all over the world. We're seeing cooperation among groups from Asia, Russia, Eastern Europe, as well as traditional Sicilian and American La Cosa Nostra criminal groups.

RO: Is the Commission still active?

TF: We don't believe the Commission is still active. In the case of many of the American La Cosa Nostra Families, they're reluctant to even name one single boss because of the law-enforcement efforts that are made against that, particularly by the FBI. So many of the organizations are now being run by committees, and their leadership is somewhat disorganized.

RO: Does a *capo di tutti i capi* exist, and who could he be?

TF: We don't believe he exists at the moment in the United States.

RO: Is that because they tend to live undercover or...

TF: In the United States we had a landmark case in 1985 called "The Commission Case", in which the bosses of the New York Families were all convicted of being bosses of La Cosa Nostra Families and for their racketeering activities in connection with running those Families. Since then we've convicted repeatedly boss after boss in a number of cities and from the five Families in New York City. So as a result of that, they're very reluctant to even publicly name a boss, much less to have the bosses meet and conduct meetings as an organization or as a Commission.

RO: How many people at the various levels did a boss like Gotti need?

TF: A boss like John Gotti would need many levels to conduct his criminal operation. The Gambino Family during the time of Gotti – during the late 1980s to early 1990s – was the most powerful La Cosa Nostra Family in the United States. It had over two hundred full members and ten times that number in criminal associates. So there was his underboss, his *consigliere*, soldiers, *capos* and as many criminal associates, which included business people, corrupt public officials, corrupt law-enforcement officers. So there were many levels to enable him and the criminal Family to conduct their operations.

RO: So wouldn't you be able to give a number in approximate terms?

TF: That would be like trying to describe how many levels there are in a multinational corporation or a Fortune 500 corporation. This was an extensive criminal operation, and they conducted many types of criminal activities, ranging from labour-racketeering to entry into many related industries like trucking, construction, restaurants, with many things like gambling, loan-sharking, extortion, homicide, all in connection with their activities. So there were many layers within the organization, both horizontally and vertically. This would be true of all La Cosa Nostra Families, but at the time of Gotti that was the most powerful in the United States.

RO: Could you give us an idea of how many mafiosi there are now? How many bosses, associates and various levels?

TF: We estimate that there are still over 1,000 "made" members within the United States. We believe about half of those remain criminally active. Many of them are in prison, many are getting older, and the newer generations of younger criminals in the Families are taking their places, but they're not as effective. Our operations, not only the FBI but other federal, State and local agencies within the US, as well as our efforts with our Italian colleagues, have helped to significantly reduce their operations. So the actual numbers of memberships are similar to what they've been over the years, but the quality of their membership is dramatically lower, and we're continuing to disrupt their activities.

RO: They aren't more than they were in the past?

TF: No.

RO: When was their number the highest in the US?

TF: We think the strongest period was probably during the 1960s. In 1968 and 1970, the United States enacted very strong legislation against organized crime. It enabled US law enforcement to conduct electronic eavesdropping, or wiretapping. In 1970 the passage of the Rico Statute gave law enforcement in the US very powerful tools, both investigative and prosecutive, to address La Cosa Nostra in particular, but other organized-crime groups as well. Over time we learnt how to apply the legislation, use those tools, conduct the investigations and follow that with successful prosecutions. So we began to have a serious impact around the late 1970s to early 1980s. So during the 1960s and 1970s they were the most powerful, and since then we've continued to increase the pressure, become more successful in our prosecutive efforts and obtain cooperative informants within La Cosa Nostra to penetrate the code of *omertà* in order to be able to reduce their activities.

RO: Is drug-trafficking still the main business of the Mafia today?

TF: In the United States we don't believe drug-trafficking ever was their single most important activity. They engage in a wide range of activity. We've felt that labour-racketeering, control of major labour organizations and the industries related to those organizations was more important to them as their base of power and source of income. By controlling labour unions, they were able to control the trucking industry, the construction industry, the docks along the eastern seaboard, and many other areas that were very lucrative over the long run, along with traditional racketeering, such as gambling, loan-sharking and extortion. Drug-trafficking was done in the US on a freelance basis without the permission of the Commission or the bosses from many Families. But there was so much money in drug-trafficking that individual components within the organizations engaged in it on the side. In many cases they would face a death sentence within the Family if they were caught. The Sicilian organizations that were allowed to operate here were engaged primarily in heroin-trafficking for many years, and they reached an accommodation with the American La Cosa Nostra – their "cousins" – that they would be allowed to operate, but they would have to pay a percentage to their "cousins". They were not strictly engaged on a daily basis in partnerships, with the exception of the Bonanno Family in the US, which was engaged in joint drug-trafficking activities. But most of the other American Families were not engaged in drug-trafficking on a daily basis.

RO: This would be true even today?

TF: Today we're seeing what we believe is a resurgence of the Sicilian Mafia engaged in drug-trafficking within the United States, and an increasing partnership with some of the American La Cosa Nostra members involved in drug-trafficking. So we're seeing increased drug-trafficking, but also increased criminal operations, including home invasion, robbery and extortion, as joint ventures with individuals from Sicily as well as members of American La Cosa Nostra Families. So we're presently conducting a series of very important, very sensitive investigations with our Italian colleagues to address this fact.

RO: And was there a special cause for this resurgence?

TF: They're always looking for new ways to make money. During the 1960s, '70s and '80s, we saw the Sicilians primarily importing heroin into the US, being one of the key distributors of heroin in the US. Now we see the price of cocaine in Europe is nearly double what it is in the US, so in addition to trafficking drugs into the US, they're now trafficking cocaine back to Europe and to other outlets, where it is gaining more money for them than heroin is by itself. We think that's had a great deal to do with it. We also see increased activity by other criminal organizations in Europe interacting with Sicilians, 'Ndrangheta, the Camorra and Sacra Corona Unita in mainland Italy. They are primarily Albanians, and other organizations, that are conducting extensive criminal operations in Europe with a connection through the Sicilians to their Italian "cousins" in the US.

RO: Perhaps drug-trafficking was changed by the Balkans.

TF: Right. And it has resulted in new partnerships among international criminal organizations. As I mentioned earlier, we are seeing increased cooperation throughout the world. This is a very disturbing trend that we have observed for the last three to five years, where there is very little conflict. These organizations are entering into agreements with each other on a wide range of criminal activities: the illegal trafficking of human beings, of women and of children, drug-trafficking. Criminal operations are also affecting the global financial network and international securities markets. There are many criminal operations that are being engaged in cooperatively by organizations from all over the world, and they seem to be doing this on a very strong partnership basis.

RO: What is the relationship today between the Sicilian Mafia and the American Mafia?

TF: The Sicilian Mafia continues to engage in cooperative efforts with the American La Cosa Nostra. There has always been a connection with the Bonanno American Mafia Family, and we see this continuing today. There is, in a sense, a resurgence of Sicilian activity within the United States. This is primarily being caused by the fact that the price of cocaine is nearly double in Europe what it is in the United States, so instead of merely trafficking heroin from Europe to the US, they are now trafficking cocaine back to Europe from the US. So this is giving them new opportunities to make money and increase profits, particularly in the drug-trafficking area. But we're also seeing this in other criminal activity, including home invasion, armed robbery, extortion, murder and a number of other activities being conducted jointly in both countries.

RO: Any new activities that weren't specific to La Cosa Nostra in the past?

TF: No, I think they're continuing to engage in their primary sources of income that they always had. They're attempting to maintain control, although they no longer have it, over the labour organizations. We've addressed that very strongly within the US. But they're continuing to expand into new areas where they can. We've seen that in the securities markets, where they try to manipulate stock prices for financial gain, and engage in money-laundering from a variety of criminal operations.

RO: Why did that *pentito* claim that the Mafia had won? Could it be because the Mafia is changing and penetrating the legal world?

TF: I'm not sure exactly what he was referring to. I think the fact that they still exist would be a good indication. I wouldn't say they've won, but they haven't lost either. They still exist, they're still conducting extensive criminal operations in both of our countries. We're continuing to fight that, and we're continuing to develop additional partners in many other countries in addition to Italy and the United States.

RO: The Italian Judge Falcone said that "One dies when one is left on his own". Would you agree, and what does it mean to be left on one's own as an investigator?

TF: I think he clearly recognized that no one agency or country could face this threat alone. These are extremely powerful, violent, vicious individuals that control these operations, and that no one country alone could address it. Very early he worked closely with his American counterparts, and to this day we continue to carry on the fight since his murder.

RO: We believe that a global vision of the Mafia throughout history is needed in order to fight it. Would you agree, and why?

TF: It has required a global effort. These criminal organizations are operating all over the world. We see Sicilian Mafia operations not only within the US and Europe, but also in Canada, the Caribbean and South America. There are alliances not only between the Sicilian Mafia and the American La Cosa Nostra, but the Sicilians are also forming alliances with the South American drug-trafficking organizations, and in some cases smuggling organizations throughout the world. So this cannot be merely addressed by the United States or Italy or Canada alone, we need to have a global effort. Most of our efforts every day are attempts to gain partnerships with our counterparts throughout the world.

RO: What about the global knowledge of history? Would the knowledge of history help to retrace the main characteristics of organized crime and help you to fight against it? Does knowing history help?

TF: Knowing history tells us that we have to fight them as aggressively as possible, and that we need strong investigative tools in order to address it, and strong prosecutive laws in order to attack them. We cannot just sit back and ignore it, or they will continue to grow and expand their operations globally. In the case of weaker countries, they are a threat to the very existence of democratic countries. History teaches us that we have to fight them as much as possible.

RO: Does the role of the "godfather" still exist, like the one modelled after Carlo Gambino and described in the movie *The Godfather*?

TF: I think that the role typified in the movie *The Godfather* has never existed. It was a highly romantic view of what many people say was modelled after Carlo Gambino. But every Mafia Family in Sicily and the United States are vicious criminals, vicious murderers, they're not the romantic family individuals portrayed in the movie. Many aspects of *The Godfather* movies are extremely accurate in terms of how they conducted their business and the types of activities they engaged in, but the notion of the admirable La Cosa Nostra boss has never been true.

RO: Would society still have somebody who behaves like the godfather, somebody who protects the community, or is that just something that was lost with Gotti?

TF: The activities that we see in the American La Cosa Nostra are not related to protecting the community or even their blood relations. These Families exist to make money. They will resort to anything in order to continue their criminal operations, including murder. They will even murder innocent people who aren't even involved in the criminal organizations. We've seen that historically in Sicily and the United States. They are not individuals deserving respect.

RO: The Mafia is a secret society. As such, could it have a mechanism for transmitting knowledge and experience from one generation to the next?

TF: In the original structure of the organization, the bosses were very experienced criminals. They were older, more mature, and had engaged in racketeering basically throughout their lives, from the time they were teenagers through their mature years. They did pass that on to the younger generations of criminals. Today we believe we've made such an impact that there is less monitoring from "senior" criminals to newer criminals. So we don't see the strong control within the organization that used to exist.

RO: So the mafioso rituals have also disappeared, such as the blood and older rituals that were a part of the secret society?

TF: Right. In 1989 the FBI recorded a ceremony in which new members were inducted into the New England Patriarca La Cosa Nostra Family near Boston, Massachusetts. Since that time when we penetrated the ritual, recorded it and proved once and for all that the ritual does exist, since they conducted the ceremony, they have now been much more reluctant to use the formal ceremony. They've been fearful that we would again penetrate it and use it in a prosecution to show that they had joined a La Cosa Nostra Family. So we don't believe they continue to use the ritual. But in the US, not all La Cosa Nostra Families used the rituals. For instance, when Al Capone started his La Cosa Nostra

Family in Chicago, he wasn't Sicilian, so he didn't believe in the ceremony, he was very independent. He used criminals from many other ethnic origins, so he didn't strictly require that the members even be Sicilian or Italian. He went into existing ethnic neighbourhoods, used the criminal organizations and brought them under his power. So historically in Chicago there never has been a ritual to designate someone as an official member of a Family. They were used primarily in the north-eastern Families, in New York, Boston and other cities in the north-east. So the use of the ritual is not a strict requirement for membership, but it was based on the Family's tradition and whether they chose to use it.

RO: How is an undercover agent like Donnie Brasco prepared, and how do you protect him while at work?

TF: I'd rather not comment specifically on the preparation. Our agents are prepared, like many others who work extensively in order to gain as much knowledge of the individuals who are members of that Family, how the Family operates, what type of criminal activities they conduct, and who their non-member criminal associates are. So there are many aspects that we try to learn just as investigators. Specifically, for an undercover agent, I would rather not discuss their preparation.

RO: At the beginning of the twentieth century, the mafiosi often travelled with immigrants and hid drugs in the luggage of other people. Could you please talk about the relationship between the Mafia and migration?

TF: Historically, in every ethnic group that has migrated, other than the honest people seeking a new life in the United States, there was always a small percentage that were just criminals. In fact, with each wave of immigration, those criminals actually victimized their own community. We saw this with virtually every wave of new immigrants, even recently with the criminal activity of the Asian communities. The newly arriving criminals live in the same geographic area as the honest citizens, people who speak the same language, until the criminals become more oriented within the country, and spread out to other areas. This was true at the end of the nineteenth century, when there was a great deal of Italian immigration into the north-eastern United States. Within that there were criminals, and the Sicilian Mafia members themselves, who arrived and created new members within those communities. So the very first activities of what later became the American La Cosa Nostra were directed at other Italians within the community: the Black Hand business-extortion activities, murders, gambling. Everything that we see today on a more generalized basis was initially within their own communities against their own people.

RO: Were drugs brought into the country at the beginning of the century through migration or general drug-trafficking?

TF: I'm not certain that they used immigration to bring in the drugs. I think the expectation with the immigrants arriving was that their luggage would be searched and that they would be scrutinized upon arrival in the US. So I'm not aware that it was used as a means of drug-trafficking. But once they arrived in the US and moved into ethnic areas – the "Little Italys" of many of our large cities – then they began criminal operations – extortion, gambling, prostitution, many of the traditional racketeering activities within their own community. Extortion against individuals and business people within their community. So I don't think that the large immigration was used strictly as a drug-trafficking method. I'm not positive but I don't think it was.

RO: Some historians say that it was when Lucky Luciano was sent back to Italy that La Cosa Nostra became an organization. Would you agree?

TF: No. La Cosa Nostra was already an organization. Lucky Luciano had done a great deal to organize the activities of La Cosa Nostra. He is credited with establishing the system of the Commission itself to settle disputes and divide up territories among the Families. So I don't think his being deported had any effect on that. It was already in existence and very strong in the US prior to his going back to Italy.

RO: What was the Apalachin Conference and what were its aims?

TF: We believe that the Apalachin Conference in New York was mainly conducted to have the Sicilian Mafia present their plan to distribute heroin in the United States and to gain a partnership in doing that with the American La Cosa Nostra. So we believe that the main purpose was for the bosses of the American Families to decide whether or not they would engage jointly in heroin-trafficking with their Sicilian "cousins". The conference was interrupted before they made that final decision, so from that point on, the existing rule of the American La Cosa Nostra was that members were not to engage in drug-trafficking or heroin, because if the public became aware of it they would be outraged. They wanted to maintain their veil of providing services that people wanted, such as gambling, prostitution and alcohol during the Prohibition. So they did not want to get involved, at least publicly, in an activity that would bring public opposition to their criminal operations. The conference was interrupted, that decision was not made, and the rule stayed in effect that members were not officially allowed to engage in that trafficking activity.

RO: How was big drug-trafficking organized? How were the drugs hidden? It is said that heroin was the first global good. Would you agree?

TF: I think there were many global goods prior to heroin. Agricultural products, sugar, silks from Asia, many other things in addition to drugs were global products. Much of the heroin was shipped in containers hidden in other products like food. Once they arrived in the US, as was shown with the huge Pizza Connection case, many drugs were distributed with restaurant supplies being shipped throughout the country to supply restaurants making pizzas. Heroin was included in the normal products that were being used to support restaurants throughout the north-eastern and south-eastern part of the United States.

RO: With regard to the "zip" killers who travelled from Sicily to the United States and vice versa to kill somebody, is there a case that you could describe to us in any historical time, and have you captured any?

TF: We've heard many cases of when hired killers were brought in that way, where they would have no identity or criminal record within the United States. They would commit a murder on behalf of an American La Cosa Nostra Family and then return to Sicily. Over the years we've seen less of that activity being strictly for murder and more for joint criminal operations. So the activity between Sicilian organizations and their American counterparts is increasing, not necessarily involving just "zips" who come over to commit murder, but for a wide range of criminal activities.

RO: So it's difficult for the FBI to detect somebody who's just come in from Sicily to kill somebody?

TF: Yes. They would come in without a criminal record that we were aware of here in the US, so once they were in the country there would be no reason to maintain a surveillance of their activities. Once they committed a murder or a crime, they would leave immediately to return to Sicily.

RO: So there haven't been cases of capturing "zips"?

TF: Not that we would identify as a "zip". We have many joint cases with our Italian colleagues where we have made arrests and solved these murders. I think the nature of the criminal business has changed a little bit in the way they conduct their partnership between the Sicilians and the American La Cosa Nostra. Also, they're well aware that we have established the closest of working relationships with our Italian colleagues. So we are sharing the membership lists and a great deal of information continuously. So it would be much more difficult for a Sicilian to enter the United States without our Italian colleagues alerting us that this individual has come over. It would also be very difficult for the Americans to ask for a murderer or hit man to come over without us being aware of it and trying to stop it. We have a number of investigations addressing that type of criminal activity right now.

RO: Writers tend to transform people like Al Capone and Carlo Gambino by treating them as heroes. Do you think these literary treatments may in some way favour sympathy towards the Mafia?

TF: I wouldn't call it "sympathy", but they are celebrities. In many cases, criminal figures have always been somewhat romanticized by society, like the Jesse James gang in the US 150 years ago becoming popular. Back in the early part of the twentieth century, there was John Dillinger and Baby Face Nelson in the gangster era. On one hand, the public hated these criminals, but on the other hand there was a fascination, and they were celebrities in their own right because they were famous. I think that criminals like John Gotti, those that maintained a higher profile, became celebrities and attracted more attention, good and bad.

RO: How does the Mafia kill? What is the difference between the way they killed at the beginning of the twentieth century with the Black Hand and today?

TF: There isn't much difference in how they kill. They still kill with a bullet to the brain or a bomb in a car, home or office. The techniques are similar over the past 100 years, and they continue to use those same techniques.

RO: Could you talk a little about the Pizza Connection?

TF: The Pizza case is interesting from several aspects. It obviously showed the activity of heroin-trafficking by the Sicilian Mafia into the United States. The designation of the Pizza Connection was that the distribution itself within the US was used in the pizza industry. So pizza parlours were opened from the north-east to the south-east and as far as Oregon, Illinois, which is about 100 miles west of Chicago. The Sicilian part of the organizations attempted to maintain a low profile, and attempted to operate and distribute outside of the main metropolitan areas. So in the case of Oregon, Illinois, there was a small community with one pizza restaurant, and when they received their supplies, that would be the method of distributing the heroin, along with the materials that were used to make the sauce and the crust and the other ingredients. So that's how the distribution network was set up. What's interesting is that La Cosa Nostra did not attempt to control the distribution or activity of the Sicilians in the US, but attempted to share in the proceeds, and some parts of the US Families did jointly engage in the activity. They weren't allowed to do so officially by the Commission, but unofficially some of them did, because there was so much money to be made. Historically, the Sicilian Mafia has been allowed to operate in the US as long as they don't interfere with an existing criminal operation of an American

Family, and as long as they abide by the code that was unofficially imposed by the Commission and the American LCN leadership. In other words, in Sicily Family members were being bombed, along with police officers, parents, judges, siblings, children, priests, but the Sicilians were told in very strong terms that if they came to the United States to conduct criminal operations, they were not allowed to use that type of terror. They were not to attract the attention of law-enforcement officials and the American public by engaging in that type of activity here. So they had to abide by American LCN rules and various sanctions, but as long as those conditions were met, they were free to come in to operate. We believe that they consciously chose more rural areas, because there would be less attention from law enforcement itself. The police agencies and FBI would have fewer agents and officers there to address it, so they were less likely to discover these operations outside of our main metropolitan areas, where we were used to finding it in the past.

RO: Is there anything that you would like to add?

TF: I would like to make the point that we have made a strong effort against the American LCN and against the Sicilian Mafia when they have engaged in criminal activity in the United States. We have been very successful during the last twenty years or more in a number of very serious cases and we are continuing to make them. But what concerns us now is that they are very cunning, and they are recognizing that they are now able to conduct criminal operations all over the world, and that they are able to engage in partnerships with other organized-crime groups from Russia, Eastern Europe, Asia, Africa and South America. So the fact that organized crime is becoming more global is not just rhetoric from American or other law-enforcement agencies all over the world. We believe it is a very dangerous trend, because they are not fighting with each other. They are engaging in partnerships. We know that the only way we can address it is to have our own partnerships throughout the world. We want to carry on the legacy of Judge Falcone. We need to have continuing partnerships and cooperative efforts in law enforcement and among different countries so we can fight this, or they will win.

Roberto Olla interviews Bernard B. Kerik, former New York City Police Commissioner

RO: We'll start with one of the main figures from the NYPD, which is Joe Petrosino. Would you like to talk about him and explain if he is still remembered within the NYPD?

BK: I think he's very much remembered in the Police Department. He was a historical figure here. He came to the US from Italy and became a citizen once he was here. He later joined the ranks of the New York City Police Department as a patrolman. He was subsequently promoted to sergeant by Teddy Roosevelt, who at the time was the Police Commissioner and later became President. He went on to create the bomb squad and was assigned to a special investigations division within the police department that worked on organized-crime cases like the Mafia and the Black Hand cases back then. And in the early 1900s he was sent to Italy on an undercover assignment. While he was in Italy, in the process of conducting an investigation, he was assassinated. His body was flown back to the US. A funeral was held for him in Manhattan, and I think more than 250,000 people went to that funeral. He was the first Italian-American to be killed in the line of duty. He was the first New York City cop – I think still the only New York City cop – to be killed on foreign soil. He was the first Italian-American to become a detective and the first to become a lieutenant, and at the time he became lieutenant he was the highest-ranking officer in the New York City Police Department.

RO: A lot of people think that it was a mistake for him to go to Sicily, or in not collaborating with the Italian Police. Is there a thought about the real mistake?

BK: I don't think there was a mistake. I think this is a dangerous job both here and in Italy. I think we were in contact with the Italian Authorities at the time, and he was doing what police officers do, which is conducting a very dangerous investigation, and that resulted in his death. If you look at the history of the New York City, we've lost over 500 cops since the New York City Police Department began. It winds up happening as a result of the job.

RO: So you think he's still mentioned in Police Academies?

BK: He's still talked about. I remember when I first came on the Department, there was a photo of him in the academy. Unlike other police officers that were killed in the line of duty, he was and is the only New York police officer to be killed outside the United States. That in itself brings a certain amount of attention to him.

RO: Who are the other police agents who've had a relevant and symbolic role in the fight against the Mafia?

BK: These days I'd say it's the whole NYPD. One in particular of Italian descent was a young man by the name of Anthony Venditti. He was killed in 1986, he was a detective assigned to the Organized Crime Control Division. He was working on a case against an Italian organized-crime group. He was in a diner in Queens and he was basically executed by three men in that crime Family. Those men were later tried and acquitted during two or three different trials. One of those men that were acquitted at the time for his homicide was recently arrested on another organized-crime case in the last two months, so although we couldn't convict him in that case, one of the gentlemen is back in the system as a result of his continued participation in organized criminal activity.

RO: You were saying that Petrosino was part of the Italian Investigative Police Squad. Is there an Italian police squad now, or if not, are there ethnic police squads?

BK: Not really. We have what they call the Organized Crime Control Bureau, and that consists of a number of investigative bodies that fall underneath it, that look at narcotics, that look at different organized-crime groups. Basically it's across the board – it's not Italian-specific or ethnic or culture-specific, it's organized-crime-specific and that's what we concentrate on.

RO: What made New York's Fiorello LaGuardia so important that an airport was named after him?

BK: He was an important figure back in the days that he was a mayor. He was someone that came in and started to change the city and make it a better place, much like Rudolph Giuliani today. Many people today refer to Giuliani as the LaGuardia of the year 2000 or the 21st century. LaGuardia came in as the mayor and wanted to see change, he was someone that reached out to the communities. He created a change and made New York City a better place. When that happens, people take note, and they memorialize those figures in time, and one of the ways to do that is to name an airport, name a street, things of that nature.

RO: Is there anything specific about LaGuardia, a fact or specific event that stands out?

BK: In my mind? I wasn't around then, and I won't get into age of course, but I think overall, growing up and hearing stories, I think he was someone of great outreach that brought the city together, and that's what he's most noted for.

RO: In terms of NYC, is there a part of the city, like a harbour or a port, that at the time was one of the main centres for "La Cosa Nostra"? Is the harbour still such an important place for La Cosa Nostra?

BK: No, these days there are no important places for the Mafia or for organized crime. We may have organized-crime participation in different areas, but nobody has control today like they did in the past. Our intelligence efforts, our investigative efforts, the things we do today are, I would say, far more successful than they were in the past. So back in the early 1900s and mid-1900s, people of Luciano's calibre appeared to have prominence and importance, but that's no longer the case. We conduct very successful investigations, and we've been very successful at rooting out organized crime in the East Heights areas, so I don't think that's the case.

RO: I don't know if you can answer this question, but how much faster do you think your techniques have become in the efforts to root out organized crime today?

BK: The investigative ability is far better than it was. Today we have electronic surveillance, technical surveillance, that we never had before, like twenty, thirty, forty years ago. That gives us a great ability to collect intelligence and investigative information, and to put cases together and push those cases forward for prosecution. Twenty years ago, the investigative ability and technique in law enforcement was greatly different than it is today. All of those things have had a major impact on crime reduction and on eliminating the power and control of organized crime.

RO: On the basis of new technologies, how does the collaboration work between your Department and Italy, for example?

BK: I think that the coordination and cooperation between the NYPD and outside authorities in general is pretty phenomenal. We recently conducted a homicide investigation in which one of the suspects, Carmine Galante, had fled to Italy. We worked that case in conjunction with the Italian authorities, and within the last two months Galante was arrested. He was placed in the top-ten list here in New York City, we had a front-page article in one of the local newspapers, and within a few days we received information that he was hiding out in a certain spot, and he was eventually captured. The cooperation we've had with Italy and many other governments has been pretty tremendous.

RO: Would you talk about the Mafia homicides and provide a description of the ritual aspect of homicides, or the fact that in the Mafia there's a legend that men can never kill their victims from behind, but must instead face their victims, because the eye retains the image of the killer? Are there other aspects of interest?

BK: I've been in this business a while, and those things don't really happen today. There may be a continued perception in people's minds that that's the reality. But the reality is that homicides from organized crime are usually to eliminate competition, to push people out of the way so that they can take over. There's no specific ritual or method of homicide. These groups deal in violence and commit homicides, but there's no specific trait or trend, not today, not like it used to be.

RO: You were talking about business and competition, with drugs reflecting the main business of Cosa Nostra. In your opinion, is the Pizza Connection still operating, or does Cosa Nostra still rely on Sicily and Italy as a base?

BK: You're saying that drugs are a primary part of their activity. That may be the case in Italy, but it isn't the case in New York City. There are a number of other things in New York

City that they're involved in: certain criminal activities at the airports, at the ports, gambling, loan-sharking, things of that nature. Drugs are not one of the highest things on their radar charts, and I'd say we've been pretty successful in keeping the drug activity down. If you look at the total amount of people arrested in New York City, seventy-five per cent of those arrests are drug-related, but when it comes to the organized-crime group that you're discussing, I don't think they fall within that category.

RO: Probably because of the idea that Lucky Luciano started the drug business so maybe they still have that perception?

BK: Sometimes perceptions linger on for a long time. If you think of New York City in 1994, you think of it as being a very disorganized, mismanaged city. It was violent, out of control, crime-ridden. There are people today that still feel that NYC is the same, but in reality crime is down sixty-three per cent, homicides are down seventy per cent, but that perception lingers on. You always have to try to change, let people know the real facts, and I think in this case that's one of the perceptions that has been maintained over the years.

RO: What are your thoughts about Lucky Luciano?

BK: My thoughts? He was a thug. He was a bad guy. Some people gave him a position of importance. In my mind, I don't think he was important. I think he was just a bad man that should have spent his life in jail. That's what I think.

RO: Some people think of him as a hero of criminality...

BK: Anyone that considers someone a hero that commits homicide, deals drugs and commits continued criminal acts, I think they need their head examined. This man was not a hero, he was a very bad man, a criminal, and criminals deserve to be off the streets. They shouldn't be roaming the streets of this city, or any city for that matter.

RO: The New York Police were very successful in identifying the people at the Apalachin Conference, but many people think it was Lucky Luciano's anonymous tip to the police. What is your version of that?

BK: I don't know if I have an exact version. Our opinion is that Luciano was out in Italy at the time, and he was sort of jealous about what was going on. At that conference, a number of his associates didn't show up, so the automatic perception was that since his associates weren't there, they couldn't be endangered, so he was the one that gave out the information. I think that's the perception out there and that is the reason why.

RO: Who are presently the most dangerous Mafia Families?

BK: These days you can't even say they're dangerous. The organized-crime Families today are disorganized and don't have the leadership that they had years ago. The Families as we know them – the Genovese, the Gambinos, the Lucchesi – they're still around, but they're in total chaos right now. Their leadership has been taken down by law-enforcement efforts. A number of them are in jail, and a number of them are in hiding. I wouldn't say they're dangerous – they're more or less a nuisance. They're a group that we constantly focus on, but they're pretty much under control today, much better than they were years ago.

RO: Could you please talk about the business that these Families are involved in? Are they still involved in the same business that they were years ago?

BK: Their involvement has changed over the last several years as a result of enforcement efforts by the NYPD, but also by the leadership of New York City. As you know, when Mayor Giuliani took over, he was very aggressive in pushing organized crime out of the Fulton Fish Market, and out of the carting industry. Those were industries that were controlled for years and years. When the Mayor came in, he gave a mandate to the NYPD and the New York law-enforcement authorities to make sure that these areas were free of organized crime. That's what we've done. Their industry changes from time to time. Some of their prime industries have been hit hard since Mayor Giuliani took over.

RO: When Mayor Giuliani started, was that his priority in the beginning? How did it work? What did the Police Department have to do?

BK: You have to look at his overall priorities. When Mayor Giuliani took over in 1994, he was extremely concerned about crime in the city. If you look back ten years ago, we had 2,245 homicides that year in New York City. Last year we had 671. The Mayor's mandate was to reduce crime. You have to focus on crime all around, not just on specific groups. You have to focus on low-level crime, quality-of-life crime, major crimes, and we in the NYPD started to do that. Some of the areas that we had to look at were controlled by organized crime: Fulton Fish Market, the carting industry and the San Gennaro Feast was another area that the Mayor wanted to focus on. He created investigative bodies, the Trade Waste Commission, to look at the carting industry, the Department of Investigation, the special investigations units within the NYPD, and the Organized Crime Control Bureau, to look at the Fulton Fish Market. He used those investigative bodies to go after organized crime in those areas. As a result, the Fulton Fish Market, the Trade Waste, the carting industry, they're organized-crime-free today. People feel safe about working there and doing their business in the city, whereas in the past that wasn't the case.

RO: With the money-laundering that took place on Wall Street, there is the thought that the Mafia is now white-collar. Is that the feeling now, or was that just one episode?

BK: I think you have that in every area of criminal activity, whether it's one of the five organized-crime Families in New York City, or whether it's the Cali or Medellin cartels from Colombia. Today, because of the investigative and intelligence capabilities of law enforcement in general, I think organized-crime units and Families try to legalize and legitimize their money, and one of the ways to do that is to launder their money through banks, through different corporations, through legitimate companies. That isn't specific to Italian organized crime, it's something specific to organized crime in general.

RO: At the beginning of the century, there was a collaboration with the Irish. Are they collaborating with different ethnic groups now?

BK: Because we've had such an impact on rooting out organized crime within the city, you don't see that cooperation and working together like you may have in the past. The law-enforcement efforts have been so strong, people have gone underground and really haven't focused on it as much.

An Interview with Al Capone
(Originally published in *Liberty*, 17th Oct 1931)

How Al Capone Would Run This Country

Unashamed on the Eve of His Trial, the Master Gangster of America Gave This Incredible and Presumptuous Interview to Cornelius Vanderbilt Jr.

Editor's Note: When Al Capone gave this interview to Mr Vanderbilt, he was facing trial for evasion of the federal income tax law, with the prospect of several years in prison if he should be convicted. What was going on in the mind of this self-imposed dictator from the underworld? Was he sobered, deflated, as a man naturally would be in such circumstances? On the contrary, as Mr Vanderbilt shows, he was coolly holding forth on the affairs of the nation, telling the President of the United States what to do and naming his possible successor, and – to crown the effrontery of it – denouncing grafters and swindlers. The interview is published as an astonishing and salutary object lesson in underworld mentality aggrandized by prohibition riches, sensation publicity and the arrogance of a gangster, swollen with power.

"Us fellas has gotta stick together."

We were seated, Al Capone and I, in a large spacious office in the south-east corner of the fourth floor of the Lexington Hotel at Twenty-second and Michigan, Chicago. It was after 4 p.m. The day was Thursday, August 27. And this was the year.

Below us, on the sidewalks, cops and plain-clothes men bristled. Their light artillery was very much in evidence. Gangster hangouts had been brushed clean time after time during the past twenty-four hours. Hotels and apartments had been entered and raided. Pat Roche wanted the King, and wanted him badly. And Pat was the State's attorney.

Someone had been kidnapped. His name was Lynch. He published a racetrack tip sheet. Rumour had it his captors demanded "250 grand" for his release. Believing that Al Capone might know something about it, the Chicago police had asked the King to help them find him. His Majesty had graciously acquiesced, and it was not long before Lynch was found. Nor had he been obliged to pay a nickel's worth of ransom.

Al Capone does not tolerate some kinds of rackets, and kidnapping is one of them.

He leant a bit further back in his comfortable office chair and lit, for the seventeenth time, his chewed Tampa cigar. We had been talking for more than an hour.

"This is going to be a terrible winter," he went on. "Us fellas has gotta open our pocketbooks, and keep on keeping them open, if we want any of us to survive. We can't wait for Congress or Mr Hoover or anyone else. We *must* help keep tummies filled and bodies warm.

"If we don't, it's all up with the way we've learnt to live. Why, do you know, sir, America is on the verge of its greatest social upheaval? Bolshevism is knocking at our gates. We can't afford to let it in. We've got to organize ourselves against it, and put our shoulders together and hold fast. We need funds to fight famine."

Could I be hearing correctly? Was I in my right senses? Here, in front of me, in the bay of a window, behind a long, large teak desk, sat the most feared of all our racketeers. Much taller than I had imagined, and broader; a fellow with a winch-like handshake, a banker's bay window and the winning smile of all the Latin races. And yet, instead of the usual line of talk that emanates from gentry of his kind, he had been giving me a discourse the like of which it had never been my fortune to hear.

He went on:

"We must keep America whole, and safe, and unspoilt. If machines are going to take jobs away from the worker, then he will need to find something else to do. Perhaps he'll get back to the soil. But we must care for him during the period of change. We must keep him away from Red literature, Red ruses; we must see that his mind remains healthy. For, regardless of where he was born, he is now an American."

Boys were shouting "extras" in the streets below. Al "Brown", as he likes to call himself, got up from his chair and walked over to the south side of the room. He drew from a cabinet a pair of field glasses, raised them to his eyes and read slowly from an afternoon sheet's headlines: "Pat Roche Confident He Will Soon Have Capone Under Arrest".

He smiled broadly at me. "Pat's a fine guy," said he quietly, "only he likes to see his name in print a bit too often."

And, thought I, "If Pat really was in earnest about arresting you, he could do it in a jiffy."

He practically answered the thought: "I guess I'm like you, Mr Vanderbilt: I get more blame from the crowd for things I never do than praise for the good I do.

"The news gang are forever riding me. Seems as if I'm responsible for every crime that takes place in this country. You'd think I had unlimited power and a swell pocketbook. Well, I guess I got the power all right; but the bank book suffers from these hard times as much as anyone else's.

My payroll is about as big as it ever was, but the profits have done their share of dwindling. Say, you'd be surprised if you knew some of the fellas I've got to take care of."

I could have answered that I wouldn't have been surprised at anything, but I held my peace. Al Capone is not the usual type of gangster who has risen to a high place. He is a capable organizer and politician. At thirty-two he has about him the most perfectly oiled machine this country has ever seen. He is as powerful in Chicago as any Tammany boss ever was in New York. To do the many things he must do daily, he has a payroll in excess of $200,000 a week.

At this writing the Capone machine has yet to meet a defeat. Just how can a man of his youth hold together the kind of organization he has built up? I asked him. His reply came without hesitation:

"People respect nothing nowadays. Once we put virtue, honour, truth and the law on a pedestal. Our children were brought up to respect things. The war ended. We have had nearly twelve years to straighten ourselves out, and look what a mess we've made of life!

"War legislators passed the Eighteenth Amendment. Today more people drink alcohol from speakeasies than passed through all the doors of all the saloons in America in five years before 1917. That's their answer to law respect. Yet most of those people are not bad. You don't classify them as criminals, though technically they are.

"The mass feeling that prohibition is responsible for a lot of our ills is growing. But the number of lawbreakers is increasing too. Sixteen years ago I came to Chicago with forty dollars in my pocket. Three years afterwards I was married. My son is now twelve. I am still married and love my wife dearly. We had to make a living. I was younger then than I am now, and I thought I needed more. I didn't believe in prohibiting people from getting the things they wanted. I thought prohibition an unjust law and I still do.

"Somehow I just naturally drifted into the racket. And I guess I'm here to stay until the law is repealed."

"Then you believe it will be repealed?"

"Certainly," was his quick reply. "And when it is, I'd be out of luck if I hadn't arranged to do business elsewhere. You see, Mr Vanderbilt, prohibition forms less than thirty-five per cent of my income."

His next statement fell like a thunderbolt.

"I believe Mr Hoover may make the text of his December message to Congress a suggestion that the nation's legislators raise the percentage of the alcoholic content of liquor. That will be his best card for renomination. Besides, you know he has always called the Volstead Act 'a noble *experiment*'.

"In time, though, people won't tolerate even that. They'll demand a return to normal drinking; and if they exercise enough pressure they'll beat the Anti-Saloon League and the industrialists who have waxed fat and wealthy at the expense of thirst.

"The law will be repealed. There will be no further need of secrecy. I will be spared an enormous payroll. But as long as the act remains in effect and there are people left who will continue to break the law, then there must be positions for persons such as I, who find it devolves upon us to keep the channel open.

"People who respect nothing dread *fear*. It is upon *fear*, therefore, that I have built up my organization. But understand me correctly, please. Those who work *with* me are afraid of nothing. Those who work *for* me are kept faithful, not so much because of their pay as because they know what might be done with them if they broke faith.

"The United States Government shakes a very wobbly stick at the lawbreaker, and tells him he'll go to prison if he beats the law. Lawbreakers laugh and get good lawyers. A few of the less well-to-do take the rap. But the public generally isn't any more afraid of a government prison sentence than I am of Pat Roche. Things people know about amuse them. They like to laugh over them and make jokes. When a speakeasy is raided, there are a few hysterical people, but the general mass are light-hearted. On the other hand, do you know of any of your friends who'd go into fits of merriment if they feared being taken for a ride?"

Did I? That was one question I could answer, and quickly.

On the wall behind the King was a picture of Lincoln in a cheap frame. He seemed smiling benevolently down. A bronzed paperweight of the Lincoln Memorial statue of the Great Emancipator was on the royal desk. A copy of the Gettysburg Address adorned another portion of the wall. That Capone admired Lincoln more than any other American was easy to see.

I asked him how he felt about the 1932 elections.

"The Democrats will be swept in on a record vote," he declared. "The masses will think they'll get relief from the Depression that way. I know very little about world finance; but I don't think the end of the Depression is going to come like that. I think it will take longer. A series of circumstances will bring about a relief, if we don't let the Reds try to bring it about before.

"Owen Young has the best chance, in my own humble estimation. He's a swell guy, and they ought to let him get it. If not, then Roosevelt will; and I think Roosevelt has enough sense to make Young his Secretary of the Treasury. Roosevelt's a good fellow, but I'm afraid his health is pretty shaky, and a leader needs health."

Capone's *naïveté* was charming. He did nothing for effect; and I am sure he wasn't trying to show off for my benefit.

Four days before, I had been sitting in my Nevada ranch house. My Sicilian secretary, Peter Marisca, had brought me a telegram that had been mislaid earlier in the day. It read: "Appointment arranged in Chicago Wednesday morning at 11. Call my office on arrival." It was signed by a well-known Mid-Western attorney. I had just had time to pack some bags and catch a late train east.

Reaching Chicago Wednesday, I read of the kidnapping of Publisher Lynch, and of the Chicago Police's bid to Capone for his help. Nevertheless, I called the attorney who had sent me the wire. Capone was in consultation with his counsel and could not see anyone.

Late that evening I purchased an early copy of a morning paper. Headlines told of Lynch's return home, and of Pat Roche's order for Capone's arrest. It was intimated that the King knew entirely too much about the cause of Lynch's sudden kidnapping.

All hopes of seeing Capone fled instantly. I had developed a bad cold in my head, and I went to bed.

Early Thursday morning there was a telephone message: "Mr Al Capone's secretary says it will be entirely all right for Mr Vanderbilt to come to his office this afternoon at three."

Peter Marisca didn't deliver it, because he thought someone was playing a practical joke! Yet he told it to me as an aside that day at luncheon at the Drake; and I nearly burned my throat with the mock turtle.

And so here I had come through cordons of police and government agents. Down in the lobby of the Lexington we had entered an elevator, in which a coloured boy as glum as glue had taken us up.

In the hallway a well-upholstered young chap had been waiting. He was dressed in the lightest green suit I think I have ever seen. And he lost no time in asking me whom I wanted.

"I have an appointment with 'Mr Brown'," I said.

"That guy with you?" He motioned to Pete. I replied that he was. We moved down the hall and into a private suite of rooms. Pete stayed outside to talk his native tongue with any number of other Sicilians.

During the interview I was brought back from my surmises by a question Capone put to me. "In your talks with big men throughout the world," he was saying, "what have they to offer as a solution for the present depression?"

"Frankly," said I, "I've heard so many solutions, I feel as if none of them really knew anything. I think they're stumped."

"Not stumped," said Al. "They can't all get together and stick to any one thought. They lack concentrated organization. Isn't it a peculiar thing that with one of the world's greatest organizers as our chief executive we lack organization more now than ever in our history?

"The world has been capitalized on paper. Every time a fellow had a new idea, they'd increase the capital stock – give themselves so much cash and their stockholders so much paper. The rich got richer; the stockholders speculated with the paper. Someone found out it paid to keep a rumour factory going. Someone else interested women in gambling on the big board. The world was wild.

"Amalgamations took place. The more clever a fellow was with turning paper recapitalizations into cash, the greater became his vice-presidential titles. Young men who ought, many of them, to be resting behind the bars of penitentiaries for stealing paper rose overnight in the world of prosperity. Our entire prospectus of living turned topsy-turvy.

"Crooked bankers who take people's hard-earned cash for stock they know is worthless would be far better clients at penal institutions than the poor little man who robs so that his wife and babies may live. Why, down in Florida, the year I lived there, a shady newspaper publisher's friend was running a bank. He had unloaded a lot of worthless securities upon unsuspecting people. One day his bank went flooey. I was just thanking the powers that be that he'd got what was coming to him, when I learnt of another business trick that would make safe-cracking look like miniature gold."

265

* * *

"The crooked publisher and the banker were urging bankrupt depositors who were being paid thirty cents on the dollar to put their money in another friend's bank. Many did so; and just about sixty days later that bank collapsed like a house of cards too.

"Do you think those bankers went to jail? No, sir. They're among Florida's most representative citizens. They're just as bad as the crooked politicians! I ought to know about them. I've been feeding and clothing them long enough. I never knew until I got into this racket how many crooks there were dressed in expensive clothes and talking with affected accents.

"Why, when I was held the other day for evasion of federal taxes I nearly got myself into a fine pickle. Certain officials wished to make a bargain with me. If I'd plead guilty and go to jail for two and a half years they'd dismiss the charges they had against me. A pretty penny had to be paid, but I thought that that was better than the strain of a long-winded trial. A day or so before the bargain was to be struck, though, I learnt that someone was going to go to the Appellate Court and that there'd be a fly in the ointment and they'd have me in Leavenworth for ten and a half years. So I decided I could be just as foxy, and we entered a plea of not guilty, and when the case comes up we'll see what we will see.

"A little while ago in one of the Chicago newspapers it said that a local millionaire manufacturer had been found to be some fifty-five thousand dollars in arrears with his personal-property tax. A day later it was printed that this had been printed in error, and that the situation had been satisfactorily cleaned up.

"If Mr Hoover's government wants me to explain my federal taxes I shall be very glad to do so. I think I could enlighten him and several other officials a considerable bit, and any time they need any sensational matters to talk about I shall have them ready to give out."

"Graft," he continued, "is a byword in American life today. It is law where no other law is obeyed. It is undermining this country. The honest lawmakers of any city can be counted on your fingers. I could count Chicago's on one hand!

"Virtue, honour, truth and the law have all vanished from our life. We are smart-alecky. We like to be able to 'get away with' things. And if we can't make a living at some honest profession, we're going to make one anyway."

It was growing late. The setting sun's ruddy light enlivened the red-and-gold fancy plaster walls of his office. It intensified the dark-red window shades. The large moose's head on the wall; the stuffed fish and game; the short army rifle – all seemed resplendent in the afternoon's final burst of glory. The big old-fashioned phonograph case should perhaps have opened of its own accord to play some triumphant march.

"The home is our most important ally," Capone observed. "After all this madness the world has been going through subsides, we'll realize that, as a nation, very strongly. The stronger we can keep our home lives, the stronger we can keep our nation.

"When enemies approach our shores we defend them. When enemies come into our homes we beat them off. Home-breakers should be undressed and tarred and feathered, as examples to the rest of their kind.

"There would be very little need for your home town, Reno, Mr Vanderbilt, if more men protected their homes. When the prohibition law is repealed there'll be less desire for birth control. Without birth control, America can become as stalwart as Italy. With an American Mussolini she could conquer the world."

The door opened quietly behind me. Peter and "Mr Brown's" secretary were still in conversation. Al greeted Pete and they had a few words together in Sicilian.

"Remember, Mr Vanderbilt, us fellas has gotta stick together this winter," he repeated. "Last winter I fed about three hundred and fifty thousand persons a day here in Chicago. This winter it's going to be worse. I think we both speak the same language; and I think we're both patriots. We don't want to see them tear down the foundations of this great land. We've got to battle to keep free. Good luck. I'm glad I met you."

The iron study door swung to. My most amazing interview was at an end.

From the Testimony of Tommaso Buscetta during the "Pizza Connection" Trial

Q: Mr Buscetta, did you come to have conversations with members of La Cosa Nostra?

A: Yes.

Q: In the course of those conversations did you learn about the structure and function of La Cosa Nostra?

A: Yes.

Q: Can you tell us what that was?

A: The organization was divided up into Families.

Q: What do you mean by "Families", sir?

A: The group was called Families because we are or we were brothers. These Families adopted the name of the village where they were located, or of a small town where the Family was located. The Family consisted of a *capo* or boss, *sotto capo* or deputy boss, *consigliere* or counsellor, *capodecina* and *soldato* or soldier.

Q: Mr Buscetta, in that structure, what position did you have when you first joined?

A: Soldier.

Q: You told us that the boss or capo was Gaetano Filippone?

A: Yes.

Q: Mr Buscetta, you said that you were a soldier in this organization, is that correct?

A: Yes.

Q: As a soldier, did you come to learn what your duties and responsibilities were within the organization?

A: Yes.

Q: Can you tell us what duties and responsibilities you had as a soldier?

A: There is not a great deal of difference between a soldier and a boss. The only difference lies in knowing how to deal with people during a conversation, some people speak better and some people speak not so well, and as in everything, there has to be a boss, but there is no difference between the boss and the soldier as to dignity or conduct of the man.

Q: As a soldier in the Mafia Family you were part of, can you tell us what you understood your responsibilities and duties to be?

A: My responsibilities were limited. Even my very conduct... And I had to wait until orders were given to me by the boss through my *capodecina* as to whether I was to cooperate or participate in any particular undertaking.

Q. What do you mean that your conduct was limited, Mr Buscetta?

A: I am sorry, I don't understand your question. You say 'my conduct was limited'. I didn't say my conduct was limited.

Q: I think you said that you had limited responsibilities and you had to wait for orders from your boss or *capodecina*?

A: That is correct.

Q: Now, as a soldier, did you receive instructions or information about the way in which you were to comport yourself as a member of the Mafia?

A: Yes.

Q: You received those after you became a member, shortly after you became a member?

A: As a matter of fact, these qualities were required also before becoming a member of the organization.

Q: Please continue.

A: I was reminded to behave in the appropriate manner, to be silent, not to look at the other men's wives or women, not to steal and, especially at all times, when I was called, I had to rush, leaving whatever I was doing.

Q: Mr Buscetta, you said that you had to be silent, is that correct?

A: Yes.

Q: Is there a particular word that was used by the organization to describe that concept?

A: *Omertà*.

Q: Can you tell us whether *omertà* applied within the organization or as to people outside the organization?

A: Mainly within the organization, but it can be applied also outside the organization.

Q: What would happen so far as you know, Mr Buscetta, so

far as you were told, if you violated one of those principles that you just described?

A: Death.

* * *

Q: Mr Buscetta, let me now return to the time shortly after you took the oath and became a member of La Cosa Nostra as you described. I would like to ask you, sir, if there came a time when someone more senior in the Family than you told you what your obligations were as a member of that La Cosa Nostra.

A: Yes.

Q: And how was that information passed on to you?

A: By voice. Nothing is written in the Mafia.

Q: Can you tell us what that person told you about your obligations as a man of honour?

A: There are many such things. The main ones are the maximum silence, secrecy also between husband and wife or brothers, and no leak of information from the Mafia outside. There was another thing. A person of the Mafia could abstain from talking, but when he talked he had to tell the truth.

Q: Your last answer, can you tell us a little more fully what you were told concerning your obligation to tell the truth?

A: A man of honour must tell the truth to another man of honour. He may also abstain from talking. Should he not tell the truth, then he may be subject to expulsion or death.

Q: With respect to silence, *omertà*, as you described it, Mr Buscetta, what were you told, if anything, that you could say to people who were outside the Mafia about the existence of the Mafia?

A: Nothing. One cannot say anything.

Q: Mr Buscetta, were you told shortly after you became a member of the Mafia anything about the identity of other members of the Mafia and how you could be introduced to them?

A: Yes.

Q: Can you explain to us what you were told and what you understood?

A: It was explained to me that there were many Families, Families in the sense of Cosa Nostra or Mafia, in the area of Palermo, and that if I were to meet some of their members, I needed an introduction by somebody else, I could not introduce myself by myself to these people. May I continue?

Q: Please continue.

A: To continue answering your question, I may have access to any Family in the area of Palermo through an introduction by my boss, I can never introduce myself alone, and I shall always follow the directions of the *capodecina*.

Q: Mr Buscetta, you said that you had to be introduced to another man of honour by another person, is that correct?

A: That is correct.

Q: And how would that introduction take place, or how were you told that such an introduction should take place?

A: I was introduced as Cosa Nostra, or the same thing, Stessa Cosa.

Q: And what did those words mean when they were used for such an introduction?

A: That I belong to a Family.

Q: And what did it mean with respect to the other persons who were present during the introduction?

A: If there were two or three men of honour and another person who was not a man of honour, for me, I was introduced as "This is our friend", for the other person, who was not a man of honour, the introduction was "This is my friend", and it was understood, therefore, who was and who wasn't.

Q: Who was and who wasn't what, sir?

A: Who was a man of honour and who was not a man of honour.

Q: You said that you learnt these things shortly after you became a member of a particular Family, is that correct, Mr Buscetta?

A: That is correct.

Q: And were you told why these rules existed?

A: For the secrecy of Cosa Nostra, of Mafia.

Q: Mr Buscetta, you said that you became a member of a Family. Did that Family have a name?

A: Yes, Porta Nuova.

* * *

Q: And what were you told about how the *capo* of your Family was selected?

A: Through a vote.

Q: A vote of whom?

A: We voted, including himself. All the members of a Family voted.

Q: And did you come to learn whether the same procedure for electing a *capo* applied in other Families?

A: Wherever there is Cosa Nostra it is the same in every place.

Q: And how did you come to learn that information, Mr Buscetta?

A: Within my own Family and then through contacts with members of other Families.

Q: Mr Buscetta, can you tell us if during the course of your membership in the Porta Nuova Family you came to learn what the functions and duties of the *capo* were?

A: Yes.

Q: Mr Buscetta, can you tell us how it was that you came to acquire that information?

A: By the members of my own Family.

Q: Can you also give us an approximate time, how soon after you became a member you became familiar with the duties and responsibilities of the *capo*?

A: Immediately after.

Q: Now, Mr Buscetta, can you tell us what the duties and responsibilities of the head of the Family were?

A: The duties were to deal with all matters pertaining to the various members of the Family in the best possible way, to deal and interact with members of other Families, with other Families, and always to have a good word in respect to the weak.

Q: You told us about a position of the underboss, of the *sotto capo*.

A: Yes.

Q: Can you tell us if you came to learn how the underboss was selected?

A: The underboss is chosen by the boss and he is not elected.

Q: Can you tell us, Mr Buscetta, how you came to come by that information?

A: Within the Family. In the Family there are the young and the old members, and the old members instruct the young ones one day after the other.

Q: Mr Buscetta, you described the position of *consigliere* or counsellor.

A: Yes.

Q: I would like to ask you if there came a time when you received information about the duties and function of the person who had that job in the Family as *consigliere*.

A: Yes.

Q: And how did you obtain that information?

A: Always within the Family.

Q: What was the function, so far as you understood it, of the *consigliere* within the Family?

A: The word itself describes the function. *Consigliere*, counsellor, is somebody who gives advice. He is elected, just like the boss, and no boss will take the responsibility of a decision unless he has called in the *consigliere*.

Q: How many *consiglieri* would there be or were there in your Family?

A: Three.

Q: You also described the position of *capodecina*, is that correct, sir?

A: Yes. •

Q: Did you come to learn what the function of the *capodecina* was within the Family?

A: Yes.

Q: How did you come to learn that information?

A: From the *capodecina* himself.

Q: And what did the *capodecina* tell you about his job?

A: No man of honour has any particular task to carry out within a Family. Only he is – there is no specific job that somebody must do. Only I am at his orders and I must carry them out when he gives them.

Acknowledgements

I should like to thank the *carabinieri*, the "*Direzione Investigativa Antimafia*" (DIA), the Italian State Police, the "*Servizio Polizia Scientifica*", the "*Gabinetto della Polizia Scientifica*" (the forensic department of the Palermo police headquarters), the Federal Bureau of Investigation and the New York City Police Department. I should also like to thank Pasquale D'Alessandro for his support while I researched and wrote this book. Special thanks are due to Donatella Saroli for her work in American archives, to Valeria Cicala, Raffaella Cortese, Giulio D'Ercole, Acacia Dourado, Silvia Greco and Beatrice Serani for their help, and to Danila Satta for her suggestions on the style of writing.

This book is based on primary source material: written documents, films and photographs held in the archives of several countries. Over the four years it has taken to research and write the book, the helpfulness of the staff in these various archives has been essential. I should like to thank in particular the staff in the following institutions: The Library of Congress in Washington DC; the National Archives, Maryland; *Teche Rai*, Rome; *Istituto Luce*, Rome; *Archivio del Movimento Operaio*, Rome; National Film and Sound Archive, Canberra; BBC Library Sales, London; Imperial War Museum, London; Hoover Institution, Stanford, California; Columbia University, New York; *Archivio Ansaldo*, Genoa; CBS News Archives, New York; Film Bank, Burbank, California; The Image Bank, New York; Hoot Shots Cool Cuts, New York; *Cinemateca Brasileira*, São Paulo, Brazil; Huntley Film Archives, London; Australian Broadcasting Corporation; British Pathé, London.

Documentation and other information has been provided by the staff of the forensic police archives in Rome and in Palermo, the archives of the "*Direzione Investigativa Antimafia*" and the *carabinieri* in Rome, the FBI Archives in Washington and of the New York City Police Department.

Index